in the hope you
want to laugh with
me – or at me –
Read on!

[illegible] –
June '99

So Far, So Funny

So Far, So Funny

My Life in Show Business

by HAL KANTER

McFarland & Company, Inc., Publishers
Jefferson, North Carolina, and London

Frontispiece: Hal Kanter (circa 1990)

British Library Cataloguing-in-Publication data are available

Library of Congress Cataloguing-in-Publication Data

Kanter, Hal.
So far, so funny : my life in show business / by Hal Kanter.
p. cm.
Includes index.
ISBN 0-7864-0483-3 (library binding : 50# alkaline paper) ∞
1. Kanter, Hal. 2. Motion picture producers and directors — United States — Biography. 3. Screenwriters — United States — Biography. I. Title.
PN1998.3.K365A3 1999
812'.54 — dc21
[b] 98-44225
CIP

Manufactured in the United States of America

McFarland & Company, Inc., Publishers
Box 611, Jefferson, North Carolina 28640

For my daughters
and their mothers

Table of Contents

"Before I say anything, I'd like to say something."— J. Danforth Quayle

Preview

Walt Whitman's smiling phrase "gladness scatterers" aptly applied to an esoteric band of Hollywood humorists who gathered twice a month for lunch and laughter.

Our only purpose in meeting was to cheer each other up by exchanging insults, swapping jokes and arguing about why we couldn't meet for our next lunch in a less expensive restaurant.

Very infrequently, Sid Caesar, Jack Elinson, Charles Isaacs, Seaman (Si) Jacobs, Austin (Rocky) Kalish, the late Sheldon Leonard, Aaron Ruben and I accepted a visitor in our midst. Despite frequent requests to participate in our Dutch treats, there were few outsiders accepted: comedians Andy Griffith and the late Morey Amsterdam, writer Mel Tolkin and a visiting publisher from Connecticut, my brother Bill.

In 1995, when we toasted Sheldon on the publication of his autobiography — a book consisting of "a bunch of antidotes," as someone told our colleague Max Wilk — Morey Amsterdam announced he was writing his own autobiography and Sheldon asked him, "Who's it about?"

Morey said, "I won't know 'til I finish it."

Morey never did.

This is my autobiography, and by the time you finish it, I hope we'll both know who it's about.

More importantly, I hope that you will have laughed.

Filmmaker Alfred Hitchcock vigorously suggested his screenwriters quickly present the Who, Where and When of a story, then — before going on to the What of it — make the audience laugh.

Hitchcock reasoned that people enter the forbidding darkness of theaters seeking escape and solace. Isolated and apprehensive, they grope for seats among strangers of whom they are usually as suspicious as was Hitch himself. The sooner they find something to laugh about, the quicker they relax, sensing commonality, and coalesce into an attentive community.

For over 60 years, I have been among the legion that practices the demanding discipline of bringing strangers together through shared laughter.

In that frequently frustrating, often laborious, seldom celebrated process, I have myself been provoked to a lot of laughter that I later shared with family and friends.

Among those friends was the folk-singing, Pulitzer Prize–winning poet and Lincoln biographer, Carl Sandburg. During one of his rare visits to Hollywood, we spent a long afternoon in fellow writer Norman Corwin's guest house exchanging anecdotes. They were both so amused by my stories of working in radio, film and television, Carl demanded I put them into a book.

"They must be preserved," he said gravely, "for scholars of frivolity!"

I take comfort that he shared with Lincoln the conviction that we are all dependent on a certain amount of frivolity to maintain our sanity.

Another friend, frivolous Groucho Marx, agreed with Sandburg, but when I asked, "If I do write the book, would you buy it?" Groucho snapped, "I wouldn't even borrow it."

Groucho never met a straight line he didn't try to bend. But I knew he was an omnivorous reader of everything he could borrow. Moreover, the cheapskate would have enjoyed many of the following pages. Especially the ones about him.

The stories on these pages were recalled from notes, diaries and letters I have been writing since my parents gave me a portable typewriter for my thirteenth birthday. Those accumulated papers attest to my romance with optimism and the sound of laughter.

I have set down these recollections for my granddaughter, other scholars of frivolity and plagiarists.

Many writers and most humorists are victims of larceny. Thieves have been stealing from me since I wrote one of my first jokes for network radio. It was about a farmer who had such a tall cow, his wife took milk showers.

At the time, I was flattered that anyone thought it was funny enough to steal. I've been flattered so many times since that I've tried to even the score by flattering others with the same degree of petty larceny.

But when I told an audience that Beethoven was so deaf, he thought he was a painter, I also told them that line was written by Pat McCormick, a rowdy gent who gave it to me in exchange for one of my favorite jokes that didn't get on the air the first time I tried it, but has been purloined countless times since.

"I was a very tall baby," I wrote. "I was born December 18th, 19th and 20th."

In this permissive age, it may seem quaint that the NBC-TV network censors refused to allow a guest on *The George Gobel Show* to read that line. They claimed it conjured an obscene picture.

As its author, I defended the joke, pointing out that Henry Fonda, the quintessential wholesome American, was going to tell it. That did not alter their stand, and because I was also the producer of the show I was obliged to explain to my guest star why the line had to be cut.

Henry Fonda stared up in amused disbelief. "Up" because I stand six feet, two inches above the carpet level and Fonda was lying down at the time.

"Damn shame," he said. "Comfortable joke."

The enduring warmth of his smile compensated for the temporary loss of a joke.

There would be many more jokes.

And a few gasps.

"Hal did a lot for our family. He left."
— my brother Bill

1. Hal Did a Lot for Our Family

There is comfortable proof that I began life as a normal-size infant. My birth certificate from the Georgia Department of Health confines my birth to December 18, 1918.

The city was Savannah, one of America's most beautiful, where the pace of life is leisurely to this day. I went home for a visit one recent October, and in Savannah it was still September.

The place of my birth was Telfair Hospital; according to that birth certificate, my parents were married. Their color was "white," the length of my mother's stay at Telfair before delivery was one day and the term of her pregnancy nine months.

I was, then, the first white child born to Albert L. and Rose E. Kanter. He was a tall, handsome, Russian-born Yankee from Nashua, New Hampshire. She was a tall, regally beautiful Savannah-born girl of Austro-Hungarian parentage. In time, they had my brother William and my sister Saralea, then retired from procreation to pursue other activities.

My birth certificate lists me as Henry I. Kanter. On the back of a sepia photograph, my mother wrote in her firm, precise hand, "Henry Irving Kanter at Tybee Island, 9 mos. old and talking!!" The exclamation marks are Mother's. She did not record what I said, but shortly after I began, Momma washed my mouth with soap because I spoke a word my older cousin Irvin Center taught me: What today's six-year-olds call "the f-word." Irvin also generously taught me and his little brother Leo how to skip, whistle and masturbate. They were talents that served Leo well when he entered Georgia politics.

It is unlikely my mother had ever heard the "f-word" until she married my father, and I'm positive that in her 93 years of life, Momma never used it, even though at one time she did drive an Essex.

Her eventual knowledge of colorful obscenities was gleaned from my father, who was liberal in his use of them with verve, style and wit—

The future Hal Kanter (identified by his mother).

although his favorite epithet was "piss pot."

"Al!" Mother would censor him with a nervous glance at the children within earshot. "Little pitchers have big ears."

"So do little piss pots," he'd say.

My father was at one time a traveling salesman and, like many of that frequently noble calling, a superb storyteller. He enjoyed making people laugh. He had a nimble, original wit and repeated stories that were considered bold in their time.

"Thank you for a lovely evening," he once said to the hosts as he and Mother were leaving a party. "I've never had so much fun with my clothes on."

When even Mother laughed, Dad repeated that line for 30 years, every time he left a party. And a few times at funerals.

My interest in the theater began early. Dad exposed us to comedy and Mom exposed us to music, literature and poor cooking.

We moved from Savannah to Miami, Florida, where Dad flourished for a time selling real estate. We shared our duplex stucco with a jocular man named Lehr who had been in vaudeville. He, his wife and small daughter had left the poor pickings of their uncertain career as troupers to join Daddy in his equally uncertain real estate venture. But show business lured Lehr back to the theater, where he became the commentator in Fox Newsreels as Lew (*Monkies Is De Cwaziest Peoples!*) Lehr.

Eventually, through Lehr I would meet my first professional joke writer and take some tentative steps on the winding road to my showbiz career.

That road began at a Saturday matinee in Miami. Comedian Eddie Cantor, one of Ziegfeld's greatest stars, was appearing — In Person! — at the awesome Olympia Theater downtown. Daddy took me as a reward for my record as a door-to-door salesman of *The Saturday Evening Post.*

Eddie Cantor filled that cavernous house with his personality. Watching the energetic Banjo Eyes cavorting in song and joining in the laughter at his jokes, I was, from that Olympian afternoon on, hooked for life on laughter.

When our economic status was changed by the Florida real estate market's swift decline, Daddy moved us from our summer home in Hendersonville, North Carolina, to Long Beach, New York. I loathed the place.

But it was there we became devoted radio listeners, as were most Depression era Americans. We preferred comedy and variety programs to the dramas of the time, and a favorite show was crooner Rudy Vallee's *Fleischmann's Yeast Hour*. (Why don't we have catchy program titles like that any more?) I resented Vallee because Mother made us eat that detestable yeast. I patronized his show only for the comedians he introduced.

In those days before organized pressure groups drove minorities off the air, we had the luxury of hearing the dialects of comedians like George (*The Greek Ambassador*) Givot, Lou Holtz and his Yiddish stories, Jack (*Baron Munchausen*) Pearl's Dutch exaggerations and a whimsical black monologist called Eddie (*Fumadiddles*) Green, all brought to his audience by Vallee, whose singing Mother enjoyed. Daddy said he was "an adenoidal piss pot."

Despite my fascination with radio, living in New York was a distinct disappointment. When Daddy brought us north, I was anxiously looking forward to seeing, of all places, New Jersey. I had read all of Albert Payson Terhune's books and pictured New Jersey as a vast paradise of rolling green hills and romping golden collies. As we drove through the Jersey flats in 1932, however, I saw no romping lads or their pups, and the noxious aroma from the marshes sickened all of us.

We had spent our summers in Hendersonville and I felt my father had betrayed us by snatching us from that sweet mountain area and into the mean metropolis of New York. I disliked the little resort town of Long Beach and the brash, rude kids who teased me about my Savannah drawl. I felt cramped in the oceanside cottage we occupied and the room I had to share with Bill and Saralea, unable to accept the fact that our father had fallen on hard times.

I determined to lose my drawl but, at the same time, make sure that I'd never adopt the harsh accents of the New York boroughs that were as disconcerting as a scream from surgery.

So I ran away from home.

I managed to get back to Savannah, to stay with my Aunt Hannah and cousins Irvin and Leo. My uncles — Hannah's brothers, Freddy and Harry — saw to it that I was sent back to Long Beach, only to flee again. It was a pattern I repeated, causing my parents a lot of grief. Nor did my widowed aunt exult when she saw me arriving again. Aunt Hannah made good sweet potato pies, but she was never a natural exulter.

My escape from the drudgery of school came through my interest in theater. In a high school assembly program, I was conscripted by our music teacher, stern Mrs. DeVanney, to fill in while the stage was being set for her baritone protégé, Autumn Monro. A few years later, Autumn's rendition of *Old Man River* would start a race riot on Guam that would eventually result in the landmark television series *Julia*, starring Diahann Carroll. But on that distant afternoon in Long Beach, I performed my imitation of Will Rogers talking to Blue Boy, his prize hog, in the movie *State Fair*.

And why would I remember that?

When 20th Century–Fox made the third version of the Phil Stong novel in 1961, I contributed to the movie José Ferrer directed. Pat Boone and Ann-Margret co-starred, and Tom Ewell played Will Rogers' part (even better than I had) for producer Charles Brackett.

After working with Ferrer on script changes, Charles invited me to lunch, where he confided that he was apprehensive about José's ability to handle something as frothy as *State Fair*. He wanted reassurance from me. The best I could honestly offer was the opinion that if he were giving a party and asked Ferrer to bring the balloons, José would bring them.

"They'd be made of leather," I said, "but they'd be balloons."

Months later, I got a note from Charles that said, "Please join me for supper before we sneak preview our leather balloon."

I don't know if the picture earned me any points, but my high school performance won me at least two friends in Long Beach. Upperclassmen Bert Gold and Ken Hart were the campus stars of an act in which Bert wore a painted mustache to play Groucho Marx and Ken employed an Italian dialect to approximate Chico. They invited me to join them in a new act.

We spent many hours in Bert's basement rehearsing a routine of jokes we'd stolen. When we thought we were ready, we went to Manhattan to audition for a local radio amateur hour hosted by gentle Harry Hershfield.

The cartoonist kindly urged us to find more original material than the jokes we had taken from *College Humor* and invited us to come back when—and if—we improved the act.

Bert and Ken kept trying. I decided to go the route Mr. Hershfield had taken and began to peddle my jokes as a freelance cartoonist (a skill I had picked up from my pal in Miami, Bob Lamme).

I was 14 years old, a part-time student at New York's Art Students League and had the nerve of a toreador.

Many magazine editors considered my work beneath their standards.

Some others paid for the ideas that were submitted in rough sketches and assigned the final work to established artists like Reamer Keller or Peter Arno. A few editors who were either adventurous, myopic or had lower standards accepted my drawings. I was published often enough to finance my escapes to the Deep South from the Shallow North.

On one return to Savannah, I met a friend of Leo's whose distant relative, a famous cartoonist named Ving Fuller, was then living in Long Beach. He suggested I look up Ving when I got back there.

I found Fuller only after I went to work as a columnist and cartoonist for *The Long Beach Independent*. It was a weekly newspaper published by Edward and Elsa Denham, an elderly English couple who had covered World War One for a London paper and smelled like they had not changed their British woolens since. I thought perhaps all newspaper people stink. I discovered only a few do.

Ving Fuller was one.

He was a short, petulant but talented man who shared his small house with an Irish terrier and a tiny woman he called "Flop." She was his mother. Flop was cowed by her bullying son and yearned to see her younger one, Sammy, who had gone off to wild Hollywood. Sam Fuller had been a cheeky young reporter on the old *New York Graphic*, a paper where Ving was a star. By 1936, Sammy was a novelist and a working screenwriter. He went on to become a film director with a cult following. A volatile showman, instead of calling "Action!" to begin a scene, he would frequently fire a pistol in the air. His crew changed their underwear often.

It was apparent even to a teenager that Ving was jealous of his kid brother's ascending star while his own was rapidly sinking from view.

Ving accepted me, probably because he had few friends. He was at least 25 years older than I and bitter that he had been reduced to ghost-drawing a comic strip called *Joe and Asbestos* for Ken Kling. The feature enjoyed its popularity on sports pages because each day's strip contained a horse racing "best bet." Kling was not much of an artist but he was a respected handicapper.

Ving helped me improve some of my cartoons, and we worked out an arrangement for us both to earn extra money. I provided the gags, Ving drew the pictures, and I took them to editors in Manhattan. We split the proceeds — unevenly. The smaller portion was mine.

My former schoolmate, Bert Gold, was also a struggling artist who spent time with us. One day I suggested a funnier joke for *Joe and Asbestos* than the one Ving was drawing. He wouldn't dare change it without Kling's permission, so he called him at the Friars Club in New York, where he knew Kling would be playing cards.

Kling approved the joke. Bert and I wrote several more, which Ving submitted when he took the week's batch of strips for Kling to sign as his own work. The handicapper liked the jokes and, relieved that he wouldn't have to interrupt his card playing to write comic strip dialogue, gave Ving that additional chore for which he paid him an extra $50. Ving was decent about it; he gave us ten. Five dollars each, thereby establishing a pay scale for an unusual vocation: Ghost writer for a ghost.

Emboldened by this triumph, we planned a strip of our own. Bert and I would write it, Ving would do the drawings, and Bert would do the lettering, which was one of his talents.

In the fall of my seventeenth year, Ving, Flop, Bert and I set out in Ving's DeSoto for California. My parents approved the move. It was the first time I'd asked permission to leave home. I did not reveal Ving's promise that his brother would see to it that we would meet beautiful starlets and get laid in the wicked city.

Tempers often flared during the cross-country trip and by the time the DeSoto chugged into Hollywood, Ving was having second thoughts about how his brother would receive us.

I don't know how Sam received his mother and brother but he was definitely not pleased to greet the young strangers accompanying them. While Sam fascinated us with tales of Hollywood and his exploits as a reporter, it was clear he felt Ving was squandering the ten dollars he was paying us.

Sam was living in a small apartment near the RKO studio, with no sign of naked starlets anywhere and certainly not room for an orgy. Bert and I found lodging in an even less commodious rooming house three blocks away.

A week after our arrival, Ving severed his relationship with us. He gave us our five dollars and told us to go home. He offered no satisfactory method of transportation that would get two boys from California to New York for five dollars. He did suggest we might appeal to our parents for funds, but neither of us would. We were determined to seek gold and glory on our own.

Bert's reach for glory extended to the public library. He brought stacks of books to the room we rented from Mrs. Dahlin, a part-time seamstress at the RKO studio. Her daughter was a movie house usherette and sometime film extra. Bert and I felt we were now citizens of the cinema community.

To support ourselves, we canvassed homes for a photographer, selling baby photos door to door. Bert did some sign painting and we both wrote jokes for a grocery market bulletin. I also continued to submit cartoons to

Eastern magazines. I found a Hollywood slick-paper publication called *jones*, published as a hobby by Grover Jones, a screenwriter. I sent him some cartoons, an article and a short story. To my delight, he printed them all. To my dismay, he did not pay for any of them. His hobby was also his contributors'.

One evening in Mrs. Dahlin's living room, I was having my only meal of that day, a fistful of walnuts she had gathered in the San Fernando Valley. We were listening to Eddie Cantor broadcasting from a radio station ten blocks away.

"I've got funnier jokes than those," I said to Bert, who was engrossed in a Ben Hecht book. "I'm going to show him some."

By the time the program was over, I was at the stage door of the Lux Radio Theater on Vine Street. I sent Cantor a request to show him examples of my brilliance. The doorman told me to wait in the alley. While I did, I struck up a conversation with a dapper gentleman named Howard Snyder. He asked me what I did.

"I write," I said. "Comedy."

"What've you written?" he asked.

"My senior show," I said. "I just graduated from N.Y.U."

"Oh?" Snyder said. "Uptown or downtown?"

I didn't know N.Y.U. had two schools.

Fortunately, Howard said immediately, "I went downtown and I wrote our senior show the year I graduated."

I changed the subject before he could ask me a question I couldn't answer. I thought *high school* was interfering with my education so I had dropped out a few months before my class graduated.

The stage doorman returned and told me Eddie Cantor had no interest in talking to me. He did want to talk to Snyder.

"Call me tomorrow, fella," Snyder said. He scribbled a number on a match cover. "If you can write jokes, maybe you've got a job with us."

"Who's us?"

"My partner. Hugh Wedlock, Jr. That's his number. Call after ten."

When I called at 10:01, Wedlock told me to come to his apartment for breakfast.

Hugh was an affable, black-haired Irishman who spoke Yiddish, laughed easily and liked my jokes. Margaret, his young bride, served us fresh orange juice, eggs and coffee. When Snyder arrived, the partners offered me a job for ten dollars a week. I became a ghost for ghosts again.

But, at last, I was in show business!

"The advantage of being on the bottom is that you can't fall." — old losers' maxim

2. The Advantage of Being on the Bottom

Wedlock and Snyder needed help because they were writing two radio shows a week. Eddie Cantor's was their primary job and *The Camel College* was a recent assignment. It required less writing because Benny Goodman and his band shared the half-hour with Jack Oakie and his featured sidekick, Stu Erwin.

If I walked to Wedlock's apartment, I flew back to Mrs. Dahlin's. My roommate was so excited, he went to the library to check out a volume of Proust. Mrs. Dahlin was so pleased at the prospect of getting her rent, she gave me another handful of walnuts. She even allowed me to use her nutcracker.

The next day, Hugh had bad news for me. Cantor had discovered he and Howard were moonlighting for Oakie, so he fired them. With only one show to script, they did not need my services. But they knew another writer who wanted a protégé who could type and spell accurately. They gave me my week's salary of ten dollars, and arranged for me to meet an inventive wild man named Eddie Davis.

Davis, *né* Danziger, a former New York taxi driver, was a legend. The short, wiry man had trapped Eddie Cantor in his cab and bombarded him with original jokes that were so good, Cantor employed him. Davis rose rapidly to the top ranks of comedy writers. Davis couldn't type, which was no hindrance to him because he couldn't spell, either. A frenetic, excitable clown who would do anything for a laugh, he spewed jokes like a corn popper. Davis was writing a screenplay with his partner, Matt Brooks, for RKO. A studio secretary typed their movie script but not the radio material they were concurrently writing for the weekly *Jack Haley's Log Cabin Jamboree*. Davis wanted me to type those scripts and suggest any jokes I could, so he urged Jack Haley to put me on staff as a junior writer.

The day after Thanksgiving 1936, I got the job. I was 17 years old and my salary was an unbelievable $50 a week. I wired my parents the good news. It was the first telegram I'd ever sent them that didn't arrive collect. Mother wept.

So did the Western Union man. Mother didn't tip.

The following day, I squandered my savings — over $20 — for a new wardrobe. On Hollywood Boulevard, I bought a pair of blue slacks with white checks, a maroon corduroy belted jacket and gum-sole, sand-colored suede loafers. I thought I was dressed like a Hollywood writer. Bert said I looked like a Filipino pimp.

On Monday, I walked from our room on Waring Avenue to a house five miles away. In 1936, smog hadn't been invented, the California air smelled of orange blossoms and honeysuckle, a substantial breakfast of freshly squeezed juice, bacon and eggs, toast and a bottomless cup of coffee at Thrifty Drug Stores cost 19 cents and it was safe to walk anywhere. Even in my garish new wardrobe.

The house in the Wilshire district was the residence of Hal Fimberg. Eddie Davis had instructed me to report to him because he was the writer who worked on the first draft of the Haley scripts. Fimberg was tall, thin, tanned and 30. He was not pleased to have a scrawny kid in blue and white pants sharing the writing budget. His orientation lecture frightened me. He told me that Haley was a very demanding boss.

"When you meet him," Fimberg warned, "don't open your mouth unless you're damn sure that what you say is funny!"

He drove me to a Hollywood apartment on Franklin Avenue that served as the writing office for the radio show. "Don't forget, kid," he said, "when Jack gets here, be funny or be quiet."

I followed him inside, brimming with trepidation. The script secretary, an Amazon named Thelma, was already there. She was dark-eyed, hairy-armed and grossly overweight. Now I felt not only afraid, but threatened.

"Thelma," Fimberg said, "explain to the kid how we work."

"In the nude," Thelma said. She started to unbutton her bodice. "Go ahead, kid — strip!"

My hands were unable to move. I was petrified by the thought of being naked in the room with that woman; surely, when she unsnapped her bra, those monumental breasts would fly out and knock me senseless to the floor.

"Well, Kanter?" Fimberg demanded.

"You first," I croaked hoarsely.

Only Thelma's giggle relieved me. I realized they were teasing me. We began working fully clothed. Fimberg paced the living room, suggesting lines. Thelma sat with a shorthand pad, taking down everything he said.

When I expressed an idea, Thelma would look at Fimberg and he would shake his head.

"No, kid. Not funny, kid. Try again, kid."

I got tired of the word. But I kept trying, pitching ideas, lines, suggestions. Fimberg analyzed them all before offering criticism.

"Bullshit!" was his most frequent critique.

Jack Haley arrived, owl-eyed, freshly barbered, soberly dressed in a suit and tie. He looked more like a stockbroker than a comedian. He greeted me with guarded suspicion. I'm sure my youth was a surprise to him. Certainly my clothing was. He tried to avoid me after our initial eye contact and addressed himself to Fimberg.

"Next week," he said, "we've got a new girl we want to try out. She's good-looking and they say she's funny."

"What's her name?" Fimberg asked.

"Lucille Ball."

"Let's give her a bounce," Fimberg smirked.

"I hear everybody else has," Thelma snickered. To Haley's credit, he changed the subject. He wanted to know what we had written.

Fimberg described a circus routine in which Haley was an elephant trainer who falls in love with the tattooed lady. The elephant gets jealous and stampedes. We were now looking for a way Haley could stop the animal, be a hero and get a laugh.

"Call Davis," Haley suggested.

"I'll get it," Fimberg insisted.

Still stung by the earlier warning not to speak in Haley's presence unless I had something funny to say, I remained silent while he and the comedian discussed the jokes. When they could not find an ending for the spot, I decided to reveal the funny notion that I had in mind.

"How about this?" I began, and they all turned to me. Haley was hopeful, Thelma expectant and Fimberg doubtful. I swallowed a lot of trepidation and plunged on: "Mr. Haley runs in front of the elephant, tears open his shirt and the elephant stops when he sees the tattoo on Jack's chest — a mouse!"

Haley stared at me. Fimberg and Thelma stared at each other. "Elephants," I explained, "are afraid of mice."

Now they were all staring at me. Fimberg filled the awkward silence by saying, "So long, kid."

I was fired the next day.

What Haley did not learn until years later was that I continued to write for him. Eddie Davis hired me himself, when he saw what a speedy stenographer I was; I could type almost 60 errors a minute. Davis paid me

$25 a week, but Matt Brooks decided he did not need my services and refused to match his partner's offer.

I didn't mind because we worked in an office on the RKO lot, a block from my rooming house. It was the first time I was ever inside a movie studio. I had lunch in the commissary where James Stewart, Ginger Rogers, Cary Grant and other stars dined at various tables. I ate at the counter where I could see them whenever one of the doors to their dining room opened.

In addition to the Haley scripts, I also made a few suggestions for the screenplay, a rather obvious steal of *Three Men on a Horse* called *Radio City Revels*. None of my suggestions was accepted. A major course in a writer's education is Rejection 101.

Their musical comedy starred Jack Oakie, Bob Burns, Milton Berle, Victor Moore, Helen Broderick and a 16-year-old tap dancer named Ann Miller. In those days, her hair moved when her head did. The writers were still submitting new lines to the director, Ben Stoloff, while he was in production. Whenever I could, I sneaked down to the stage to watch.

When the shooting was completed, Eddie thought I should live closer to his home in Beverly Hills. His sweet wife Helen found an apartment for me on Wilshire Boulevard. Bert remained at Mrs. Dahlin's. He found enough work (sporadically) to exist but not enough for carfare home, where he decided he belonged.

At the end of the Haley season, Brooks and Davis went back to New York to write *Hold On to Your Hats*, the musical comedy that was a triumphant return to Broadway for its star, Al Jolson. Eddie, Helen and their baby, Evelyn, rode on the Super Chief. Brooks went along so he and Eddie could work en route. Matt wanted his new Pontiac in the East and gave me $40 to drive it there. I accepted with the proviso that Bert come along to spell me at the wheel.

We drove past Ving Fuller's apartment house and thumbed our noses at his old DeSoto, parked in front. Bert never saw Ving again. Unfortunately, I did. But it would be three years later, when I had a steady job on Broadway making people laugh.

How many people get instant validation that their work succeeds, their aspirations realized? Not many. Some surgeons, perhaps; an occasional teacher, a few performers, athletes, hairdressers, hangmen.

And comedy writers, when they find work.

"Life is the Happy Hour of eternity."
— a drinking buddy

3. The Happy Hour of Eternity

The earliest volume of bound scripts in my home library is *The Joe Penner Show*, to which I contributed in 1938. I was again ghosting for Matt Brooks and Eddie Davis. Their collaboration on *Hold On to Your Hats* was a Broadway hit with Jolson and Martha Raye. Most of the credit for the book was not assigned to Matt and Eddie but to Guy Bolton, a veteran librettist who spoke English very clearly although he was British.

When the opportunity to return to Hollywood to write *The Joe Penner Show* came to Brooks and Davis, they offered me a position on their staff, again at $50 a week.

Joe Penner was an innately funny, sibilant product of burlesque who had ridden his catch phrase, "*Wanna buy a duck*?" to enormous but neverlasting stardom. We wrote his radio scripts in an apartment that I shared with a fellow junior writer, an older man named Harry Crane. He was often very funny as the passenger when I drove Matt's car back to California. Harry didn't drive at the time but he kept me amused, and when he said he wanted to save money for his wife and starving child — as he put it — I accepted his offer to share expenses by living together. We found a walk-up apartment on Yucca Street in Hollywood, one spacious room with a Murphy bed, bath and kitchenette.

Early every day, before the bed was made and pushed back into the wall, Eddie Davis arrived. He stripped down to his shorts and lay in the sun burning through a large window in those crystalline winter days. As we worked on the script, Matt Brooks remained aloof, glibly promoting his own career in steam rooms where film producers gathered to lose weight and in delicatessens where they regained it.

Matt wrote only one spot in which he played a dialect character with Penner. Brooks was a former Catskill mountains entertainer, an unctuous sartorial dandy who considered Noël Coward the British Matt Brooks.

Davis had no self-delusions. When he applied for membership in a

Hollywood health club, he pointed to a word on the application and asked me what it meant.

"Occupation. What you do for a living," I explained.

"Oh," he said and wrote, "*Orter*." I asked him what that spelled. Eddie gave me a withering look before he said, "Author, stupid!"

That's me outside the window Eddie Davis crawled into in Beverly Hills.

An orthodox sun worshipper, Eddie had another consuming passion: He'd do or say anything to get a laugh. His most frequent method of getting one was to drop his pants in public. Sometimes he went beyond that. While I was working with him in the den of his Wilaman Drive home one day, his gentle wife Helen was entertaining a group of women in the living room. For no apparent reason, Eddie removed all his clothing, left the den and strolled out as naked as a plucked chicken. Instantly I heard Helen shriek, "Eddie!" over a chorus of soprano yelps. Five minutes later, there was a rapping on the den window. I opened it to allow Eddie to climb in. Helen had locked him out of the house.

Before Brooks and Davis formed a writing partnership in New York, Eddie teamed briefly with a gentleman named Abe Lipschutz. Shortly thereafter, Abe changed his name to Allen Lipscott, moved to Hollywood and established himself as the dean of comedy writers, still working productively at an age when most men had retired.

Lippy was the first professional comedy joke writer I'd met. I was 14 when Lew Lehr introduced me to him. He was living in the Mayflower Hotel, facing Manhattan's Central Park, and earned a comfortable living writing for both Lehr and bandleader Ben Bernie. In Philadelphia, where he had written vaudeville material, he was a friend of my mother's cousins, the Ehrenreichs. The coincidence evoked an avuncular attitude and he advised me to seek other areas of vocational pursuit. Comedy, he maintained, was a dicey game that should be played only as an avocation. His true work, he said, was writing plays. And indeed he had written one play, which succeeded only in keeping him in radio.

Among his colleagues, Lippy is remembered with affection and some envy for at least one widely quoted line. It was spoken at a dinner in his honor, organized by our gregarious friend Si Jacobs. Fifty or so of Lippy's California associates were invited to a Dutch treat stag banquet in a private dining room at Chasen's restaurant. The veteran writer was hilariously attacked by a platoon of original wits whom I, as master of ceremonies, called up to speak. When the all-male audience had laughed itself into exhaustion, Lippy rose for his rebuttal. Peering through his thick glasses into the crowd, the bald pixie (who looked like a lascivious Methodist missionary) lied to us.

"I've never been to one of these stag affairs before," he said. "In order to say something fitting and not make the complete *schmuck* of myself these other bastards would have you believe I am, I called my old friend George Jessel for some advice. He said there are two essentials if you want to be a hit at one of these affairs. One, drop big names; and two, talk dirty.

"So, fellow writers — fuck Hemingway!"

In the winter of 1940 while we were writing the Penner show, my roommate spent a lot of time after work meeting women. When Harry brought one to our flat, I had to leave for a few hours. I saw a lot of 25¢ movies. One of the women he brought up was a young, pretty dancer who asked me not to leave. Marti believed there was safety in numbers. Later, I walked her home. When I returned, Crane was waiting for me.

"Did you score with her?" he demanded.

"Gentlemen," I said, "don't discuss such matters."

"Gentleman!" he snorted. "You'd screw anything with hair on it — including a barber shop floor!"

Before the Penner series completed its brief season, I met the show's producer, Paul Monroe, an Ivy leaguer who urged me to look him up in New York. He was going back there to take over production of a dramatic series called *Grand Central Station*. He encouraged me to try writing something more serious than gags for the Joe Penners of the world.

Monroe flattered me by saying I was "too intelligent to waste time on comedy." It did not occur to me to ask why he was wasting his time on the same commodity. I had not yet discovered that comedy is a more exacting, demanding and rewarding discipline than any other writing for the theater.

I did return to New York, I did look up Monroe and I did write some dramatic scripts for *Grand Central Station*. It was sponsored by Listerine.

Through their advertising agency, Lambert & Feasley, they bought all rights in perpetuity and for a half-hour script paid $100.

Several of my scripts were rebroadcast four and five times. Over the years, each broadcast had different casts and new producers, but the writer never earned another dime. That's one good reason we formed a guild.

Thanks to the Writers Guild of America, its members enjoy one of the finest health plans in the nation. I know that from personal exposure to its benefits.

But before we get into that, let's go back to 1940 when, foolishly, health was not a priority.

"Did W.C. Fields drink? Do ducks waddle when they walk?"—Paul Jones

4. *Do Ducks Waddle?*

One difficult aspect of the craft of creating comedy material is convincing others that what you have written is funny. Even among collaborators, there is frequent and often bitter disagreement. The English satirist Evelyn Waugh never understood how two people were able to collaborate; he said it's like three people having a baby.

Matt Brooks and Eddie Davis had one disagreement too many and ended their partnership. Brooks sailed to England "to do two musicals in London." On Broadway, he was derisively called "Two Musicals Brooks," as in the seldom-asked question, "What ever happened to Two Musicals Brooks?"

Eddie invited me to work with him on a play he called *Pooh Pooh Pulitzer*. I don't know if I would share billing with him as co-author because we never finished the farce. Gainful employment came our way. Actually, it came his way. Not many show business people knew I was in their business.

Eddie suggested that I work with him on the assignment. His offer made it clear that I was not to share equally either the credit or the check. Someday, as I learned my craft, we might become equal partners, Eddie promised.

My first lesson under our new agreement was a rare challenge: Material for the cantankerous clown W. C. Fields. The legendary comedian was employed by American Tobacco for a weekly five-minute spot on their popular radio show *The Lucky Strike Hit Parade*. Fields had written the first script himself and the sponsor, an irascible man named George Washington Hill, was furious at the comedian. How dare that arrogant old souse talk about his son, Chester Fields, on time paid for by Lucky Strike! Mr. Hill wanted to fire Fields but his advertising people pointed out that Fields had given the show a huge increase in Hooper ratings. Mr. Hill relented. He'd give Fields another chance, but only if the script was prepared by writers on whom they could rely.

Somebody considered Eddie Davis reliable enough to do the job. We returned to California where we wrote a script that met the ad agency's approval. It was also our task to present our work to the Great Boozer himself for his approval.

A nervous minion of the agency showed up in gray flannels to escort us to Fields' home. We were ushered into his presence. Let's dispense with the question of whether or not W. C. Fields drank adult broth. Yes. And constantly. Either that or he used gin as a room deodorizer, after-shave lotion, breath freshener and underarm deodorant.

The agency man presented us to Mr. Fields and, in his parlance, tossed the ball into Eddie's court. Fields sat in a huge, throne-like rattan chair, sipping from a goblet, watching beady-eyed as Eddie opened the script I had typed. He began reading enthusiastically and I tried to be a one-man laugh track. Fields ignored me. He also ignored the ad man who was searching the star's face for any sign of amusement or approval.

When Eddie finished reading, Fields said, "A missionary in Africa came to a cannibal village and announced, 'I've been looking high and low for my brother. Have any of you seen him?' And the cannibal chief said, 'Ah, yes — I passed him in the jungle this morning!'"

The ad man chuckled and said, "Droll, Bill. Very droll."

"Droll, shmoll," Eddie said. "What about this?" He handed our script to Fields.

The agency man quickly assured Mr. Fields that we would stand by to make any changes he might want before, during or after rehearsals. Fields nodded and said, "Don't be surprised, boys, if I can't use any of this rancid bat shit."

And he didn't.

Nor did he use any of the next writers' scripts.

Nor did he and Chester Fields last beyond three weeks on the air for Lucky Strike.

Eddie and I went back to New York on the Super Chief in a drawing room paid for by the advertising agency. We resumed work on *Pooh Pooh Pulitzer*.

We were not at it long when Davis was called in to write two radio spots for Olsen and Johnson. The comedy team was breaking all records on Broadway as the stars of *Hellzapoppin'*. It was the crowning achievement for the veteran vaudeville headliners who always shied away from radio because they realized they were not very effective without their visual props.

But now they were forced to appear on the Kate Smith variety program to replace Abbott and Costello, the team that had become prominent on the singer's weekly hour. Olsen and Johnson were co-producers of *Streets of Paris*, a Broadway revue in which Abbott and Costello were headliners.

The show went out of town for tryout performances and shrewd Ted Collins, Kate's manager and producer, allowed them to be absent only if Chic and Ole, the hottest names on Broadway, filled in for two weeks.

Collins, in turn, engaged Eddie Davis, and Eddie — true to his word and to his need — brought me into the assignment. We saw *Hellzapoppin'* and went backstage after the show to meet the stars. Chic Johnson shook hands and disappeared. Ole Olsen spent the rest of the night with us and a chorus girl of his choice.

We tried to get the essence of their whirlwind two-hour show into a six-minute radio spot. I was certain that I had a grasp of what made the show such a hit: incredible tempo. If you didn't like one gag, wait a second. Eddie agreed. "You're learning, boy," he said.

I was at last out of the ghost's closet, talking with the producer, the stars and attending rehearsals.

We had one joke Ted Collins did not like in the first script. He asked Eddie to take it out. Eddie insisted it was "the best joke in the show."

"It's an old joke," Collins said.

"It's a brand new joke," Eddie argued. "I wrote it last night. Ask the kid. Didn't I write it last night?"

As far as I knew, he had. I'd been up most of the night typing the script from notes and lines Eddie hurled at me.

"Take it out anyway," Collins demanded. "I don't think it's funny."

"'Not funny'!" Eddie exploded. "It's one of the biggest laughs Jolson ever got!"

We took it out.

For Chic and Ole's second appearance, we wrote two bit parts into the spot. Eddie played one of them and I played the other, for which we received an extra few dollars. Our spot played well and Davis was offered a steady writing job for *Hellzapoppin'*. He turned it down on the basis that $50 a week was less than he tipped cab drivers. Instead, at his suggestion and with his blessing, I got the job.

In 1939, I went to work for Olsen and Johnson writing topical jokes and new bits for the show that opened September 22, 1938, and ran for 1,404 hysterical performances on Broadway.

My run was shorter. But for almost a year, my office was Ole's dressing room in the venerable Winter Garden theater. I had been in that upstairs room on a previous occasion when I came to interview Fanny Brice for the Long Beach High School newspaper, *The Tide*. I arrived early during a matinee and Miss Brice's maid took me down to the stage where I watched the star from the wings. She was performing a scene with the outrageously funny Bobby Clark. What a thrill!

I ached to be a part of that wonderful world I was seeing so close and from such a privileged perspective.

In her dressing room, Fanny was amusing and gracious to the skinny kid, smiling at the whisper of Savannah in my speech that I was desperately trying to overcome. She showed me with pride a painting by her young son Billy, who is now recognized as one of America's finest modern artists. I thought she was the kindest lady I had met. Not many important people had so much patience with kids. Especially on two-show matinee days.

My job for Olsen and Johnson was providing topical jokes to *Hellzapoppin'*, new bits as often as I could and also prepare material for their charity appearances. At those benefit affairs, they seldom did any of my jokes. Like most comics, they were distrustful of any new material they had not tried out themselves or heard others get laughs with. When they were introduced, Chic would stand for a bow, giggling infectiously, Ole would get up and pour a glass of water on Chic's head then both would sit down. Soggy pants comedians.

After trying out a new bit at the Winter Garden, they would keep it in the show for one or two performances before it would mysteriously be taken out.

"Why, Ole?" I finally asked my boss.

"You're getting paid to write new stuff," was his only explanation. What I didn't know until five years later was that all of those bits and gags were being filed in his bulging loose-leaf notebook to be used in their next show, *Sons o' Fun*.

With my new position of importance in the world of theater and the heady income of $50 a week, I was able to move out of the Belvedere Hotel on Eighth Avenue and into a bachelor flat. I also played host to an older man named Lee Sands, who had offered me shelter and girls in his room at the Belvedere. My new apartment was on West 58th in a building occupied by the successful actor George Tobias.

"Come up and see my collection of neckties," he invited me. "I have over 1600."

"I'm impressed," I said. "You have such a short neck."

George later went to Hollywood and played parts that seldom called for him to wear ties.

Lee Sands, a tall man with posture as erect as a question mark, was a comedy writer who had not only fallen but impaled himself on hard times. He was writing a play with a sad-faced taciturn veteran of World War I, Fred Rath, who lived on Staten Island. He and Lee labored over a farce they called *Bigger Than Barnum* and subsisted for three years on small advances from shoestring producers, none of whom ever got their play on the Rialto.

The two men used my apartment as their writing room. When Lee was evicted from the Belvedere for overlooking several months of rent payments, he moved in with me. We shared the fold-out bed.

Another part-time resident was Lee's childhood playmate, Joe Erens, a round, pleasant cigar smoker who earned money selling jokes. Anybody's. Joe lived in Brooklyn with his mother but used my apartment as his Manhattan office. Sometimes he spent the night, sleeping in an armchair.

My one-room domain became the headquarters for many unemployed friends and their friends. As much traffic passed through it during a week as went through Ole Olsen's dressing room in an evening.

"I do all of my work sitting down. That's where I shine."— Robert Benchley

5. *I Do All of My Work Sitting Down*

Happiness is the momentary absence of pain, and by avoiding the news from Europe for a few months in 1940, I was enjoying that absence.

Ole was a gregarious man who was the official greeter for the team and his dressing room in the Winter Garden theater was always open before and after performances. Chic Johnson was far less convivial than his partner. He sat reading his Racing Form in a room that was a flight above Ole's where his only visitors were his family and a few of his immediate bookmakers.

A constant stream of dignitaries poured in and out of Ole's, and there I encountered senators, governors, mayors, actors, athletes, business executives, Congressmen and, just when I was old enough to cast my first vote, a presidential candidate.

Wendell Willkie, "the Barefoot Boy from Wall Street," shared Indiana nativity with Ole. He was a florid, ham-handed, vigorous and outgoing man with an aura of destiny and bourbon about him. His presence filled the room with electric energy. He had a booming laugh, a vigorous handshake, exuded power, wealth, confidence, and inspired awe. I voted for Roosevelt.

One worshipful night for me was the Actors' Fund annual charity event, a midnight marathon that followed the performance of *Hellzapoppin'* on the Winter Garden stage. Among the many stars who contributed to that dazzling event were Laurence Olivier and Tallulah Bankhead.

Tallulah barged into Ole's dressing room earlier than expected, while he was still onstage. Her mink coat and a platoon of admirers trailed her as she entered, barking loudly for something more potent than bathwater to drink.

Although Olsen was then part owner of a small bistro he called Another Place — because people were always saying, after a few drinks, "Let's go to another place"— he seldom had liquor in his dressing room. Ole had two good reasons: Liquor costs money and he did not like to spend it.

Miss Bankhead scoffed when I told her that Ole kept a dry room. She insisted that was uncivilized and that there had to be a dram of *something* on the premises. Chattering constantly, she rummaged through drawers and chests and trunks until she found a bottle of brandy hidden on the top shelf of a closet. With a cry of "Eureka!" that may have sexually aroused a bull moose as far away as Manitoba, she broke it open.

When Ole came up from the stage, glistening after his final curtain call, he was alarmed to find a woman he did not know sharing the contents of his precious bottle with her friends. I was not among the privileged but Ole whirled on me to demand, "Is that my Napoleon brandy?"

The gallant Miss Bankhead instantly defended me by admitting guilt.

"I found it squirreled away," she purred, "obviously long forgotten."

"That bottle was given to me by the mayor of Terre Haute," Ole grumbled. "I was saving it for a special occasion."

"Daaaahling," Tallulah exhaled in her deepest croon, "this *is* a special occasion. I'm in your house!"

I fell in love.

A frequent visitor to Ole's room was his pleasant and considerate daughter, Moya, who seemed to dote on her daddy and he on her. Moya's brother J.C. was a cadaverous member of the *Hellzapoppin'* cast who appeared in several sketches on-stage but whom I seldom saw off. He would seem to vanish when the curtain fell.

I thought maybe he went to warm his hands because every night in the second act, J.C. sat on-stage holding a 25-pound block of ice.

Moya was an unaffected, pleasant young woman who fell in love with a large, hearty, down-to-earth man she brought to the theater several times. He seemed to me an unsophisticated, simple soul although he had invented some sort of radio for use in aviation. But it was I who was simple. He was William Lear. Moya married him.

Ole insisted their first child be named Chanda. He thought it would be amusing to have a granddaughter named Chanda Lear. I don't know if Moya and Bill agreed or not. I do know that after Lear's death, Moya took a firm grasp on the affairs of the man who gave the world the Lear Jet.

Other daughters who were backstage almost every night were the motherless children of Dewey Barto, the astonishing acrobat and engaging gentleman who was the short half of Barto and Mann, *Hellzapoppin*''s classiest act. Nanny Barto and her sister Betty Lou waited patiently for the final curtain to accompany Dewey home. Miss Barto later changed her name to Nancy Walker and it went up in lights over Broadway.

Chic's son-in-law, Gene, was also a member of the cast. His job was to wander into the theater carrying a small folding chair and a newspaper, move up and down the aisles, disturb as many people as possible while pretending to look for his seat, mount the stairs stage right, cross to stage left on the apron, unfold his chair and sit against the proscenium to read his paper. He sat there in silence throughout the show, reacting only to one bit with Hal Sherman, an eccentric dancer who worked stylishly in front of a drop depicting Number 10 Downing Street, for some reason that was never clear to anybody.

One night, Gene became ill and Ole asked me to fill in for him. I enjoyed that. Ham was still lurking in my heart. After several performances, I complained to Ole that Sherman never did the bit with me that he always did with Gene.

"Don't fret about it," Ole said. "We've got enough laughs."

He was right. He was also cagey. Sherman was the Actors Equity representative for the company. He knew I was not a member. He also knew that his job would be in jeopardy if he reported the production to the union, so he chose to ignore my presence on the stage.

I resented Gene when he recovered and had the gall to return to the show.

One afternoon, Ole and I sat on the bare stage waiting for the errant Chic to rehearse some new bits I'd written. As we sat in the silent house, I mentioned what a thrill it was for me to walk through that stage door every day.

"Ole," I asked, "how do you feel being on the same stage where Will Rogers appeared, the very boards that've supported Al Jolson and Ed Wynn and Fanny Brice and Bobby Clark and Willie Howard and all those other immortals?"

Ole snorted. "Not one of them ever did the business *we're* doing!"

Ah, Theater! The smell of the greasepaint, the roar of the cash box!

When Simon and Schuster's inventive editor, Jack Goodman, thought Olsen and Johnson could write a novelty book and cash in on their extravagant success, Ole assigned me the task and I spent several stimulating sessions with Goodman to figure out how to capture the essence of *Hellzapoppin'* in print. Goodman embraced my idea to issue the book sealed in a can.

While we wrestled with various notions, King Features newspaper syndicate offered Olsen and Johnson immediate money for a daily comic strip to be called *Ellza Poppin*. Ole scrubbed the speculative book project for the certain cash.

He had seen some of my doodling and suggested I draw the strip. I demurred. Drawing a comic strip is a full-time job. Ole said they'd pay me an additional $50 a week. But the editors at King Features understandably wanted a more accomplished cartoonist than I, so I settled for $25 a week to write the strip, no matter who would draw it. While they were auditioning artists, I was startled to see a face from my recent past.

Ving Fuller approached me sheepishly on Seventh Avenue and asked if I could afford to buy him a hot dog. He told me he was unemployed, broke, alone. He was remorseful about his treatment of Bert and me in Hollywood. He blamed it on Sammy. He was bitter about his little brother. Sam had urged him to go back to New York because there was nothing for him in California.

Ving confessed all this as he devoured two Nedick's hog dogs. I told him to come to the Winter Garden stage door after the evening performance and to bring along some samples of his work. I gave him two dollars to get a haircut and was embarrassed by the intensity of his gratitude.

Ving's name was, of course, known to the editors at King, and when I urged Ole to give him a shot at the strip, he agreed. Ving quickly drew three or four different faces of "Ellza." Ole, Chic and Dick Hyman of King Features picked one. I typed out a week's worth of comic strip dialogue, advanced Ving money to buy a Whatman board, India ink, pens and gum erasers and production began on *Ellza Poppin.*

Ving's work was fast, crisp, funny and quickly accepted by newspaper editors. The strip got off to a flying start. Two weeks later, Ving repaid the money I'd advanced him and confided how much he was being paid to draw *Ellza Poppin.* More than Ken Kling had paid him for *Joe and Asbestos.* He asked what I was earning. It was none of his business, I said, but he surmised that we were both being underpaid.

Naively, the alarm bells went unheeded.

Another week or so went by. Ving said that we should demand more money. He knew from sources at the syndicate that Chic and Ole were being paid at least a thousand a week just for the use of their names. I was reluctant to ask for a raise.

A few evenings later, Ole told me that Ving had lodged a complaint with him; I was giving him old material, he said, jokes I had stolen from other cartoons.

I was shocked by the accusation and furious with my accuser. I called Ving and demanded a confrontation. He claimed he was too busy to see me and hung up.

A few days later, Ole told me that Ving was unhappy with my scripts and he was drawing his own jokes he considered to be better. I asked for a showdown in Vic and Ole's presence.

Instead, the comics met with Vic alone and after a chat (during which the artist drew flattering caricatures of them), Olsen and Johnson fired me.

Stunned, saddened and disillusioned, I turned from comedy to write drama. Freelancing, I sold scripts to the long-running *Grand Central Station*, *Lincoln Highway* and *Star Spangled Theater* radio series. It was a struggle to pay the rent for me and Lee and find enough for our staples — beer, cigarettes and cantaloupes.

A few months following my bitter departure from the Winter Garden, Olsen and Johnson's lawyer called me. Ving Fuller was suing them, demanding a share of their royalties and ownership of *Ellza Poppin*, charging them with various forms of malfeasance in their agreement. Would I, the attorney asked, testify for the defense?

My testimony satisfied the defendants and their attorney. The judge threw out the case and gave a stern lecture to Fuller on mendacity, greed, treachery and gratitude.

The comic strip was turned over to another artist and Ole offered me my old job. I turned it down. I had to register for the impending draft and if my number were drawn, I wanted to avoid being sent to Fort Dix. I remembered the aroma of New Jersey.

When I collected my last check for a *Grand Central Station* script, I packed my valise, my portable typewriter and my friend Lee Sands and we flew to California. On a Greyhound bus.

"Our romance deteriorated into marriage."
—Larry Rhine

6. *Romance Into Marriage*

Before my employment was terminated by Olsen and Johnson, I realized I was in love with a girl I had known since high school. Her name was Doris Prouder, which her business school advisor suggested she change when she left for the work force and college.

In Long Beach High, I was considered the class clown, and while Doris was in a grade below mine, we shared a history class where my jokes annoyed her. She successfully ignored me but I could not ignore her because she was the prettiest Yankee I'd ever seen. She was also the wittiest. I was determined to win her hand and other parts of her body.

It took me a few years of romance but just before sundown on Friday, September 5, 1941, we stood before Rabbi Manuel Laderman in Denver, where I said, "I do." Doris said, "I'll see."

She has stubbornly remained my severest wife, best critic, funniest friend and the mother of practically all of my three children.

The serious part of our romance was also the least expensive because it was conducted by mail, when postage was three cents. Doris was employed as an assistant editor at *Parents Magazine* in New York and I soon obtained work when Washington invited me to report to an Army recruiting center where officers would test my ability to serve for a year as a $21-a-month soldier. With no other immediate prospects for gainful employment, I accepted the government's offer.

Lee Sands was too old for Selective Service, so while I prepared to defeat the enemies of democracy, he went to work in a delicatessen to defeat hunger on Sunset Boulevard.

The night before I reported for induction, Lee catered a very liquid farewell party for me that lasted too many hours.

Before six the following morning, I arose with an elephantine hangover, stepped over the sleeping bodies of some party leftovers and into a new and rapidly changing world. With my throbbing head and forlorn apprehension, I was inducted into the U.S. Army in Hollywood on April 5, 1941, the morning that Jackie Coogan, the celebrated former child star, enlisted.

Doris and Hal Kanter (September 4, 1941), the day before their wedding.

Coogan had convinced his amusing friend Tommy D'Andrea to enlist with him. I don't know what D'Andrea did for gregarious John Coogan, but Tom's presence ameliorated my anxiety, for I had known him in New York. He was an attractive, glib chap from Chicago with some vague relationship to "the boys" he hinted were his *paisans*. We had met a year earlier when D'Andrea was writing for a comedy team known far and narrow as Shaw and Lee.

Coogan, the most famous child star the silent films ever exploited, was then recently separated from Betty Grable, his blonde wife who became the definitive pin-up girl of World War II. Press photographers wanted shots of this first film star to enlist in the Army and Jack insisted on posing with Tommy and me. We became immediate celebrities among the fruit pickers, cab drivers, real estate salesmen, undertakers, carpenters and dairymen who were our fellow recruits.

We were sent to Monterey that afternoon for processing at the Presidio, where newsreel cameras covered Jack's metamorphosis from civilian to soldier. From Monterey we were shipped back down to Camp Roberts for our 13 weeks of infantry basic training. Every day, I wrote to Doris and was the envy of every literate man in the company because I got at least one letter from her every day.

After being shuttled from Hollywood to Monterey to Roberts, one of her letters began, "*Romeo, o Romeo, at what fort art thou?*"

Coogan's celebrity resulted in an invitation to a party at the quarters of our Battalion Commander, thoughtful Col. William L. Tydings. Among the colonel's guests was a Paso Robles businessman who had the camp's lucrative laundry concession.

"I'm delighted to meet you, Private Coogan," the man said. "I've been a fan of yours since you were in silent movies."

Hal Kanter (left) and Tom D'Andrea at Camp Roberts, California, 1941.

Before Jack could say anything, D'Andrea stepped up and demanded, "Never mind him, pal — what happened to my socks?"

The long hours Uncle Sam demanded for hearty food and ill-fitting clothes were not to Coogan's liking, so he appealed to Col. Tydings for a better way of life. Jack volunteered his, Tom's and my services to entertain the troops with a company show. Tydings accepted with alacrity, thus ensuring exemption from extra duty for the three of us.

My khaki career as a writer, producer and performer began, as it did for D'Andrea. Our show was such a hit, the Battalion Morale Officer, Capt. Alex Ruth, wanted one every week, but we were nearing the end of our training period and Jack was particularly anxious to move on.

Coogan had not joined the Army to do what he'd been doing all his life — and for higher wages — so he volunteered for the glider corps. In time, soaring over the combat zones in the China-Burma-India theater, Jack covered himself with glory for distinguished service.

When we completed our basic training and I had qualified as a marksman with both the Browning Automatic Rifle and the new Garand, I feared assignment to some remote outpost to which others were already being

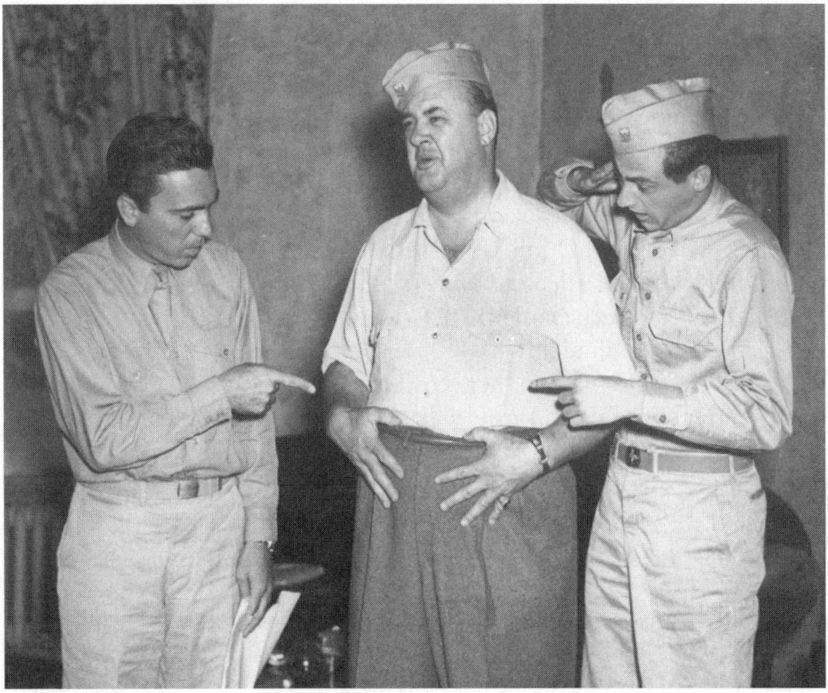

Tom D'Andrea (left) and Hal Kanter (right) call attention to civilian Don Wilson's waistline in Denver, 1942.

dispatched. But D'Andrea wangled a transfer for both of us, through one of his low friends in high places. From the Infantry to the Air Corps, we were assigned to the Public Relations office at Lowry Field, Colorado, where one of our first assignments was to produce a morale-raising show for the opening of the new post theater.

Our show was broadcast by radio station KLZ and featured Jack Benny's popular announcer Don Wilson, a native son who was visiting Denver. The music was volunteered by the band leader then appearing at Ellitch's Gardens, Ted Weems. He had two singers we would remember, a barber named Perry and a near-sighted blonde called Marvel. She later became known as Marilyn Maxwell in films and he is still known as Perry Como everywhere else.

Tommy and I worked hard on the script but we argued over one of his lines that I did not feel was funny. He said I was wrong. He argued that he was more experienced and the line would stay whether I liked it or not. I let him have his way; I have always disliked contention and Tommy was not only older he was given to inflicting physical inconvenience when sufficiently provoked. I have always disliked physical inconvenience even more than contention.

Our show was considered a success even by the wary GIs who populated the PR office and had kept us "Hollywood types" at arm's length. Our commanding officer had appeared on the show and wanted to hear how he sounded, so we were sent to his office to play the air check recording for him.

Col. Early E. W. Dunn was a formidable old aviator who was purported to have said he wanted officers around him "who can fly and fight all day, drink and fuck all night." Fortunately, I wasn't an officer because I never could drink all night.

The colonel listened to the recording and never smiled even when the audience responded philanthropically to our jokes. The moment came when Tommy read the line we had disputed. There was no laugh. Philanthropy had its limits. Tommy turned to me and said, "I told you that line should've been cut, asshole!"

If I were prepared to respond, the look the colonel shot at me kept me silent. And quite damp. I was shaken beyond Richter scale measurement.

After a restless night, I asked our immediate superior, Lt. Aubrey O. Cookman, to relieve me of my collaboration with D'Andrea and assign me to other chores. Cookman surprised me by immediately obliging. I began writing news stories for general release and also features, columns and editorials for the post newspaper *The Rev-Meter*, in addition to drawing a comic strip, *Pvt. Reginald Rookie.*

Tommy continued doing an occasional radio spot for the office but spent more time pursuing a local society girl of means, despite his contention that the last time he had seen a face like hers, "it was stuck in a bag of oats."

She was one of two sisters we had met in town. "The older one's bowlegged and the younger one's knock-kneed," Tommy described them. "When they stand side by side, they spell ox."

Nevertheless, Tom urged me to encourage the younger one. She was tall, skinny and usually smelled of Vick's VapoRub. The sisters invited us to spend a weekend at their luxurious sheep ranch in Chama, New Mexico. There was money in that family and the girls were vulnerable. But I was not interested. I was in love with my gorgeous Yankee, Doris Prouder.

D'Andrea married the older sister. He remained in the barracks at Lowry, however, and when he was eligible to leave the pre–Pearl Harbor service because he was over 28, he refused unless his bride's wealthy father establish him in business. Tom wanted to own a nightclub but his cagey father-in-law was not interested in furthering Tommy's career.

His bride filed suit for divorce and Tommy escaped Denver by getting his high-placed friend to intervene again and he was transferred to Santa Ana, California. Eventually he appeared in *This Is the Army*, signed a contract with Warner Bros., became an actor, remarried and enjoyed success in television until he sank out of sight in the '70s.

Over the Labor Day weekend in 1941, I had a three day pass. I spent them with Army pals fishing in Wyoming and returned to Lowry to learn that Doris had arrived that morning from New York and was at the Shirley-Savoy hotel in downtown Denver.

I rushed into town, where the dark-haired beauty had come, she said, to tell me to stop writing letters to her every day, that our romance was over.

So we got married.

Two wars were about to begin. Doris and I have managed to keep ours going merrily long after the other hostilities ceased.

"I often quote myself. It adds spice to my conversation."— George Bernard Shaw

7. *Spice to My Conversation*

Doris had a round trip ticket which suggested to me that her intention was to return to her job in New York. She entrained for home to face both our families and several gentlemen, all of whom were as disappointed as our families in the news of our wedding.

One of her suitors, a lawyer, wired her, "Colorado marriages are not recognized in the state of New York."

The new bride sat in the railroad coach, sobbing over what she had done on impulse, alternately weeping, sniffling and blowing her nose between sobs. A gentleman behind her leaned forward to ask, "Is something wrong, miss? Can I help you?"

Any man would want to help the dark-haired, fair-skinned young beauty. Doris began to blurt out her remorse and anxieties. The gallant stranger took an empty seat beside her and listened sympathetically, consoling her with clucking sounds and paternal pats on her hand.

"We've been writing letters," she moaned, "and that's the extent of our relationship."

"He must write a hell of a letter," the man said. "What's he do in civilian life?"

"He's a writer," Doris sniffled.

"I know lots of writers," he said. "I write myself. What's his name?"

She told him.

"My God!" the man gasped. "You're Doris, the girl Hal always talks about!"

"But I really don't know him," she wept.

"Hal Kanter," he said soothingly. "You'll *love* him!"

The solicitous stranger was a struggling entrepreneur named Irwin Allen. He was to discover profit in disaster as the Academy Award–winning producer who gave audiences such movie adventures as *The Poseidon Adventure* and *The Towering Inferno.*

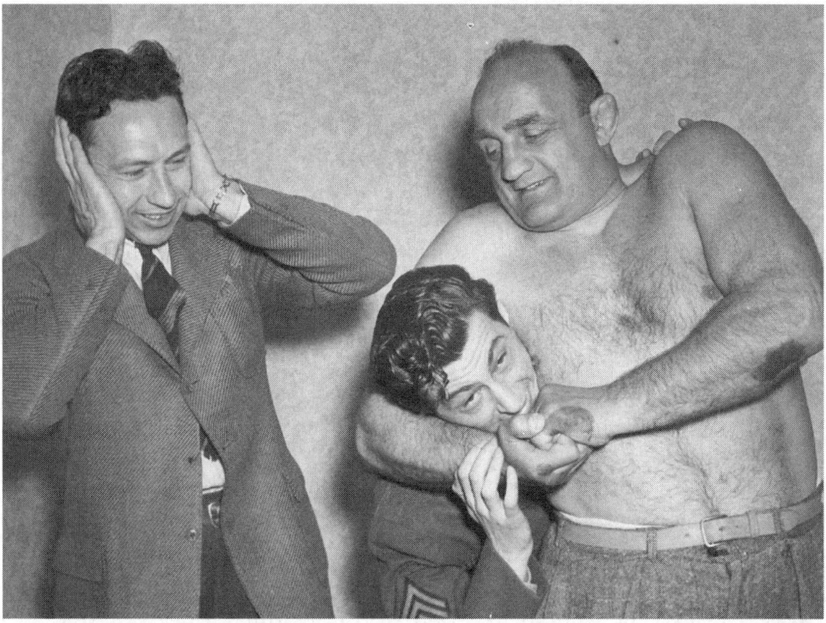

Wrestler/promoter Johnny Atkins is amused by the headlock wrestling legend Vladek Zybysko has on Sgt. Kanter, circa 1942, Denver, Colorado.

His kindness to Doris at that time I was to recall years later at a bachelor dinner for Irwin before his marriage. It provoked from Fred MacMurray the wistful comment, "Gee, I never suspected Irwin could be such a nice guy."

While Doris was in New York deciding to resign from her job and move West to begin life as a married woman, my radio work led me to public speaking. I would appear anywhere for anyone who could get me a pass from Lowry and pay me for talking. As a married man, I felt obliged to augment my Army wage beyond the few extra dollars I picked up as the Denver correspondent for the trade papers *Variety* and *Radio Daily*.

The energy at my disposal at that time astonishes me today. In addition to the several stories a week I turned out for the Army's PR office, I did Army-slanted pieces for the *Denver Post* and the *Rocky Mountain News*, wrote others for the *Rev-Meter*, continued my comic strip, wrote a humor column, ad-libbed a disc jockey show on KMYR, wrote, directed and appeared in 45 weekly dramas broadcast via KOA as *The Lowry Field Theater of the Air*, hosted a half-hour weekly game show called *Canteen Quiz* and did an anonymous book review show as *The Bookworm* every Sunday morning for KOA.

When Doris returned from New York, having resigned from her *Parents Magazine* job, I had only another six months to serve in the Army—so we thought—and she found part time work typing a manuscript for Mari Sandoz, a novelist I had interviewed on the book show. Mari was finishing her acclaimed *Crazy Horse*, that definitive history of the Oglala Sioux.

We became good friends. Doris asked Mari to read a short story I'd written. Mari suggested I submit it to a *Story Magazine* competition for servicemen. It came in second. First prize was won by a soldier named Norman Mailer.

Mari was an encouraging supporter of Doris' and my work through the years until her death. We treasure the autographed copies of her books in which she drew little sketches for us.

A friend from New York was stationed at nearby Buckley Field. Willie Bauer was smooth-talking, witty, forceful and, despite the wiseguy patina of Broadway, a compassionate and tender companion. Doris and I introduced him to a warm and generous divorcee we had come to know well, Helen Kleinberg. Willie and I took our ladies to dinner one evening at Denver's vaunted Navarre restaurant. We were in uniform, the girls in sweet dresses. The four of us stood in line behind the velvet rope and watched in growing annoyance as the *maitre d'* ushered in one party after another, never asking either soldier how many there were in ours.

Willie, who had managed the Pic-a-Rib on New York's jazz-famed 52nd Street, became quietly irate. Taking Helen's arm, he beckoned us to follow as he unhooked the rope and walked to an available booth. The *maitre d'* rushed over, bristling with territorial imperative and unctuously snarled, "How can I help you, soldier?"

"Buy war bonds!" Willie snapped at him.

We had a nice meal. A few weeks later, we served as best man and matron of honor when Helen married Willie.

I had moved up the organizational table to sergeant when Lowry Field got a new commanding officer, Col. Harvey Burwell. A bulldog-faced, two-fisted drinker with little patience for administration, he took a liking to me. I wrote his public speeches and his weekly message to the troops for the *Rev-Meter*, and told him bawdy jokes he could repeat at the Officers Club.

Burwell had "Hollywood connections"; after World War I, he and Cecil B. De Mille established a flying company. When it failed, Burwell returned to the Air Corps and De Mille continued making films, but they remained friends.

De Mille arranged for a new draftee to serve under Burwell at Lowry. He was the actor John Carroll. MGM had groomed him to replace Clark Gable, but nobody ever did.

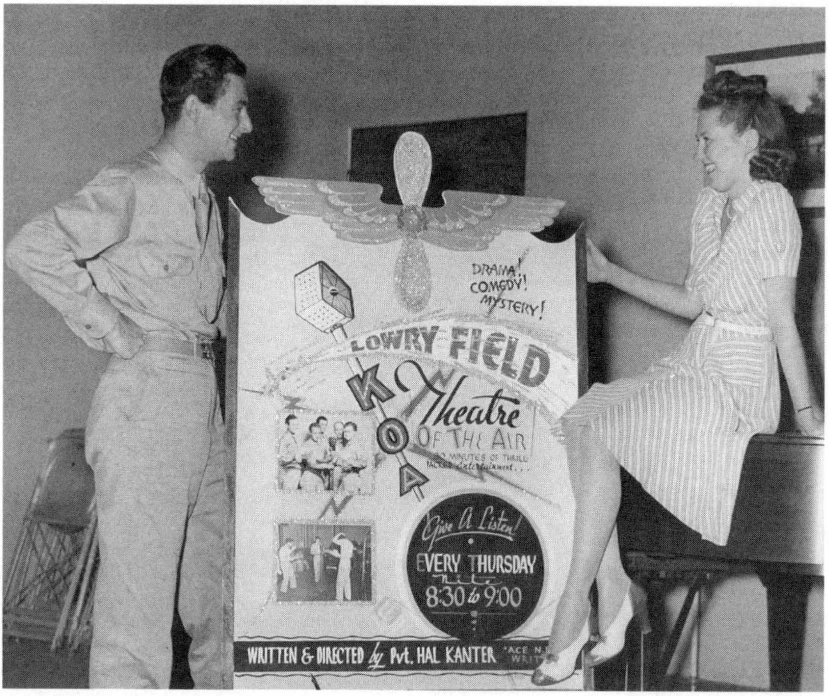

Kanter and an unidentified woman with the poster for *Theatre of the Air*, a radio program Kanter wrote and directed.

The big, blustering Cajun arrived as a buck private in Denver. He spent more time at the Brown Palace Hotel than he did on the post. Burwell was his pal. He assigned Carroll to me, promoted me to staff sergeant and charged us with producing a documentary film about the aerial photography school at Lowry Field.

Our cinematographer was Major Guy Newhard, a special effects cameraman in civilian life who had worked on the original *King Kong*. He assembled a crew of professionals now in uniform and we went to work. In several weeks, we wasted a lot of taxpayers' money, due to the excesses of our director, Pvt. Carroll. It was an omen of the money studios would squander on pictures he starred in after the war. Those films were all released. Ours never was.

Newhard and I did make one short film that was exhibited. It was in answer to a request to Col. Burwell from Denver's Harry Zinn, a politically active, civic-minded gentleman who asked that we figure some way to help the city's War Chest Drive.

Burwell agreed to that, but insisted that his adjutant, Col. Charles

Private John Carroll , Major Guy Newhard, Staff Sergeant Hal Kanter circa 1942 at Lowry Field, Colorado.

Pearcy, also appear and, to engage the attention of enlisted personnel, I represent them in the film. I was happy to. Khaki can't hide ham.

We flew to California in a bomber and, somewhere between Denver and Burbank, Col. Pearcy stepped from the cockpit to the cabin. I became alarmed. Pearcy was the pilot and the co-pilot was already sitting with us!

The dapper colonel smoothed his mustache, smiled and opened a sandwich. I looked at Col. Burwell, who read the stress in my face.

"We're on automatic," he said. I relaxed. But only for a moment. He then ordered me to go forward and take the controls. I broke into a sweat, one of my least favorite endemic reactions when panicked. I had — and still have — less knowledge of operating any aircraft than I have of Norwegian adverbs.

Burwell followed me into the cockpit and gave me some simple instructions, then settled in the co-pilot's chair as I took the wheel. I actually flew the plane with a sense of power I had never experienced, overcome only by terror, until the sweat slicked my hands too much to hold the wheel.

Taking over, Burwell said, "If anyone asks what you did in the service, son, you can now honestly tell them that you were a bomber pilot."

Mr. De Mille's friendly arm around my shoulder was as sincere as an undertaker's "get well" card. Left to right: S/Sgt. Kanter, C. B. De Mille, Gen. Harvey Burwell, Col. Charles Pearcy.

Fifty years later, I'm no longer surprised how many people never ask me.

After our arrival in Hollywood, while Burwell and Pearcy were sequestered with Mr. De Mille in his office at Paramount Studios, I waited in the reception room and struck up a conversation with a ruddy-faced, pudgy gentleman named Dr. Wassell, a hero I'd never heard of then. I thought he might be De Mille's dentist.

When I was summoned into the presence of the Great Epic Maker, I found his huge office cluttered with drawings of Gary Cooper in various costumes. De Mille was preparing his next picture, *The Story of Dr. Wassell.*

"The gentleman I met outside?" I asked. "He doesn't look anything like Gary Cooper."

"When my film is made," De Mille assured me patronizingly, "Coop's exactly who he'll look like to the world."

We got down to business. De Mille had gone over the script I'd written in Denver. He approved all of it except one line, "Children in Greece are crying for food." That annoyed him. He called in three men, two screenwriters and a publicist, and read the offensive line to them. There was spirited discussion. My senior officers and I listened in silence. Was this how Hollywood made movies? Ten minutes of debate over one phrase?

"It sounds like the slogan for Fletcher's Castoria," De Mille argued. "'Children cry for it.'"

His employees agreed, of course.

I suggested that children weren't crying, they were begging, and we adjourned until the following day's filming on a stage at Major Newhard's old studio, RKO. It was a short walk from the De Mille gate, abutting the Paramount lot. Today it is part of Paramount, the De Mille gate gone. *Sic transit gloria movie.*

Newhard had lights, camera and a small set prepared when we filed onto the stage. De Mille was first, as always, followed by my two officers and De Mille's staff. I brought up the rear. As De Mille passed, a stagehand removed his hat in deference. It was a gesture that impressed me and a moment I never forgot.

Several years later, when I directed my first feature on that same RKO lot, one of De Mille's old assistants, Eddie Salvin, was assigned to me. He was a large, boisterous, skillful assistant director who showed his deference to his former boss in a more amusing way. When I was ready to go for a take in a scene involving as few as five extras, Eddie would invariably tickle me by shouting instructions he claimed to have used on several De Mille extravaganzas: "This will be picture, so adjust your togas, light the torches on the wall and back, you Christian dogs, or we'll burn your Holy Man!"

Our War Chest Drive film turned out well, thanks to the commanding presence of De Mille. Burwell was promoted to Brigadier General and, before being transferred to another command, he called me to his office to thank me for all I had done. He offered to send me to Officers Candidate School but I demurred as tactfully as I could. I had only a few more weeks of duty before discharge from the service. I had had offers of civilian employment in both Denver and New York and, even more exciting to me, an offer from Mr. De Mille to contact him when I became a civilian. As an officer, I feared, I might be obliged to remain in the service for another few years.

The day Roosevelt promised "would live in infamy" arrived and the events of that December 7 extended my tour of duty beyond my desire.

"When I was younger, I could remember anything—whether it happened or not."
—Mark Twain

8. Whether It Happened or Not

World War II happened.

It took the fun out of Army life.

When I was assigned to the 80th Training Battalion in Camp Roberts, California, we were lined up in descending order of height for assignment to bunks. I was the fourth tallest in our barracks so I slept within sniffing distance of a towering merchant seaman who argued that he was more valuable at sea and vowed to get out of the Army in a month.

"How?" a San Francisco fireman asked.

"I'll piss my way out!"

Every night, the tall salt wet his bed. Our barracks began to smell like a kennel until he was transferred to the camp hospital where he continued his urinary campaign. Within the month, the Army did release him.

The memory of that soggy sailor would visit me years later, during a discussion in Hollywood with Prince Michael Romanoff, about our mutual first attempts to invade California.

Mine began when I was 15, thumbing rides, and got stranded in Tonganoxie, Kansas, where I found work in a roadside motor court-service station-cum-cafe. I started by drawing murals on the cafe walls and stayed on for three months as an apprentice handyman known to my boss as "Thumbs."

It was there I lost my virginity. While the boss was cheating with his waitress in one cabin, his wife came into theirs, where I was babysitting their two-year-old son. Angry at her husband, she got even by indoctrinating me in the mystery of the vulva, which, to my delight, was not a Swedish car.

When those steamy sessions threatened to become dangerous, I moved on. I got as far west as Albuquerque, where I was arrested on a charge of vagrancy. I spent the night in a holding tank full of menacing drunks until my parents wired me bus fare they could ill afford at the time. I was warned by a judge never to return to the city. It took me 50 years to get up the nerve to disobey him.

My friend, His Royal Self-Appointed Highness, Prince Michael, had more nerve than I.

The ingenious little crew-cut impostor of irascible charm and courtly deportment who could scathe a prime minister with a glance or create a Mardi Gras with a smile, befriended me at 20th Century–Fox, where the impish gentleman drew a salary from the ruling Zanucks in exchange for his civilized presence at the studio.

Exchanging confidences one afternoon in my office, I told Mike my adolescent experience. Hitchhiking in New Mexico, I was picked up by a well-dressed young man who learned that I was "an artist." He took me to the home of a white-bearded, robust old man who lived in Albuquerque with five hound dogs, three young people of indeterminate sex and a printing press. He was the editor of a local "labor paper." In exchange for room and board, I drew several editorial cartoons he demanded. I was as politically naive as the old man's hounds.

One day, the police took the old man away, the young people fled and I was hauled off to jail. The next day I faced the abrupt and menacing judge, who ordered me out of Albuquerque.

Romanoff enjoyed the account enormously and, with a wicked smile, suggested that I now return as he had done, for he, too, had been apprehended on the same charges in the same city where he was banished under the name of Harry Gerguson, not Prince Michael.

"Many years later," he said, "I was driven across country in the company of a lady of quality, a guest in my Rolls-Royce. When we arrived and the lady was suitably registered in a hotel, my man drove me to the local airport where I engaged the services of a pilot and small craft. High above the wretched place, I ordered the pilot to cut the motor and as we stalled aloft, I urinated outside.

"I returned to the hotel, rang the mayor's office and introduced myself to his secretary. His Honor immediately came on the line to welcome me and I said, 'Sir, I have returned to do to your community what your scabrous courts once did to me. I have just pissed on Albuquerque!'"

At Camp Roberts, the third tallest man after the soggy sailor who peed his way out of the Army, was my immediate neighbor, a bulldozer operator from Firebaugh, California, named Willie G. Eppler. Originally from the Ozark country, Willie was a country boy given to such thoughtful analysis as "Don't believe this shit they're tellin' us that this's a peace-time Army. I'll gar-and-tee you that before we get out, we'll be in a shootin' war!"

"Really, Willie? Who do you think we'll be fighting?"

Willie thought before he replied, "I can't say right off, but this is for sure — it'll be one of them God-damn foreign countries!"

While rough-housing in the barracks, Willie and some other country boys angrily accused each other of being hog-polers. I asked what a hog-poler was. Willie was astonished. To his antagonists, he yelled, "Hey! Jew don't know what a hog-poler is!"

"Hogs love acorns," a boy named Earl was eager to explain. "When a hog has et up all the acorns on the ground, the hog-poler takes a long pole, shoves it up the hog's ass and holds him up so's he kin eat the acorns off'n the tree."

"Hot damn!" I said. "That explains why your armpits are full of hog shit!"

The others hooted with admiration. From then on, they remembered my name was Hal, not Jew.

Small victory, large solace. But when we were called into the company clerk's office to state our religious preference, I said, "Jewish." The puzzled clerk frowned as he thought for a long beat before he asked, "Is that Catholic or Protestant?"

"Put down H," I told him, "for Hebrew."

"Oh," he said, then muttered, "all you Hebes are alike. You think nobody else can spell."

"That's not true," I said. "A lot of you who had Jewish teachers can spell very well."

Those incidents stayed in the back of my mind. They were joined by another, shortly after war was declared. I was doing *Canteen Quiz* at Lowry Field, broadcasting to the entire Rocky Mountain region. A contestant asked me on the air, "Did you hear about the Jew who volunteered?" and when I cautiously said, "No," he said, "Nobody else did, either."

I was too stunned by the laugh it got from the audience to think of a retort. Then I was angry at myself for allowing the remark to go unchallenged.

With Willie G.'s prediction that we'd be in a shooting war come true, I grew more and more ashamed that I was safely far behind the lines of fire while so many of my fellow Jews were in the battle. My brother Bill was preparing to ship overseas as a second lieutenant. Cousins Irvin and Leo were in the Navy, Leo on a destroyer in the Pacific and Irvin doing his lethal work as a cook in the Atlantic.

This was at a time when my father had borrowed some money to realize his dream of publishing a contemporary form of the classic literature he had devoured as a youngster. His idea was to illustrate the books in public domain and put them out as *Classic Comics*. Later, he changed the name to *Classics Illustrated* and, in time, Dad's books became known throughout the world. They were translated into many languages and are today treasured collectors' items.

Postal regulations required that the books — sold as magazines — contain a percentage of prose, so I wrote several articles for Dad under the nom de plume of Hal Kane.

As a soldier in Colorado, I wanted to become more involved in the war effort and asked to be sent overseas. I was transferred immediately. To downtown Denver. In the headquarters of Major General John Curry, I was put in charge of publicizing the area's recruiting for the Women's Auxiliary Army Corps.

It was there I met a soldier who became a lifelong friend. He was a dark-bearded, heavyset dynamo from New Jersey, Irving B. Kahn. He was named for his successful uncle, Irving Berlin, and before the war he was employed by 20th Century–Fox in New York.

Kahn was assigned to help organize the campaign to recruit WACs and one of his first ideas was to get every radio star to record a pitch for us. The glib corporal convinced our general to fly us to Hollywood, where he talked us into the NBC studios on Vine Street and an office for me to write while he prowled the halls, ambushing stars to read what I wrote.

The first was easy: Bob Hope. I had met Bob in Denver and gave him some lines about Lowry Field, so he remembered me and was happy to record for us. Bob also got Jerry Colonna and his announcer, Bill Goodwin, to do the other spots I quickly provided.

Bing Crosby, Bob Burns, Red Skelton, Louella Parsons and Dinah Shore were among others who took the time to read copy I was tailoring for them. While some of them edited their copy, only Bing rewrote a few lines, which made me sound better.

With a stack of recordings, Kahn and I returned triumphantly to Denver, where we began putting together a troupe of G.I. professional entertainers for a show we called *The WACaravan*, to tour the Rocky Mountain region. The company consisted of singers, dancers, jugglers, comedian Lew Slavin (known professionally as Lew Black) and a young ventriloquist named Richard Cohen whose dialect dummy, Velvel, later brought him fame as Ricky Lane.

The company commander was Lt. Harold T. Hastings, a handsome bomber pilot who had completed enough missions over Germany to be sent back for rest and recreation. "Ace" Hastings got little of it shepherding that group of show folk who attracted hordes of women wherever they played.

Spencer Tracy came to Denver on a war bond tour. Kahn convinced him to do a radio show for us. The only catch was that I had to write it and the great movie star had to approve it. I had less than one day to come up with a 15-minute script.

Tracy was sequestered from his public in a suite at the Brown Palace Hotel, where Irving and I were admitted to present my script. The star was accompanied by a press agent from MGM whose primary job seemed to be keeping Tracy's glass replenished with amber liquid.

Within the hour, we were calling him Spence and Spence was calling us names. But he did approve the script and we agreed to meet at nine the next morning to rehearse the show, which was to air that night. By the time we got back to our post, 15 minutes away, there was a message for Kahn. The MGM press agent insisted he return to the Brown Palace.

Tracy had abruptly decided he didn't want to do the show. He hated the script.

Both Tracy and the press agent, Irving told me, were too drunk to listen to reason. He said we should show up at the hotel tomorrow anyway and see if we could change Tracy's mind. I said that I'd rewrite the script and present a new, shorter version to him in the morning.

Which I did. I cut out a part I had written for myself. I stayed away from the hotel until Irving called me to come to rehearsal. When I arrived, Tracy was suffering a hangover but was willing to read the lines.

He greeted me with congratulations on the rewrite but thought I should put myself back into the scene I had cut. I thought not and Irving agreed. He had become the producer.

Dress rehearsal at the Denver Civic auditorium was a shambles. Tracy, who had been drinking all day, could hardly stand. He asked what happened to the first script, which he decided he wanted to do. Irving and the press agent got him into a dressing room to try and sober him up with hot coffee while I attempted to get mimeograph copies of the first script made.

At show time, with a packed house out front, Tracy was introduced to an eager audience who never suspected he had been imbibing. He picked up the script Irving handed him in the wings, acknowledged the applause and, on cue, read the words of the second script. He got a standing ovation.

When he came off stage, I was in the wings to congratulate him. He didn't recognize me.

"Yes," Katharine Hepburn told me long after his death, "Spencer could be a trial."

Irving B. Kahn was sent to Officers Training School and I was sent overseas via the Armed Forces Radio Service.

"Everybody knows it's raining but he knows it better." — Jerry Hausner

9. *Everybody Knows It's Raining*

One of the most amusing and interesting mammals I ever knew, actor/writer/artist/photographer/cynic Jerry Hausner, was the first soldier I met when I reported for duty at the Hollywood headquarters of Armed Forces Radio Service in 1944.

The AFRS was then located on Western Avenue, in the home of the original Fox Studios, and was perhaps the most loosely run military unit of World War II. If all our armed forces were made up of servicemen as ill-prepared for combat as the men of "Fort Fox," our national Thanksgiving dinners today would be sushi and sauerbraten.

The commanding officer of that disrespectful company was personable Lt. Col. Tom Lewis, an experienced radio executive whose famous wife was Loretta Young, a radiant film star with a deceptively delicate demeanor who could give orders on her set as well as any officer in combat. Her glamorous contemporary Marlene Dietrich called her *Miss Dove Shit*.

Few of the colonel's enlisted men had any basic Army training. Upon induction, they were grabbed by Col. Lewis and immediately began writing and producing radio shows for a salary that would not keep most of them in cigarettes and aspirin.

Pvt. Al Lewis, a comedy writer, had so little time to adjust to Army life, he said he needed a three-hour pass to go up and down Sunset Boulevard and practice saluting.

"I saluted every uniform I saw," he said. "Army, Navy, Marines, policemen. I even saluted a streetcar conductor. He didn't salute back but he gave me a transfer to a second lieutenant."

Cpl. Bill Danch and I were assigned to write a comedy spot for Fibber McGee and Molly. (Bill worked on their program before entering the service.) A native of Hammond, Indiana, Bill had recently married the beautiful, laughing Margene and brought her to Hollywood for their honeymoon.

In a supper club where John Barrymore was dining with friends, the young bride was thrilled to see the great star at such close range but blushed at his clearly audible colorful vocabulary. Attempting to protect Margene's delicate ears, Bill slipped their waiter a dollar and asked him to request Barrymore either censor his talk or lower his voice.

When the waiter whispered something to the actor, the famous profile turned and the waiter indicated Danch. Barrymore rose, tottered over to their table, leered at Margene, then snarled to Bill, "What seems to be your trouble, horse cock?"

Bill said Margene enjoyed the evening a lot more than he did. He regretted he tipped the waiter a dollar. A quarter would have sufficed.

There were no barracks at Armed Forces Radio. We were all on separate rations. Bill and Margene had a small house off Sunset. Their neighbor was Humphrey Bogart. He drove Bill to Western Avenue every morning. I walked there from my hotel room.

Bill said it was a shame that I was going overseas; we could make some good money as a team if I could stay in Hollywood.

"How?" I asked. He grinned. Didn't I know that every writer on the post was moonlighting for civilian shows? There were precious few comedy writers who escaped the draft and their services were at a premium. Many of those G.I. writers were being paid more under the table than they had earned over it.

A high wire fence surrounded an empty lot where we did calisthenics now and then — when Capt. Vic Pettito was in the mood — and where groups of men sometimes policed the area. One day, a group was picking up cigarette butts and pop bottles when an agent tried to hire a writer for the Cass Daley comedy program. He managed to engage Al Lewis' attention. Al listened to his impassioned plea for help, which ended with the offer, "And you can pick up an easy, unreported 600 bucks a week!"

"What?" Al asked indignantly as he bent to pick up a candy wrapper, "and give up all this?"

Sgt. Jerry Hausner shared several duties, among which was acting, announcing, and some writing; he was also official photographer. Jerry's camera art was a hobby he had perfected to rival the best. One day he was shooting stills of the cast of *Command Performance*, our most prestigious hour, in which the dignified Greer Garson figured. She wore a dress with properly demure decolletage, and as she put her arms around her co-stars for Jerry's camera, the impertinent soldier looked up from his finder and called, "Greer, baby — bend over more! This is for the boys overseas and they miss their mothers!"

As a civilian, Jerry was one of radio's most versatile performers; he would do as many as four or five shows in a day. One of his weekly roles was as the newsboy who opened each episode of a newspaper drama in which Edward G. Robinson played a crusading editor.

Robinson, theater-trained and film-oriented, worked hard at his radio rehearsals. Jerry often skipped rehearsals when he had a conflict on his schedule. He would race in at the last minute to read his lines flawlessly. Robinson was infuriated by Jerry's nonchalance.

During a summer hiatus, Jerry — who studied art in Paris on the G.I. Bill and was a fair hand with a paint brush — was visiting the New York Metropolitan Museum of Art with his wife Velma. They encountered art patron and collector Robinson, who snarled, "What are you doing here?"

"We are enjoying the great masters," Jerry said, "unlike you, who is shopping!"

That active, energetic scholar insisted that his mission in life was "to spread a little hatred wherever I go."

With respect for his judgment and vast theatrical background, I once suggested he become a director.

"Are you kidding?" he protested in alarm. "A director has to read the *whole* script!"

Jerry did serve as a casting director for the animated cartoon house that gave the world the nearsighted *Mr. Magoo* series. It was Jerry who cast Jim Backus, his childhood friend from Cleveland, as the voice of Magoo. Jerry himself did Magoo's nephew as well as many other voices.

There was no more stimulating person to spend time with than Jerry Hausner, a friend I treasured for half a century. Another amusing friend I met the same day I met Jerry was the soldier named George Rosenberg, who was to play a larger role in my life.

It started with my first encounter with that suave pixie, Prince Mike Romanoff. Rosenberg, one of the original investors in Romanoff's first watering hole, drove me from Western Avenue to Beverly Hills for lunch. Entering the swank establishment, I was goggle-eyed to see Irene Dunne, Cary Grant, Orson Welles and other familiar faces at various tables — and even more impressed when they all greeted Pvt. Rosenberg with affection.

I knew very little about Rosie other than that his job at AFRS was booking talent for the many radio shows the unit produced. He, Lester Linsk and Barron Polan were the three soldiers who apparently had access to everyone in show business. All had been agents before being drafted. Barron once asked me if my postwar plans included representation, implying he would be interested in signing me to his old office. I assumed Rosie had invited me to lunch with the same idea in his mind.

If he did, he never mentioned it. Rosie just wanted to have lunch and show me how he lived. That was the Rosenberg style.

I offered to pay my share of the bill when it was presented, but Rosie wouldn't accept it. He signed the tab, dropped some cash on the waiter's tray and waved him away. It was then that His Highness glided to our table, where Rosie introduced me. Romanoff shook my hand firmly and said, "Despite the company you are in, I trust you have been treated with common civility?"

Much later I learned that as long as Rosie was in uniform, he was never obliged to pay any of the tabs he signed in his friend's elegant emporium.

It was no surprise to me to learn that George and Barron left their respective employers after the war and formed their own agency. Polan and Rosenberg employed one secretary — Dorothy River, a compassionate woman with the world's sexiest telephone voice — who served them for the rest of Rosie's life. They began the firm of Polan and Rosenberg by representing writers exclusively and I became their first client.

But before that happened, I had to spend 18 months in the Pacific, following those several months of training on Western Avenue and in Camp Irwin, California's desert outpost where Gen. Patton had trained his tank corps for the invasion of Africa.

While I was being prepared for overseas duty, Doris returned from Denver to New York for a position at the Book of the Month Club. Our romance resumed by mail.

When training was complete at Camp Irwin, I was granted a furlough before being shipped to an unknown destination. I went east with farewells to bid my folks and to bed my wife.

Our daughter Lisa was born nine months later.

When I got the news on Guam, Lisa was five days old. Don't think I didn't count the months I'd been away.

According to a notebook I've kept, a truckload of broadcasters in khaki, 22 enlisted men and three young officers left AFRS's newly relocated headquarters on Santa Monica Boulevard in Hollywood at 1930 hours the afternoon of May 20, 1944. Col. Lewis congratulated us and gave his blessing. We were the first group to be sent overseas from AFRS headquarters.

We rumbled through Los Angeles to the Union Station and were herded onto a troop train. It is not the most elegant way to travel. We suffered the inelegance until 0630 the morning of May 23 when we arrived in Seattle, where another G.I. truck bounded us to Fort Lawton. As the ranking noncommissioned officer, I was appointed NCO in charge. We enlisted men were assigned to one barracks, our officers to another.

Lt. Garnett Marks, Pfc. Reuben Reich, Sgt. Russell Beggs, Lt. Sam Roley, T/Sgt. Hal Kanter at Station SSCY, Camp Young, California, February 1944.

We spent an intense period of processing at Lawton and in such secrecy we had no idea where we'd be shipped. We were also back in the real Army, not the country clubbish AFRS of Hollywood; rousted from our bunks at dawn, we engaged in rigorous calisthenics, sweated out chow lines in a steamy mess hall, drilled, went through gas mask exercises in chemical warfare chambers, fired rifles, sat through hours of orientation lectures, took "abandon ship" drills and more physicals, received shots, were issued clothing one day that would be recalled the next and other outfits issued.

"Is the Army trying to keep us guessing," Sgt. Russell Beggs, a pale, sad-eyed Detroit broadcaster who resembled a peach with glasses, asked, "or is the Army itself guessing?"

My guess was that *they* guessed. That's why it's called an Army.

Compiling data for our Personal Affairs reports, I felt the seriousness of our impending journey when I had to list each man's next-of-kin. Had I accepted Gen. Burwell's offer, I thought I might now be a shavetail with a snug Stateside job instead of facing the unknown from which my next-of-kin might soon get a tragic telegram.

On the historic day of June 6, 1944, under cover of darkness, hundreds of G.I.s were rudely roused from deep sleep and swiftly loaded into long lines of government trucks. We sensed this was no rehearsal. It was the real thing; our mail had been censored for several days.

Ignitions exploded into action and our convoy snaked out of the post and through the silent, dark streets of Seattle toward the waiting troop ships. We sat huddled among our gear in those harsh trucks, each with his hidden fears that were compounded by the secrecy of our departure and the news of allied losses in the war we were heading into as participants.

The convoy turned onto the streets of downtown Seattle where we suddenly found crowds of early morning and late shift workers lining the sidewalks, waving, applauding and shouting at us: "Go get 'em, Yanks! Get the Japs!"

We sensed then that we were not going to Sicily.

"If I'm not drowning, why is my life flashing before my eyes, and if I am drowning, why aren't I wet?"—Carleton Alsop

10. *Why Aren't I Wet?*

As the sky turned from licorice stick black to gumdrop gray and the chilling wind swept in from Puget Sound to drop our body temperature as low as our spirits, Seattle Red Cross volunteers served a steaming brown liquid to thousands of shivering G.I.s at dockside that grim morning of June 7. The gracious ladies called it coffee. It tasted like stained bilge water that could shine a brass buckle.

"Kee-rist!" Sgt. H. Ashley Simms groaned as he spat his out. "What violence they've done to a defenseless bean." Simms was an epicurean gourmet who carried bottles of exotic sauces in his barracks bag.

As the sun broke through, we labored up the gangplank to our cramped quarters below decks where we stowed our gear and abandoned comfort.

Among the rules laid down by the commanding officer of our crowded bucket was one loudly blasted over the public address system: "Now hear this! There will be absolutely no gambling on this vessel for the duration of its voyage!"

A groan went up. We were then summoned topside for the ship's chaplain to hand each man a ditty bag that contained a comb, a toothbrush, a Bible and a deck of playing cards. A marathon poker game began immediately.

Shortly after we were at sea, the P.A. system crackled with another announcement. It was D-Day in Europe. Across the world that very morning, Allied forces had landed on Omaha Beach.

Some passengers cheered. Others shivered. The chaplain offered a prayer. As broadcasters, our group had written about the war, reported on it, bringing education and information about it to our troops around the world and making jokes about it. Now we were in it.

The destroyer escorts for our convoy took on a paternal, protective coloration as they zigged and zagged the long line of troop-laden *Liberty ships* across the desolate Pacific, as alert as every tense man on our deck for enemy submarines and aircraft. The ships followed in what seemed to be an endless conga.

We wore life jackets at all times during 11 miserable, sweltering days. We stood to eat, the food salted by Niagaras of sweat that ran down our chins and into our mess kits. We sweated out lines leading to the ship's store during the hour it was open each day, buying cigarettes for five cents a package and ten-cent "Air Force beer," so called because "you drink ten and you P-38."

To conserve water, we were allowed one brief shower every three days; we quickly became a gamey herd.

"Dante Alighieri," scholarly Russ Beggs surmised, "must've done his research on this boat."

Lying in the bowels of the ship one afternoon, Jim Fox said he heard a strange metallic *clank* inside the bulkhead every night.

"That's just a welder," I comforted him. "They build these tubs so fast, he's still in there finishing the hull."

The distant thunder of Navy guns brought us topside one morning. Fast. If light travels faster than sound, we came in second. Miles ahead of us, we saw the smoke of the destroyer's artillery and the shells strike before we heard the explosions. We were never told their targets. Everyone advanced his own theory; subs, Kamikazis, enemy gunboats, bombers, merely target practice.

"Those bastards!" Clarence Cato said. "They fired at a USO ship that was bringing us some relief pussy!"

Relief came on the sunlit morning we sailed serenely into the harbor of Paradise, which, at that point, could have been Death Valley. But we were in Hawaii.

At Oahu's Fort Shafter, we were reoriented by Lt. Col. True Boardman, who had arrived from AFRS in Hollywood earlier. Our group was divided into units to be dispersed through the Central Pacific to build American Expeditionary radio stations and provide I(nformation) & E(ducation), entertainment and some comfort to our land, air and sea forces at war with the Japanese.

Col. Boardman, a popular radio writer in civilian life, realized our own need for some recreation after the harrowing voyage he had avoided by flying to Hawaii. He arranged passes for us to explore Oahu, the storied island we'd been led by movies to believe was the languorous frontier of romance.

Oahu was Newark with tattoo parlors.

Waikiki was Far Rockaway, strewn with candy wrappers, beer bottles and condoms.

Downtown Honolulu was a brazen hussy of a city where the indigenous population seemed out to cadge, steal or con every serviceman out of very dollar he had — dollars which were called "invasion bucks" because they were overprinted with the word *Hawaii* against the day the Japanese might invade that island carnival.

In 1944, the Hawaiian gentry was secluded behind garden gates as the business area was given over to a non-stop orgy of drunken, leering American males and their multi-blooded Polynesian playmates.

True Boardman broke us into four-man units, each under a commanding superior, to be scattered to Makin, Palau, Tarawa, Kwajalein and Pelelu. I was assigned to the sixth, commanded by Lt. Jack Wormser. We were sent to a pile of coral that history would never forget: Eniwetok.

Jack was a handsome, soft-spoken, sensitive man who acknowledged even the most subtle humor with a giggle. He was quietly forceful, doggedly determined and had a strong sense of family. His enlisted men would follow him anywhere.

Among them was Byron Palmer, who would be Ray Bolger's co-star in *Where's Charley?* after the war. Byron had been a radio announcer before they could find a uniform to fit his skinny body. Thirty years later, in Century City, I thought I recognized the handsome, distinguished, gray-haired fellow during a theater intermission and approached him. "Excuse me," I said, "but aren't you Hal Kanter?" He broke into a toothpaste-ad smile and said, "No, but you are. I'm Byron Palmer."

He introduced me to his wife, who was not the same wife I had met at a reunion a year after we emerged from our khaki cocoons.

Another member of our crew was Sherman McFedries, a bald gentleman older than any of us who had volunteered to serve out of patriotic fervor. His peacetime position was an executive one with the Union Oil Company and he had a radio background as a sponsor's representative.

One evening as we sat on the bank of the lagoon, marvelling at the colors of the Pacific sunset, Mac mused, "Several hours ago, that sun was dipping over my beautiful garden in Pasadena, showering its golden rays on the roof that protects my beloved wife and precious daughter..."

I swallowed a lump of emotion.

"...and here I sit, on *Eni-fuckin'-wetok*!"

The fifth member of our team was a sandy-haired, lantern-jawed, whistling young engineer from the Midwest, Bill Lannan, on whom we depended for all mechanical and technical aspects of installing and operating the broadcast equipment, from the generator and transmitter to turntables and microphones. Lannan was indefatigable, inventive and so cheerful nothing seemed to irk him.

Eniwetok is a skimpy, desolate arc of coral. Navy guns had shot off the tops of every palm tree when we took the Japanese stronghold.

We arrived in a C47 called *My Devotion*, a cargo ship that was decorated with pictures of a nude Noel Toy, an Asian showgirl. Our pilot was a young man from Iowa and we marveled that he could find so tiny a speck of rock in that vast expanse of ocean. Eniwetok was so small, I announced, that when the tide came in, we all got submarine pay.

Our mission was to establish station WXLE, originally slated to be broadcast from a pyramidal tent until Jack Wormser convinced the SeaBees that we should have something more substantial than a plywood floor and canvas sides. The Navy's remarkable Construction Battalion poured a deck of concrete and built a snug Quonset hut for our use.

As the foundation was being laid at the edge of the lagoon, one of the cement workers asked me what kind of programs we'd broadcast. I told him that our schedule included everything from the cheerful *G.I. Jill* in the morning through all his favorite Stateside shows, news, music and variety programs we would originate ourselves, a late news wrap-up and a closing prayer. Something for everybody.

"How about jukebox records?" he asked hungrily. "You got some of them?" We had stacks of them and there would be more coming every two weeks from Hollywood.

"Reckon you could play my favorite?" he asked. "Roy Acuff singing 'The Great Speckled Bird'?"

I promised him that would be one of the very first we'd put on the air—and dedicate it to him.

"Hot damn!" he crowed. His eyes grew misty as he said, "If I could hear ol' Roy Acuff singing 'The Great Speckled Bird' just one more time, I wouldn't feel no fur from home than I been up in a balloon!"

I knew then why the Army, in its ultimate wisdom, had sent us overseas.

Before enough receivers arrived to accommodate all the personnel, SeaBees strung up loudspeakers so that our programs could be heard throughout the atoll. We had a captive audience. Only the few with their own sets had a choice: WXLE, Eniwetok—"On the road to Tokyo!" or the Japanese propagandist, Tokyo Rose. I was told that one evening, while the SeaBees were working in feverish secrecy to widen the airstrip on our atoll, Tokyo Rose said with a nasty laugh, "Confidentially, boys, your strip is showing."

I took the first available break in our program to say, "Don't look now, Rose, but your show is slipping." That remark was repeated often and not only by me.

In November 1945, *Collier's* magazine published an article called "The Plucking of the Rose" that extolled our endeavors. It was written by combat corespondent Sgt. Jack Sher and documented the efficacy of our operations in driving the Japanese propagandist off the air.

One of the programs Wormser suggested we try was an interview show with celebrities. What celebrities? Henry Fonda? Lt. Commander Fonda declined to appear. He had put his public image aside for the duration and wanted no mention of his presence in the Pacific. He was not there to rehearse for *Mister Roberts*.

Bob Hope came through with his troupe and he was more than cooperative. He and Jerry Colonna came to our hut for an interview and later posed for photographs with the horde drawn to our station by their voices.

With so few celebrities to interview, we had to fill evening time in other ways. I began a late show called *Sack Rat Serenade*. A sack rat was a man who spent a lot of time in his bunk. Late in the evening, everyone had retired. There was more night life on an Eskimo ice floe than on Eniwetok.

I played ballads, read poetry, spoke in a soft whisper of families back home, emphasized the importance of our crusade against the Axis, and waxed optimistically about the future and our individual potential for rebuilding it as free Americans.

If it was heavy-handed, it was also sincere. That quality, combined with the sweet voices of ballad singers Dinah Shore, Jo Stafford, Helen O'Connell, Doris Day and a host of others, made the program one of the most popular on our schedule. As Senior Sack Rat, I became an island celebrity and issued Sack Rat identification cards. A SeaBee artist made a woodcut logo and printed up thousands of them. I still have mine.

One day, an officer from a Navy hospital ship lying in the lagoon came ashore to thank me for *Sack Rat Serenade* and asked if there was anything he could do to show his patients' gratitude. I said if they had any fresh fruit, we'd appreciate it.

For three months, the only food our mess served had been powdered eggs, Vienna sausages and K-rations. I had become so skinny, I could have discarded my belt and tucked my pants between my ribs.

Two hours later, three swabbies came ashore with a gift from the crew of the ship: a crate of oranges, 20 pounds of red meat, tomatoes, onions and a gallon of ice cream. Never in my life before — or since — have I been so handsomely paid for a radio show. We gorged ourselves and enjoyed residuals by burping for the next 12 hours.

After working 18 hours a day, seven days a week since we went on the air, Jack insisted I take a furlough by visiting our sister station on Kwajalein. I could examine their operation as a comparison shopper while cutting up touches with my buddy Russ Beggs. An Army transport flew me over the next day and I found Kwaj to be a pleasant change of coral. It was warmer than Eniwetok, equally desolate, but the broadcasters did have a reefer — the Navy term for refrigerator — in which they managed to keep cold beer.

Beggs was the NCO in charge and had created a popular afternoon show called *Kwaj Lodge* which he supervised as Rock Happy Roger. Russ had pulled off a broadcasting coup by recording some questions to a new movie sex symbol, Lauren Bacall, sending the platter to Hollywood where Bacall recorded her answers. When it returned, Russ played the record and the station was besieged by tumescent servicemen who wanted a go at the lady.

Russ showed them the long-playing disc on which only her voice had come to the Pacific, then fled for his life into the lagoon.

He took time off after one *Kwaj Lodge* on which I appeared as the visiting Sack Rat to show me the enchanting sights of his island, a tour by Jeep that took up the better part of 15 minutes. Before going back to Eniwetok, I bought some authentic Japanese Army souvenirs which I later learned were all made by industrious Yanks on Kwajalein.

Flying back on another ATS aircraft, I met an absorbing civilian named Loomis Dean, of *Life* magazine, who had been the official photographer for Ringling Brothers. He regaled me with stories of circus life which had intrigued me since reading *Toby Tyler* as a child. But oh my! Toby never indulged in the grotesque sexual activity Loomis graphically described as commonplace under the small tops behind the Big Top!

A few years later, I sat in front row seats at the circus in Los Angeles with my wife. When the show began with its procession of elephants, I watched a pretty girl riding atop one of them (and wondered which of the beasts she was doing nasty things with) when Doris leaned far back and fanned herself with her program. The fragrance of elephants close by is overwhelming.

"Now I know how Sabu died," she whispered to me. "Holding his breath."

Over Eniwetok, as our plane circled to land, I looked down to see the most impressive panorama of military hegemony ever assembled; during my three day absence, Task Force 58 had rendezvoused in our lagoon. My heart soared at the exultant spectacle of carriers, battleships, destroyers, escorts, minesweepers and supply ships as far as the eye could report — the massed might of Allied sea power. How thrilling it was at that moment to be an American!

As our transport touched down on the widened landing strip, along which were fighter planes from the carriers and assorted other craft being readied for the impending assault, I was eager to get back to our microphone; I was a communicator, grateful to God and our taxpayers for the *audience* that had suddenly arrived!

That night, after we had signed off and retired, we were blasted out of our cots by the loudest explosion any of us had ever heard. Palmer screamed in alarm. McFedries crawled under his cot, whimpering.

Lannan stared at me, eyeball to eyeball, as both of us lay on the deck, and croaked, "Did you just shit in your drawers, or was it me?"

We both ran to the lagoon and plunged into the water while a series of bone-rattling, teeth-jarring, spine-freezing explosions continued from the flight lines, ablaze with fire.

Wormser appeared to coax us back on land and explain what happened: A cargo plane had fallen short on takeoff and touched off the first explosion which was spreading along the lines of armed aircraft. Jack wanted to make sure that we didn't attempt to go on the air and report what was happening lest it give comfort to the enemy that monitored our wavelength.

The atoll had sprung to life through the frequent bursts of bullets and bombs and fuel tanks exploding over the roars of tractors. Those intrepid SeaBees were plunging their huge Cats into the cauldrons of fire to shove the aircraft into the sea. I marveled at the physical courage they displayed, the dexterity with which they maneuvered those enormous bulldozers while ducking tracer bullets and deadly shrapnel.

Not all of them ducked in time. We had grievous losses in human life. That night also cost us a lot of metal, most of which was eventually salvaged by our enemy and returned to America as Datsuns, Toyotas and Hondas.

Task Force 58 was rapidly replenished and set out for the attack on Guam, to make that island safe enough for AFRS to move in.

Wormser and I had our orders. We left Eniwetok to establish a bigger station with a new crew that would follow.

My Yankee chauvinism was about to suffer a few hard blows.

"My C.O. was such a complete ass, his dentist was a proctologist."—John A. Ruge

11. His Dentist Was a Proctologist

The British officer looked like a bored Sean Connery as the Jeep in which he, Jack Wormser and I bounced through the Guam jungles from the landing strip to what was left of the capitol city, Agana, skirting the detritus of native Chomorro compounds.

Hordes of small brown children darted in and out of the foliage along the way. I wondered aloud why there were so many kids on the lush island.

"Long rainy season," the poker-faced Englishman explained.

He was reporting for duty as a liaison officer for the British fleet to the staff of Chester A. Nimitz. The white-haired admiral was establishing CINCPAC HQS on a hilltop overlooking Agana. CINCPAC is the acronym for Commander in Chief, Pacific. We Army men were again under Navy jurisdiction.

I was billeted with a Marine company at Island Command. The next morning I awoke and strolled across a barren area in my shorts, with a towel and bar of soap to take a shower. The Marines had rigged up a contraption of oil drums and pipes, an amusing but welcome addition that stood on an open platform in the middle of the compound of pyramidal tents.

While I was lathering my pathetically bony body, I heard some squeals. I turned to see three grinning Chomorro girls watching me and discovered how difficult it is for even a skinny man to hide behind a bar of soap.

I chided the Gyrene topkick about allowing women to wander around the area. "Dogface," he said, "those girls come by every morning, look over the men, pick the one they want and crawl into that man's tent at night. Don't knock it!"

The only thing that ever crawled into my tent was one of Guam's giant land crabs. And that one brought his extended family.

Before our staff arrived, I had time to become acquainted with the terrain. An accommodating SeaBee drove me to a village where he bartered

This was once the U.S. Navy's Officers Club. We built our first radio station on Guam in the basement (Hal Kanter, left; Jack Wormser, right; Guam, 1944).

for jugs of *tuba*, a powerful cure for sobriety the natives made from coconut palm hearts. He exchanged necklaces made of human teeth for the liquor, which had more bite than the macabre jewelry.

"Jap teeth," he told me. "Gyrenes pull 'em out of dead Nips."

I shuddered. *Our* boys? Those Eagle scouts and YMCA basketball players who eat Mom's apple pies, feed wild birds, adopt stray kittens and help little old ladies cross their legs?

"Those God-fearing American boys pull teeth out of dead men to make necklaces?"

"They don't always wait 'til they're dead," the SeaBee said grimly. "You've got stars in your eyes, Sarge. America's a violent nation, torn from the Indians by violence. If you think pulling teeth is bad, what would you say about the sweet American God-fearing kids who chop off Japs' heads, boil the meat and hair off them and use the skulls for radiator ornaments on their trucks?"

I couldn't say anything. I'd seem some of those skulls on island vehicles. Now that I knew how they'd gotten there, I was nauseated.

These are the men, I thought, for whom we are going to open our broadcasts each morning with Kate Smith singing "God Bless America"?

Our new staff arrived. Shy, intense, very young Jimmy Schell, a fellow Southerner, was our engineer. Towering, bulky Bill Ramsey taught radio courses in a small California college. A wide-beamed, waddling Hawaiian-American named Kani Evans had been an Islands newscaster. They were all made welcome by Wormser and me. Kani Evans quickly wore out his. He was acidly critical of the programs produced by our Hollywood colleagues and a chronic complainer about everything from the Marine mess to the equipment we were issued by AFRS.

The day arrived when Jimmy Schell, seated at our new console, nodded his head at Evans, whom Jack had selected to announce with great pride and baritone bravado, "THIS IS STATION W.X.L.I., ARMED FORCES RADIO ... ON THE ROAD TO TOKYO!"

We were broadcasting from the basement of an American Navy officers' club. The single room was all that was left standing of a concrete building. In retaking the island, our bombardment had reduced the area to rubble. There was no door to our airless studio so we hung Army blankets over the open entrance to shield the outside noises, more of them on the walls to deaden the sound. There were occasional bursts of gunfire from the hills where Japanese holdouts were sought out, captured or destroyed as they continued sniping at us.

There were also the incessant motors of bulldozers and trucks, the lowing of caribou and barking dogs, aircraft overhead, shouting men and shrill children just outside our broadcast room. We endured the heat by ingesting great quantities of salt tablets washed down by warm chlorinated water from the Lister bag standing at the entrance.

I seldom miss it.

Guam was the nerve center of the Pacific war. The top brass of all the

Left to right: Jim Schell, Bill Ramsey, Hal Kanter, Kani Evans in their studio in the officers' club which was reduced to rubble.

Allied services as well as journalists, entertainers and Washington political figures came and went; we were able to bring many of them to our microphones. Among the journalists was Quentin Reynolds, who had established himself as a headline-making war correspondent. Wormser got him to the studio for an interview.

Reynolds was not inexperienced at self-promotion. He was glib, garrulous and his breath smelled like a bar rag. He spent most of his time on Guam drinking at the officers' club. Enlisted men of the combat correspondent corps had little admiration for Reynolds. One was particularly derisive of the star journalist with the face full of broken veins.

"The man's a fraud!" he sneered. "I turned in a piece on hand-to-hand combat with some Nips in the boonies and that glory-grabbin' *goniff* snatched it, tacked on a two-line lead, filled it with personal pronouns and wired it to New York!"

We suffered the concrete steam room until Jack Wormser made a move. He obtained two large Quonset huts which were placed in an L shape on a grassy knoll where we built the finest radio station in the Pacific, complete with an auditorium studio that could seat 100.

Charles Butterworth and Luella Gear performing my radio adaptation of the Ephrons' play *Three's a Family* in our new studio on Guam.

We inaugurated it with a special event: A USO troupe had island-hopped to Guam, playing the Henry and Phoebe Ephron comedy *Three's a Family*, starring two amiable old pros, Charles Butterworth and Luella Gear. The film version of the Broadway play was also being shown on our island. I got a copy of Miss Gear's script and did a one-hour radio version which the cast enjoyed playing one Saturday afternoon to a packed auditorium. *Variety* duly noted that it was the first—and perhaps only—time a work was presented on stage, screen and over the air on the same day in one location.

I called that to the Ephrons' attention over lunch at Paramount a decade later. Phoebe recalled reading about it. Henry wondered why they'd never gotten a royalty check.

Bill Ramsey emceed a series of concerts that featured Navy musicians under the baton of an obliging and talented conductor named George who also played the violin. George spoke of his kid brother in Milwaukee, taking piano lessons.

"You'll hear about Lee some day, for sure," George Liberace said with fraternal pride.

A young Marine officer with a keen sense of humor dropped in to play the piano for us and sing some of the songs he wrote before he became famous. His name was Bobby Troup.

When amateur boxing began, Jack set up a ringside blow-by-blow remote and discovered a portly actor with enough knowledge of the sport to provide color between rounds. His name was Sam Messer, he came from Cincinnati and after the war he changed his name to Robert Middleton and appeared in many films.

A contingent of sports stars in Navy uniforms toured the Pacific. One of them was a middleweight boxing champion who invariably drew a laugh when the group entered a hospital ward and he announced brazenly to the wounded, "I'm Freddie Apostoli and I can lick any guy in this room!"

Bobby Riggs was another sports celebrity but he didn't get laughs when he claimed that he could beat anyone at tennis. Bobby wasn't joking.

Among the baseball players was a New York Giants infielder, Bud Blattner, who began hanging around our station. He was welcome because of his engaging personality and his access to cold beer.

Talking of the future one evening, Buddy said that when his playing days were over, he'd like to get into broadcasting. I urged him to start there; we got fragmentary scores via short wave and he could fill in with knowledgeable commentary to do a daily sports show. With our guidance, he began. Bud went on to become a popular St. Louis broadcaster who shared the microphone with legendary Dizzy Dean, the former pitcher who retooled the English language and "slud" into folklore.

One evening on Guam, Johnny Mize, the Giants slugger who would go on to hit a record 51 home runs in 1947, brought up the subject of table tennis. Riggs claimed he was as unbeatable in that as he was on the courts. Mize scoffed; he said Blattner was a better player. Riggs laughed.

"A shortstop!" he jeered.

Wormser and I joined Mize in goading Bud into a match. Riggs was eager to prove himself if Blattner was willing to make a cash wager on the contest. Bud was, so the time and place were set: the Red Cross hut at noon the following day. Word spread through Island Command. By noon, the hut was packed. Side bets were made, with Riggs the heavy favorite.

Before a cheering crowd, to Riggs' increasing annoyance and frustration, the underdog won handily. After money changed hands all through the area, Bud grinned at Riggs and admitted something of which we were unaware but which Mize did know.

"If you'd taken the trouble to ask, little hothead," Buddy told Bobby, "I'd have told you that I was captain of the men's United States Olympic Ping-Pong team."

One of my programs was a daily listing of all the movies being shown on the island and a review of each new film that arrived. Our theaters were all open-air with coconut logs or empty gasoline drums serving as seats. If our audiences were not dedicated film fans, they soon became hard-assed moviegoers.

My reviews were usually scathing. It is easier to get laughs by rapping anything than by praising it. I try to remember that whenever I read an indictment of my own work, but it doesn't always soothe the sting of rejection.

Our most popular local show as the noon hour called *The Daft Board* over which I presided as the chairman, Dr. Jungle Jolly Gerald. He voiced the gripes of the enlisted majority five times a week between jazz records and the scripted adventures of an ever-changing cast of outrageous characters, all of them played by me, Wormser and anybody who might be in the studio at air time.

It was egregious nonsense, studded with dreadful puns and frequently appalling jokes, but Jungle Jolly Gerald became a celebrity. One of the attentions he attracted was that of Sgt. John A. Ruge, the illustrator prowling the forward area on assignment by *Yank* magazine. A broad-shouldered Irishman with red hair, glasses, a hearty laugh, discerning eye and unique vocabulary, Jack sought me out and we became instant soulmates. He was one of the most original people I have ever known; we were close friends from that evening on Guam until his death in New York of a heart attack in 1982.

Jack's colorful speech and written prose assiduously avoided cliché, as did his excellent drawing. When Big Red or Old Jake (as he alternately referred to himself) was feeling good, he said he was a *gemhole*. A devoted film buff, he called movies "ball busters." He once praised a film as "an absolute Tchaikovsky." When I didn't decode that, he explained: "A Nutcracker Suite!"

To Ruge, a telephone was either "the ameche" or "the don" ever since Alexander Graham Bell was portrayed by Don Ameche in the inventor's filmed biography.

"Gimme a growl on the ameche," was Jack's request for a call, or, "Last night, Jane was yammering on the don..."

Jane Chenoweth, the watercolorist, was his second wife. The first was Martha Blanchard, a cartoonist during the postwar period when they both freelanced and Jack boozed. He was a prodigious drinker whose monumental drunks alarmed his friends, who frequently had to pick him up in an eye dropper and deliver him home in a sponge.

He tapered off when he married Martha but continued to fall off the wagon often enough for her to insist he join Alcoholics Anonymous. Jack attended only two meetings.

"A flock of Bible floggers," was how he described the group. Jack was a lapsed Catholic with little patience for any organized religion.

On one visit to New York, I found him in a midtown hospital where he had come to realize that he could not single-handedly clear the Western hemisphere of J&B Scotch.

When he and Martha ended their marriage, Ruge did stop drinking. He enjoyed a flurry of profitable assignments, married Jane and did not touch alcohol for the next 20-odd years. But his speech pattern never changed. Talking about an Army organist we had known, he said, "He's still a Spam-handed God-box flogger."

Nobody ever died in Jack's lexicon. People "left no forwarding address." Maria Ouspenskaya died in a fire started while smoking in bed and Ruge said the old Russian actress had "gone up in a cloud of Luckies."

Strolling through Manhattan's Museum of Modern Art with Jack, Doris and I stopped at a piece of sculpture formed in twisted metal with shards of shattered plexiglas. While we were debating what it was supposed to represent, Jack offered his vision: "That's James Dean's windshield."

When the creator of *Believe It or Not* died, Jack suggested an epitaph for his tombstone: "Here lies Robert L. Ripley. Believe it."

Following Ronald Reagan's first few months in the Oval Office, Big Red asked in a letter describing his struggles to survive on an artist's income, "Did you ever think you'd wake up some morning and actually miss Jerry Ford?"

I wake up missing John A. Ruge.

"Odd things, animals. All dogs look up to you, all cats look down on you; only a pig looks at you as an equal."—Winston Churchill

12. *Only a Pig*

When I read that Mary Coyle Chase had won the Pulitzer Prize for her comedy, *Harvey*, I made a note to get limber enough to kick myself in the ass.

Two years earlier, in Denver, I had gotten a call from Bob Chase, an editor of the *Rocky Mountain News*. He told me his wife was writing a radio series for the Teamsters' Union and was unable to find an actor to play a talking horse. Could I do it? I told Bob if he got me a pass, I'd leave Lowry Field to do anything legal or fattening.

Mary Chase was a beaming, bright-eyed suburban housewife who wore a print dress, white gloves and a flower-laden straw hat. She was pleased with my performance and impressed with my background. She asked timorously if I would read a play she was writing; she was having trouble with the second act and thought I might help her work it out.

"What's your play about?" I asked. She said it was a comedy about a man who has a *pookah* for a friend. I had never heard the word.

"Harvey is a white rabbit," she explained. "He's six feet tall, but only Elwood can see him. Elwood P. Dowd drinks, you see..."

"And the rabbit talks?" I asked the lady who had written a talking horse years before Francis the Mule had said a word to Donald O'Connor.

"Yes," Mary said, "Harvey talks, but Elwood's the only one who can hear him."

"Sounds nifty," I probably said. "I'm pretty busy right now, but maybe some other time," and retreated hastily from the lady with the straw hat, white gloves and chattering animals. I had other fish to fry, never suspecting Mary would wind up eating caviar.

On Guam, I wanted to make up for my youthful gaffe and intended to send congratulations to the Chases for Mary's Pulitzer surprise, but I delayed writing when something more momentous occurred. The evening of April 11, 1945, I worked past midnight preparing for an interview with Walter Davenport, a distinguished editor visiting from Washington. I awoke late the morning of April 12 to experience the most severe shock of my life.

I was standing in my shorts, shaving at the outdoor wash basin in front of our tent, when a Marine officer passed and said, "Well, we finally got rid of that son of a bitch!"

"Who's that, sir?"

"Roosevelt. Haven't you heard? He died."

The razor dropped from my hand, sudden tears from my eyes. I had to grab the metal tub to keep from sagging; my lungs collapsed, and if my heart didn't stop, it certainly hesitated. It was the loss of our president, our leader, that buoyant man who had sustained us through the most devastating depression and global conflict our country had known, that agonized me. It was only hours later that I would react to the officer's pleasure at the death of Franklin Delano Roosevelt.

I threw on my clothes and raced to the station, where our little staff was in a frenzy. Jack had canceled all recorded programs and both he and Ramsey were searching the short waves for any information they could gather to feed to Kani Evans. They had been too busy to call me and my appearance was welcome by Evans, who had not yet had breakfast. I took over for him and asked Ramsey to go out and get a cross-section of America's feelings for FDR. Jack went to the Marines P.R. offices to gather any information coming through and get some details on the background of our new president, about whom we knew little. One advantage of being overseas during his campaign was being spared most of the charges hurled at Senator Truman by the opposition who found him an easier target than the president.

With only coffee and cigarettes to sustain me — I had not had breakfast yet, either — I talked myself hoarse until Ramsey relieved me. I raced our Jeep up to CINCPAC for my meeting with Davenport.

The gray-haired newsman had been shaken by the report from Warm Springs, Georgia; he had covered FDR for years and knew him well.

"Our problem at WXLI," I told him, "is getting more information about Truman. People keep asking us questions I'm ashamed to admit we can't answer."

"You have a grave responsibility," he said. "It's important that everyone realizes that our system is infallible — and that Roosevelt was very careful in his choice of Truman. Harry will be more than a good president; he'll be a great one!"

Davenport went on to fill me in on the former senator's background. I covered several pages of my notebook and sped back to write what turned out to be a 45-minute piece the island listened to and, judging the reaction, felt vastly relieved.

But I could not forget that Marine officer, any more than I could the

Army colonel I had met a few months earlier who was cut from the same bolt.

One of the servicemen we put on the air was my Long Beach High fellow alumnus, Autumn Monro. The handsome baritone often sang for the troops. One evening he performed for an audience of the few Army men stationed on Guam. Some of those soldiers were black. Whether he was insensitive or was just being faithful to Oscar Hammerstein's original lyric, Autumn began "Ol' Man River" singing, "Niggers all work..."

Reaction was immediate and intense. It erupted into a bitter, bloody race riot.

Within days, President Roosevelt sent a personal emissary to Guam to investigate the incident and root out the causes of the conditions that brought it on. The president's investigator was the executive secretary of the National Association for the Advancement of Colored People, a soft-spoken, mild-mannered, polite but firm gentleman named Walter White. He was no darker than his surname.

After a morning of interviews with Navy personnel, Mr. White called on us at WXLI. Jack and I provided him with all the information we had. Mr. White asked me to accompany him to the commanding officer in the Army area and serve as a witness to his interview with the colonel.

I introduced Mr. White as the president's representative and the colonel was expansively cordial. At White's suggestion, I had not mentioned the NAACP.

"Colonel," he asked, "can you recall any instances of racial unrest prior to the incident here last week that resulted in the bloody—"

"Oh, Jesus!" the colonel groaned. "Those god-damned niggers!"

Mr. White darted a look at me, stood up and said, "Thank you, sir," then crisply walked out of the building.

"What the hell's griping him?" the colonel asked me.

"Sir," I said, "Walter White is a Negro."

The colonel whistled and said, "That sneaky bastard, Roosevelt! He would trick us with a pink one!"

I never saw Walter White after he left Guam but I did have a vivid flashback of him the night Johnny Mercer and Henry Mancini won the Academy Award for their song, "Moon River." At the Governor's Ball after the Oscar presentation, Mercer stopped at our table and grinned, "Hey, buddy, you know what NAACP stands for? Niggers Ain't Actin' Like Colored People!"

Fortunately, he didn't say that on the air. Johnny waved his Oscar and said, "Martinis for everybody!" By the time I saw him that night, I think he had already had everybody's.

After my encounter with the racist colonel, I wrote to Doris describing the degree and extent of stupidity among officers in an effort to express my profound disappointment with them. The letter was returned to me by the censor because I wrote it on the back of a newscast I had delivered on the air the day before. I protested. There was nothing in the news that the enemy was not already aware of or that would aid and comfort them. And what I had to say about our military was a comfort the enemy already embraced.

When I wrote Doris to explain why she hadn't gotten a letter the previous day, I blamed it on the jackass who censored our mail and went on to describe him in what I considered to be amusing satire. It did not amuse him.

Jack Wormser went out of his way to find a sympathetic lawyer to defend me when the Marines insisted the Army court-martial me. I was brought to trial on the charge of insubordination.

The court returned a verdict of not guilty. Later, the judge said that when the charges against me were filed, the Army routinely published parts of my letter the Marines considered subversive and, to their amazement, they had to mimeograph dozens of those charges because they were ripped off bulletin boards and mailed home!

Despite the ignorance of our military, we somehow managed to expand our forward area. We had taken Saipan, where another AFRS station began operation. Soon thereafter, Jack Wormser was promoted to captain and determined I needed another change of scenery. I didn't argue. He arranged for me to fly to Saipan and exchange programming notes with the AFRS personnel. I was greeted by Howard Duff, Ashley Simms and their part-time announcer, Lt. Tyrone Power. He and Duff spent hours discussing their craft, conversations Duff would refer to when he moved from radio (as *Sam Spade*, among other roles) to screen stardom.

"Gene Tunney was just here," Howard told me. "Did you see him on Guam?"

"No. I had enough of him in Denver," I said. "He was recruiting for the Navy and we met in a radio station where a woman named Maida Severn was going to interview both of us. The Champ gave me a stern lecture on my filthy habit of smoking cigarettes."

"And did you," Duff asked archly, "give him a lecture on his filthy habit of prizefighting?"

Our living quarters on Guam were superior to those on Saipan, so I was happy to get back to my home base. But my pleasure was short-lived when Wormser and I were separated by the Army. He was rotated to Honolulu and replaced by a hulking, brooding National Guard major who was the owner of a small radio station in Kentucky. Life at WXLI changed almost immediately under the officer who had definite ideas and strong opinions.

One of his first orders prevented me from poking fun at radio commercials, a running gag on *The Daft Board*. Advertisers' commercials were the life's blood of broadcasting, he insisted, and we would not bite the hand that pays us.

"The War Department pays me," I said, "not Sal Hepatica." He warned me not to argue that point or any other as long as he was in command.

The humorless major also insisted on programming more religious music and at least one "inspirational chat" every evening. Our studios played host to more chaplains than the BYPU. The Fundamentalist Kentuckian ran a rigid, God-fearing station and we did not get on with felicity.

I seized an opportunity to cover our first fire raids over the Japanese mainland for the Army news service and the major, delighted to get rid of me, allowed me to take a portable wire recorder and fly to Iwo Jima.

It was a wretched place when I arrived. Our men were still fighting in the hills and on the black volcanic ash beaches. We were subjected to air raids two and three times a night. I never did see all of *Rhapsody in Blue*, Robert Alda's film biography of George Gershwin, because the week it was shown on Iwo, the movie was cut off every night by screaming sirens, the blackout and the scramble into foxholes until the Japanese dropped their deadly loads and moved on.

Huddling in those shelters, we traced the aircraft arrivals as their bombs exploded in the distance, coming closer, screaming overhead in paralyzing fury before trembling in recession.

During one raid, three of us trembled together in a ditch as we listened to bomb, BOMB, *BOMB*—a loud THUD!—followed by *BOMB*, BOMB, bomb and then that eerie silence before the "all clear." When it wailed mournfully in the night, one of my ditchmates crawled out to see an unexploded bomb was stuck nose down in the gritty black sand ten feet in front of us. The soldier slithered to it on his belly, reached out to pat it and crooned affectionately, "You gold-brickin' son of a bitch!"

There was a happy reunion on Iwo Jima with a colleague from Lowry Field. Maston Jacks, a former Arizona newspaperman, had left our PR unit in Denver to attend Officers Training School. The day we met in the Pacific, Maston had just been promoted to major and, in a brief ceremony in the mess tent at the foot of Mt. Suribachi, gold leaves were pinned on his collar.

Later that afternoon, Maston and I ran into another Denverite, Starr Yelland, a KOA staff announcer who was now a Navy officer. He greeted us warmly and asked if we'd join him for drinks at the officers' club. Only the Navy would have established one that quickly in a combat zone.

"Hal," Yelland cautioned me, "wear your bars."

"Stripes," I corrected. "I'm a tech sergeant."

He was visibly annoyed. "Well, sorry, Kanter. See you at six, Maston."

Maston, who always had a built-in chickenshit detector, exchanged a grin with me. It was the last time either of us saw Starr Yelland.

But I did think of him two years later when I ran into his boss in Hollywood. I was walking down Vine Street with George Gobel and encountered Lloyd Yoder, the affable man who had managed KOA during my Lowry Field Theater days. I stopped to say hello and introduce him to my friend George.

Yoder put his arm around me and said, "Mr. Gobel, you're very fortunate to have this fine man with you. Not only is he talented, he's one of the best-liked young men we ever had in Denver. Why, if he came back, he could run for mayor!"

"Could he win?" George asked.

"Hands down!" Yoder said with a chuckle. He shook my hand firmly and said, "It certainly was good seeing you again, Charlie!"

As he walked briskly toward NBC, I don't know if Yoder heard George slapping the side of a building in hysterical laughter, but I'd seldom seen my iddy-biddy buddy so amused.

I was not amused on Iwo Jima. If we had experienced terror on Eniwetok, I went through a night of hell on Iwo. The island was socked in by a heavy ground fog when our bombers returned, nearly empty of fuel, after dropping their payloads on Yokohama. In the control tower, a commanding officer was desperately talking his pilots down as one aircraft after another plunged into the sea or beyond the landing strip.

Sirens blared, horns moaned and rescue vehicles wailed around me as I stood at the foot of the tower with my wire recorder, trying to describe the carnage. I could hear the colonel above me, screaming directions in a voice shrill with panic one moment, choked with emotion the next. Some made it safely. Many did not. Men wept openly. It was a bloody nightmare. I broke into tears. Disaster was not my journalistic beat.

When I got back to Guam, I was eligible for the journey home. Major Redneck gladly signed the papers that relieved him of my presence and I was trucked to an evacuation depot to await transport. There were many men ahead of me and few ships. It could be a long wait.

Sam Messer came to my rescue. He was assigned to Military Police and confided he could get me to Honolulu by air if I would escort a prisoner to Oahu. I snatched at the offer and was airborne the following day.

My prisoner was a short, frightened kid from West Virginia. I was armed with a rifle and sat next to him in a cargo plane filled with homeward-bound fighting men. When we stopped at Kwajalein, I brought the prisoner to a Lister bag for a drink of water. We had to drink from cupped hands because there was no glass. He obligingly held my rifle for me while I drank.

Aloft again, my angry pilot summoned me to the cockpit and asked me why in God's name was I usurping the seats of good soldiers to fly a damned prisoner and why the hell didn't I put the bastard on a slow boat instead?

"Captain," I said, "I'm no M.P. but the only way I can get back myself was to bring the man."

"Say!" he said with an abrupt change of attitude, "you're Jungle Jolly Gerald!" He asked me to sign his Short Snorter bill. Then he asked me why the prisoner was arrested. I told him what the kid had told me earlier.

"He stole an officer's radio."

"Jesus H. Christ!" the co-pilot exploded. Both flyers despised the idea that their fine airplane was being used to transport a petty thief.

"Personally," I smiled, "when he told me, I was flattered."

When we landed on Oahu, four burly military policemen relieved me of my prisoner and the rifle. As they roughly slapped handcuffs on the terrified boy, I protested.

"Take it easy," I admonished. "Can't you see how frightened he is? He's really a sweet kid."

"Sweet kid, huh?" the sergeant snarled as he signed my receipt for the prisoner.

"So he stole an officer's radio," I shrugged.

"That what he told you?"

"Yes, why?"

"What he shoulda told you," the M.P. said, "was that when the sumbitch officer caught him, he shot the sumbitch's brains out!"

It took me the rest of the day to get my stomach back up out of my combat boots.

"You must not suppose, because I am a man of letters, that I never tried to earn an honest living."— G. Bernard Shaw

13. *An Honest Living*

One broiling California afternoon in 1942, a perspiring Louella O. Parsons, the doyenne of Hollywood columnists described by John Barrymore as "that quaint old udder," patted my knee and said, "When you get out of the Army, young man, come see me; you have a future in Hollywood." I thanked the soggy fat lady and made a note to add her offer to others if I ever did get back to civilian life.

In the spring of 1945, that prospect seemed remote. I was reunited with Wormser, bivouacked in a Chinese school the Army had taken over in downtown Honolulu to house elements of Armed Forces Radio to which we were still attached.

Compared to the work load we carried in the forward areas, duty at Chung Shan school was a vacation that gave me time to recuperate and replenish my body weight. I arrived from Guam weighing a wraithlike 128 pounds. I looked like a mustache held up on a stick. So every day I ate three sturdy Chinese meals.

As servicemen, we had access to the Outrigger Club at Waikiki and the Royal Hawaiian Hotel which the Navy had taken over. I spent a lot of time at the beach in the company of friends, first among them Bob Crosby, the Man Who Would Be Bing.

Bob won our affection when he came through Guam with his Marine band, wearing a sign on his back that read, "Don't shoot. Bing's brother."

The self-effacing, talented Crosby and I formed a bond of friendship that endured until his death 50 years later.

At Waikiki we were often joined by another band leader, Art Jarrett, and Ensign Fred Benson, the C.O. of a Navy band directed by Ray Anthony and featuring Larry Storch, a versatile comedian.

Fred was at that time married to Jean Holloway, Kate Smith's prolific young writer I would later meet and work with within the year.

During the time we were in Hawaii, Gertrude Lawrence was headlining a USO trio that comprised the sophisticated songs of John Hoysradt, who later shorted his name to Hoyt and lengthened his career as an actor, and the dancer, Paul Draper. Their act, designed for the swank supper clubs of Mayfair and Manhattan, completely bewildered 98.7 percent of the Yanks in uniform.

Another international star on the island was then a major in the United States Army. His name was Maurice Evans and there is a reason why I smile when I remember him.

During one of my subsequent semesters at 20th Century–Fox, David Karp, an Emmy-winning author, arrived from New York to write his first screenplay. Intrigued by the mechanical aspects of filmmaking, my passionate colleague gained entrance to the stage where *Planet of the Apes* was being shot. David did not write that fine screenplay but he was a vociferous champion of all writers and defender of most.

He came bursting into my office in a towering state of Karpian outrage, thundering, "That Limey son of a bitch!"

"Who?" I asked, startled.

"Maurice Evans!"

It seems Evans was sitting with Kim Hunter and Roddy McDowall, all three of them wearing the laboriously applied ape masks, going over dialogue for the scene director Franklin Schaffner was lining up. After reading the lines, Evans tossed his script aside and said, "It's certainly not Shakespeare, is it?"

"How *dare* he!" David bellowed. "How dare that Limey bastard criticize any writer's dialogue when he has to dress like a monkey to make a living!"

Maurice Evans, an eloquent Welsh actor, had been in America for many years and distinguished himself on the Broadway stage long before the U.S. Army dressed him as a major or Richard Zanuck dressed him as an ape.

We met when Jack Wormser was requested to produce a radio show for the American Red Cross. Jack drafted me to write it.

The request was made by E. Stanton Griffis, the Red Cross commissioner, who was also chairman of the executive committee of Paramount Pictures and later became America's ambassador to Poland in 1947, Egypt in '48, Argentina in '49 and Spain in 1950. Apparently, the man couldn't keep a job.

He had no difficulty getting two stars for his radio show: Maurice Evans and Gertrude Lawrence. Jack enlisted the services of Bob Crosby and his Marine orchestra but advised me not to write any jokes for Major Evans, a serious man and an even more serious actor.

Remembering the short drama I'd given to Spencer Tracy in Denver, I rewrote it now for Evans, with Gertrude Lawrence as a Red Cross nurse.

It wasn't Shakespeare, either, but Evans didn't say so. What he did say after the case gathered for the first reading was that he felt left out.

"Why can't I have some jokes with Gertie and Bob?" the major asked Capt. Wormser.

"Of course," Jack assured him after an embarrassed look at me. "I'm sure Sgt. Kanter can accommodate that."

The show went well and Mr. Griffis made a special point to thank Jack and me for our participation. He told both of us to call on him after the war. There might be something at Paramount for us. I added his name to the list of postwar offers.

That night, I told my roommate, Sgt. Robert Eisenbach, of his offer. Eisenbach was also a writer. He had been the youngest drama critic on a San Francisco newspaper and eventually a successful Hollywood writers' agent. I had an inkling of his future that evening when I told him my ambition was to sign a contract for $200 a week.

Two hundred dollars seemed a fortune to me. Separation from the service was imminent and I was growing apprehensive about my ability to support a wife and family.

"If Paramount offered me a contract for $200 a week," I said, "I'd sign for life!"

"No, absolutely not," Bob snorted. "You'd be crazy to do that."

"Two fifty?" I asked.

"Not for any amount. Don't sign for life," he insisted. "I won't permit it!"

"Who are you not to permit it?"

"I'm your friend is who I am who won't permit!"

Our discussion escalated into a violent argument and ended when I declared that in spite of his unreasonable friendship, I was going to sign that contract! Having made that decision, I went to sleep convinced that I was set for life.

A virus put me in the hospital, where I lay the day the Japanese surrendered to MacArthur, too weak to join everyone celebrating the end of W. W. I. I., as film executive Y. Frank Freeman called World War II.

Jack Wormser came to say good-bye. He had his orders and ship passage home. It was an emotional farewell. We had become brothers.

Bob Crosby, also on his way home, told me to let him know the moment I got back to California. He wasn't sure what he'd be doing but thought we might do something together.

The day I left Chung Shan, Bob Eisenbach asked me to call his mother when I got to San Francisco and tell her he'd be home within the month.

My trip back was on a Navy destroyer. It was faster than the trip out and more luxurious. I was berthed near the ship's bakery and awoke every morning to the aroma of fresh bread. I spent hours in my bunk reading classic novels that the War Department was printing in soft covers. If that was not the birth of paperback books, it was the time they got off their knees and began running around the world.

When I wasn't reading, exercising or sniffing bread, I was staring at the pictures of Miss Lisa Kanter, the new lady in my life. She was three days old when I learned of her arrival in a telegram from my father. It took that long to reach my APO address. My crew toasted my firstborn with glasses of *tuba*, the Chamorro home brew that has a kick like a Brazilian soccer player.

I studied those pictures of my daughter so intently, so often, her little pumpkin face was seared into my frontal lobe. I can still close my eyes and see that adorable smile.

The morning our ship sailed through the Golden Gate is now a golden memory. What seems like thousands of civilians lined the docks to welcome us home. Almost as many tears were shed by mothers and lovers on the pier as by soldiers and sailors on shipboard.

We were home. Safe. Whole. Heroes.

As soon as I was told where and when the Army could function without my services, I telephoned my father to tell him I would soon be on my way to Fort Dix for discharge. I would have called my wife but Doris was then living with her parents in Brooklyn and they had no phone. Dad said he would get the message to Doris and assured me that the family was well, my daughter was beautiful and told me to call him as soon as I got to New Jersey.

Then I remembered my promise to Bob Eisenbach and called his mother.

"What do you want?" the lady asked me.

"Your son asked me to call," I said.

"He calls me every Friday," Mrs. Eisenbach told me. "I don't know what your game is, sir, but you're not talking to a fool. Don't call me again!" And she hung up.

Welcome home, hero!

The Army was only slightly more welcoming. It seemed as eager to get rid of me as I was to leave it. It put me on a train along with other veterans and we steamed across the country. En route, there were crowds with banners and bands welcoming servicemen home at some stations but there were none when some of us reached Fort Dix, New Jersey.

An hour after I arrived on a Sunday afternoon, I called my parents in New York to announce my arrival. My sister Saralea and my Uncle Mike were visiting my father at the time. Mother was attending a meeting, so she was not with them when they acted on a sudden impulse to kiss me.

They jumped in Mike's Chrysler and sped to Dix on the chance they would find me. They did. Saralea turned out to be the best kisser.

They did not have time to locate Doris, so the reunion with my wife was delayed until I collected my severance pay on Tuesday and went to my parents' apartment in Tudor City, where Doris was waiting.

She was an even better kisser than Saralea.

Dad wanted to take us to dinner. I declined. He insisted. I resisted. Mother fussed at him for being selfish. "My son wants to meet his daughter," she said.

Doris and I did not go to Brooklyn that night. We checked into the Hotel New Yorker, me with my barracks bag, she with her toothbrush. Room service brought dinner to our room, where we had steak and wine, then brushed our teeth.

I spent my first night as a war veteran laughing with my wife. Long after Doris fell asleep, I lay wondering what my daughter's reaction would be to her father, why Doris didn't bring a nightgown, whether I had tipped the room service waiter enough and where could I buy some white shirts tomorrow?

"It ain't nothing 'til I say it is." — Umpire Beans Reardon

14. *'Til I Say It Is*

Lisa smiled the smile I had memorized.

She was a beautiful baby, sitting in a high chair, holding her teething ring, a stale bagel tied to a ribbon.

Clara, her maternal grandmother, stood by, beaming but protective, reluctant to let me hold my daughter. But when I held my arms out to Lisa, she gurgled her willingness to accept my embrace.

My father-in-law was a short, heavy, powerful man with an engaging personality and a smile to rival Lisa's, whom he adored. He hoped I would find an apartment nearby so they could see Lisa every day. To his chagrin, I reminded him that we might not remain in New York.

"You're not going to work with Al?" he asked. My father had obviously expressed his unilateral decision to have me join the family business, which already included Mike, their youngest brother Maurice and Saralea.

Dad also decided my brother would come aboard when Bill returned from Germany, where he had won a battlefield promotion to captain and was decorated for valor with the Silver Star, Bronze Star and a Purple Heart. And me? I had a Good Conduct ribbon.

Dad's vision — which often exceeded his grasp — included Saralea's husband Bart Emerson, who opted to join his own father's jewelry business in Washington, and cousins Irvin and Leo Center, who remained in Savannah, where they resumed normal behavior and prospered.

Dad's office at 826 Broadway provided me with a telephone and typewriter my first week back. I wrote to Barron Polan, Bill Danch, Jerry Hausner and Jack Wormser to advise them I was out of the brown gown. I sent letters to Louella Parsons and Cecil B. De Mille to tell them I was now available for work, then went out to look for some white shirts. They were scarce but I managed to get two at the vexatious price of six dollars each. Before the war, I had never seen a shirt that cost more than three.

Irving B. Kahn, my friend from Denver, was back at work in the New York office of 20th Century–Fox, and when I called him there he insisted I come right over. He took me to his favorite Chinese lunchroom where, over *dim sum*, he plotted my future, which included working for him when he became a producer. Meanwhile, he was going to assign an agent to keep me occupied until he was ready to leave Fox.

That settled, he reminded me that when he left Denver for OCS, he entrusted to Doris an antique pistol he found in a Larimer Street pawn shop. She promised to keep it for him and now he wanted the elegant old weapon. I promised to return it the next day, when I came back to meet the agent he had arranged for me to interview.

I remembered the appointment but forgot the pistol. The agent was Sammy Schiff, a bouncing ball who seldom sat still and was constantly looking over his shoulder. He worked for Ted Collins, so I understood his paranoia. Sammy told me that he was going to leave Collins to establish a talent agency with Kahn. I would be their client as soon as they got me a job, which, to my surprise, they did in a very short time. But not as a writer.

Hobby Lobby was a radio show that exploited celebrities who had unusual hobbies. If they didn't have one, their writers would invent something. Irving convinced the show's producer that I was not only a celebrity but, boy, what an unusual hobby I had; I collected funny animal stories! That was news to me.

But my celebrity was confirmed by an article Jack Sher wrote which gave me credit for winning the propaganda war against Tokyo Rose on Eniwetok. It was printed in *Collier's* magazine and boasted a handsome picture of me at my WXLI microphone. It gave me 15 minutes of celebrity.

The argument that convinced me to do the show was the $150 fee. That much money for a five-minute appearance impressed not only me but my wife, my in-laws and — I suspect — my father. My mother's attitude was, "You're worth more."

Doris accompanied me to the studio, met Sammy and joined us for dinner with Irving after the broadcast. More Chinese food. Also, more good news. I was to meet another agent, Frank Cooper, who represented Alan Young, a comedian about to make his first movie. Cooper was looking for a writer to join their staff for the next six weeks and Sammy felt I had a good chance of getting the job.

Before Doris and I took the subway back to Brooklyn, Irving reminded her that he was still waiting for his pistol. She said she'd have to find it in her mother's house. She never did find it, although she looked — as her mother said — far and high for it.

When my father-in-law admitted that he had given the pistol to the group of Jews collecting arms to support Israel's war for independence, Doris said, "Papa, it wasn't yours to give. That belonged to Irving and it's a valuable souvenir of the Old West."

"It's more valuable in the Old East," he said, "killing Arabs!"

"Papa," I told him, "that cumbersome old horse pistol hasn't killed anything since the last buffalo stampeded in Colorado."

"It can be fixed," he said and warned me, "Never underestimate the ingenuity of a Jew!"

When we broke the news to Irving, he laughed, "That pistol is putting holes in our enemy!"

Frank Cooper offered me a job writing for his Canadian comedian who had come into prominence while I was overseas. Cooper's offer was for a trial period at $200, saying, "If you prove yourself after two weeks, I'll pick up your option for four more at $250. Then, when we go to the coast for Alan's movie, I'll give you $300 for the rest of the season. Okay?"

Okay. Hadn't I promised Bob Eisenbach that I'd sign my life away for less? I started the next day, working in the office of the show's director, Eddie Polo.

"Oh, you're going to be great," Polo said when I came up with the punchline of a scene industrious Jess Goldstein and sleepy Norman Paul were writing. Polo said this captured the comedian's essence:

> GIRLFRIEND: Oh, Alan, how will we ever become man and wife?
> ALAN: We'll get married.

Jess was a jocular schoolteacher who was on a leave of absence to discover whether or not he could support his family by writing comedy. He could. And very well.

So could Norman, when he was awake.

Toward the end of my two-week trial period, Frank Cooper said he wanted to try out another team of writers, so would I stay on at the same salary?

I said no. He said in that case, he'd have to lay me off for two weeks, but if the other writers didn't work out, he'd bring me back at $300.

When I called my agent, Sammy was so quick to advise me to live with Cooper's decision, I knew he was not the man I wanted to represent me. I told that to Irving, who said he didn't blame me and that he was already reconsidering his plan to enter the agency business. He had met an actor who invented a prompting device he wanted to market, a gadget he called a *Teleprompter*.

I was frustrated by my first postwar assignment, discouraged by the caliber of the businessmen I had to deal with and harbored secret doubts about my chances for success. If Doris shared those doubts, she never shared them with me.

The next few days I called on old friends in Manhattan like *Variety*'s venerable editor Abel Green; comedian Jack Pearl, who played in a radio drama I wrote in 1939; and several producers I had written scripts for in 1940 and 1941. They were all pleased to see me. None of them offered me work. Except my father, for whom I wrote a few more articles.

One morning I was awakened by Katya (my mother-in-law), who was troubled that a telegram had arrived for me. To her generation, telegrams were invented solely to impart bad news. The last one she had gotten was from Doris and me, telling her that we had been married in Denver.

The telegram that arrived that morning was from Barron Polan in California. It instructed me to contact George Rosenberg at a Manhattan number immediately.

"H.K., where the hell've you been?" Rosie growled when I called him. "Get your ass up here right away!"

"Here" was a penthouse on Park Avenue, the home of Rosie's dear friend, William Randolph Hearst, Jr. When I was admitted by a butler, I regretted I didn't have a calling card to present.

The last time I had seen Sgt. Rosenberg, he was in denim fatigues, watching Lester Linsk and Jerry Hausner load musical instruments on an Army truck. I was not prepared for the civilian who greeted me now. Rosie was lying in bed under a velvet canopy, wearing a silk dressing gown over satin pajamas, being shaved by a Greek barber and buffed by a French manicurist. The butler summoned the maid, who brought me a glass of orange juice, and Rosie asked me what I had been doing since I got home.

"You stupid son of a bitch," he said when I told him my adventure with Cooper and Schiff. He asked me if I had signed anything with either of them. I had not.

"Good," he said. "Don't sign anything with anybody. Barron and I are putting together our own shop. We'll handle writers only. I assume you want to come back to the Coast, so when can you leave?"

"When can you get me a job?"

"How about now?" Rosie said. "Look over the listings, see what show you'd like to work on and get back to me tomorrow. Don't call until ten in the morning."

Doris was amused but skeptical when I reported our conversation and looked forward to meeting the debonair bachelor I had described.

I kept my own skepticism unexpressed: Would Rosie turn out to be another Sammy or Frank? The only agent I had ever engaged was a flabby fatty who represented character actress Alison Skipworth, whose wardrobe, I suspected, he also wore. When I told him in 1941 that I was leaving for

California when my draft board classified me 1A, he said I could evade Army service the same way he had done in the first World War.

"Tell them," he said, "that you're a homosexual."

"Suppose they ask me to prove it?" I asked. He patted my face and squealed, "You'll *love* it!"

I did not kiss him good-bye.

I would have kissed George Rosenberg when I called him the morning after our meeting in Bill Hearst's house. It was a phone call I'll never forget.

I made it from a drug store phone booth two blocks from my in-laws' apartment promptly at ten.

"H.K.," he said, "I've been thinking there's no reason why you should have to pay your way back to the Coast, so I've got you set with a show here that'll bring you out when they go in a coupla months. By the time you and your bride get settled with your new kid, we'll have more work lined up for you. You start tomorrow."

Wait, wait! Slow down! What the hell was he telling me? Start what, Rosie? Who? Where? How? This was all too much, too fast.

"You got a piece of pencil and a paper?" he asked. "Ritz Towers. Park Avenue. Look it up. Be there tomorrow morning to start work with Goodman Ace.

"Goodman Ace?" My heart was slamming against my ribs. "You got me a job on *Easy Aces*?"

"No," Rosie said, "they're off the air. Ace is producing the Danny Kaye show."

I could not believe what I was hearing. How did he do that?

"I told Ace you're a hero," Rosie said, "so if you can't be funny, be heroic."

He ended our conversation telling me Ace would be expecting me at ten. "I'll see you in a couple of months on the Coast," he added. "If you need us, we'll be in the book. Polan and Rosenberg. Congratulations. You're our first client."

"Rosie," I said, almost in tears, "I can't tell you how much I appreciate this."

"You'll think of something," he said. "You're a writer, aren't you? Even if you didn't ask the first question a writer should ask."

"What's that?"

"How much?"

"Oh," I said. "How much money, you mean?"

"Now that you ask," Rosie said, "you start at $750."

"Seven hundred and fifty dollars a week?"

Did I hear right?

"For starters," Rosie said. "You go to $850 the minute you get on the train. See you on the Left Coast, pal." He hung up.

I stood there, holding a disconnected line, struggling to catch my breath. I hung up and still stood there until a woman pushed the booth open and asked, "*Nu*? You're going to spend the weekend?"

I remember that I went back to deliver the news to Doris but I don't remember my feet hitting the ground. Maybe that's because I floated.

"I admit the virtue of being able to stand criticism. Unfortunately, it is a virtue I do not happen to possess."— Thomas Wolfe

15. A Virtue I Do Not Possess

Goodman Ace was a tall, stoop-shouldered, near-sighted, milk-white cigar smoker with the longest earlobes west of the Ubangi tribe. He was also a Talmudic scholar, dedicated card player, horse race enthusiast and cynic whose career began in his native Missouri where he reviewed stage shows for the *Kansas City Star*.

Shortly after he married, Ace expanded his work to include a radio report on theater. His young bride, Jane, frequently accompanied him to the studio. One night there was not enough news so Goody involved Jane in a discussion of their bridge game. Her distinctive voice and eccentric thought process combined with his acerbic wit was an instant hit with their listeners. In a few months, they were network stars, broadcasting from Chicago as *Easy Aces*.

By the time I reported for work, they had been living many years in New York's Ritz Towers, where I was admitted by the Aces' majordomo. He showed me to the den where Mr. Ace said, "Manny, bring me an aspirin. I have to shave."

Manny didn't question that, and while I was debating whether I should, Goody said, "An electric razor gives me a headache."

While he shaved with one, he briefed me on Danny and Sylvia Kaye, of whom he was amusingly disrespectful. Sylvia was the only piano player he knew who played jazz wearing opera gloves and he referred to Danny as his *Muggin' Doovid*.

His writing staff trickled in. Arnold Auerbach, who had written for Fred Allen, came in from his home in Connecticut. I don't recall how long he remained on the staff but I recall that first day when we worked together, Arnold suggested a joke which Goody rejected, saying, "It sounds contrived."

"It should sound contrived," Arnold said. "I just sat here and contrived it."

Arthur Alsberg, a tall, diffident young graduate of the University of Pennsylvania, was always late, although he lived in Manhattan. He was the son of a Wall Street broker and was described as "a wealthy socialite" by lurid scandal sheets playing up Arthur's divorce from a showgirl. In spite of the publicity that embarrassed him, he contributed much richness to our scripts.

Herbert Baker was a Yale classmate of my Army buddy, Max Wilk. Herbie — who never seemed to lose his baby fat or his temper — was a gifted lyricist whose primary chore was writing lyrics with Sylvia. And, to my surprise, the other member of the staff was Jess Goldstein, who was holding down two jobs. He confided that working for Ace was more pleasant than working for Cooper.

I earned my bones with Goody the first day on the job with this line for Danny: "I've been in bed all week with a terrible haircut."

At lunch time, those of us who did not have appointments with therapists, women or handball players had our choice of ordering food sent up or going down to the dining room. I usually chose to eat with Mr. and Mrs. Ace, at Jane's invitation. When it came to preparing food, she always knew what to order. The only thing I ever saw in the refrigerator in their apartment was a bottle of Vichy water, a jar of Durkee's dressing and half a box of chocolates.

On show day, the cast met in a CBS studio for rehearsal, Danny sitting at one end of a long table, Goody at the opposite end. We writers sat with Ace, facing the actors who sat with Kaye. Among them was Butterfly McQueen, the squeaky-voiced actress in *Gone with the Wind* who said she didn't "know nothin' 'bout birthin' no babies."

Miss McQueen, *off* stage, didn't know nothin' about a lot of things. When she didn't show up for rehearsals one week, Goody got a call from the amused stage manager of a Broadway show who said that McQueen would be late because she was auditioning for a job to replace a blonde chorus girl. McQueen was at least 30 pounds heavier than any girl in the chorus and danced like an aardvark.

Another week, she asked if I would write a radio show for her. "But I don't want to play a maid or a secretary," she said. "I want to play something else."

"What would you like to play?"

"Ooooh," Miss McQueen said, "a lady on a bus!"

When the cast finished the first reading of the new script every week, they would usually applaud the writers. One week Danny did not join them. Pouting, he said, "I'm the highest-paid straight man in show business."

Without looking up from his script, Goody said, "Jack Benny makes three times the money you do."

That did not placate Danny, although he knew as well as anyone that Benny was generous in allowing his cast to get laughs. When the time came for Kaye to start his next film for Goldwyn, Goody refused to come to California because "it's too close to Mary Livingston."

Arthur Alsberg and I were Goody's guests for lunch one afternoon when he stopped at the front desk to pick up his mail. He showed us an envelope and said, "This is a check from the telephone company, for Jane. Every three months, they send her a substantial check—and Jane doesn't even know how to dial."

Another afternoon, when I entered the elevator to their apartment, a woman shrank back in the corner and avoided my eyes. I couldn't help but stare at her: She was beautiful. We rode in utter silence to the floor where she got off quickly. I asked the elevator operator if he had any idea who the beautiful woman was. He looked at me as if I'd just arrived from Graustark.

"Miss Garbo, sir," he said.

When I reported my fellow passenger to Jane, she said, "Yes, she lives here. She talks to our dog, but not us."

The Aces had a Sealyham that Goody or Manny walked two or three times a day. Whenever Garbo encountered them, she stooped to pet the dog and murmur to him but Goody affirmed that she never spoke directly to him. Respecting her privacy, he gallantly returned her silence.

One evening, she stopped to pet the dog on Park Avenue when a car suddenly slammed on its brakes and quickly backed up. Garbo fled as a woman leaped out of the car and approached Goody.

"Is that a male Sealyham?" she demanded.

"Yes," Goody said.

"How'd you like to breed him to my bitch?" the excited woman asked.

"Madame," Goody said severely, "in Manhattan, it's against the law to pander for Sealyhams!"

I was crossing Fifth Avenue a few years after my first vision of Garbo. She was crossing from the opposite side. I smiled at her. She returned a down payment on a smile but kept moving. I stopped in front of a store window that reflected the street and saw her stop, turn and look at me. I wished I were a Sealyham because when I turned toward her, she bolted away. She never delivered to me the rest of that smile.

When I left Goody's employ to accompany the Kaye crew to California, I gave Jane a five-pound box of her favorite chocolates. A dozen years later, Goody told me that Jane wanted to sew a button on a blouse and sighed, "I wish Hal were here."

"So do I," Goody said to coax Jane through her convoluted thought process.

"You do?" she explained. "Then you remember that big box of chocolates he gave me in 1946!"

Goody waited for the other shoe to fall.

"I saved the box to keep my sewing things in and I put it on the top shelf of the bedroom closet only I gave away that little stool and now I can't reach it."

"And Hal's very tall," Goody realized.

"He could reach it without the stool," Jane acknowledged.

The last thing I remember Jane saying about her husband was that when they came back from a Florida vacation, Goody was as tan as the Jack of hearts.

"An Apology: Those sections in this book which are from my own works were made by my two assistant compilers, not by me. This is why there are not more."—Mark Twain, 1888

16. An Apology

Through Jane Ace, Doris and I found a sublease in the Mayflower, a residential hotel on Central Park West, an address her father boasted about and whose rent scandalized her mother. Doris was pregnant again, a condition my father boasted about, which scandalized *my* mother.

When we attended my brother's wedding, Bill wore his uniform because it fit better than his old suit. I bought my first tuxedo for the occasion and for the same reason. The only article of my uniform that would still fit was the necktie.

I had gained weight rapidly eating Katya's cooking. My mother-in-law excelled in the kitchen, whereas my mother's idea of a suitable dinner was a hotbed of cold cuts.

Danny Kaye had a reputation as a chef but the only food he ever served me was in Chicago, where we went to broadcast the show from Milwaukee for our sponsor, Pabst Blue Ribbon beer. The night we checked into the Ambassador East, Danny invited me to his suite.

Arthur Alsberg and Herbie Baker were already there, along with bandleader Dave Terry and announcer Dick Joy. Our star had ordered gigantic platters of shrimp, crab, lobster and Beluga caviar and poured overflowing flutes of champagne.

"Pabst is paying," he urged. "So eat! Drink! Vomit!"

When we arrived in Los Angeles with Kaye but without Ace, we had a first draft of a script we wrote on the train without the benefit of a head writer. The next day we met the man who was to fill that spot, my Army buddy Al Lewis, who had been known as "Bobaloo" Bobrick, his family name.

Lewis loved what we had written. He hoped our producer would also love it because the second thing Al hated was rewriting. The first thing he hated was having to write.

Our new producer was an older man named Willie Schorr. "His wife committed suicide last year," Al told us, "so when you meet him, don't ask 'How's your wife?'"

I assured Jess and Arthur that Al's sense of humor wasn't always so macabre, pointing out that he had once teamed with Hank Garson to write Robert Benchley's radio shows.

Jess's wife and family remained in the East, as did Doris and the baby, so we agreed to share expenses by living together for the few months we were employed by Danny. When we discovered a luxurious penthouse overlooking the ocean in Santa Monica, Arthur Alsberg became the third member of our household. They were both neat, clean gentlemen but one of us never rinsed the whiskers out of the basin after he shaved. I would never accuse anyone, but it wasn't me or Jess.

The penthouse at the Shangri La also served as our office for writing the show. By agreement, Al would come in at 10:00, work until 12:30, go out for lunch and resume work at 2:00. That was our agreement.

The first day, Al arrived after 11. And he was accompanied by Bernice, his beaming, dark-eyed wife, who was eight months pregnant and huge. She brought her knitting with her and sat in the living room with us as we tossed lines back and forth, laughing whenever Al spoke, even if all he said was, "Let's break for lunch."

The second day, Al and Bernice arrived for work at 11:45 and his first words were, "Let's break for lunch." That became his mantra and he was never on time as long as we continued to write that show.

My Hollywood debut as a public speaker began during this period. A group of writers who decided to give Bobaloo a stag baby shower persuaded me to take him and Bernice to dinner at the Hollywood Brown Derby with my collaborators. Bernice was in on the plot with me, Jess and Arthur. Before we ordered dinner, I had to convince Al to accompany me to the private dining room, where, I told him, some of our Army buddies were celebrating Howard Duff's new contract as radio's *Sam Spade* and wanted us to stop in for a drink.

Al was genuinely surprised when we joined the party and touched when he discovered its purpose. It was the first of what became a series of stag dinners, remnants of which today are collectors' items in some circles.

The master of ceremonies at Al's baby shower was the cherubic Bill Morrow, a man who was frequently guilty of premature exultation. He introduced the speakers for three-minute talks. There were two dozen of us and, with the laughs engendered, the program lasted over two hours.

Charlie Isaacs said he wouldn't get a laugh because "I'm a constructionist," which got a big laugh. Radio executives felt that comedy should be written by teams consisting of a joke writer and his more intellectual partner who understood the art of dramatic construction. Radio writers felt that executives should come in teams, too, because it usually took two of them to make a complete ass.

The night of the baby shower, Ray Singer, who had a nervous tic and outblinked the world five to one, said that he knew how babies were made and he was shocked that little Al Lewis would do that to sweet little Bernice.

Larcenous Mac Benoff borrowed from a Mark Twain essay on masturbation to advise Al how to behave.

I don't remember what my message was but I expressed my fright at being introduced by a man who was wearing Pierre Laval's necktie. The treasonous French premier always wore a white tie before he was executed. Bill wore one while executing Al that night.

Whatever I did say must have impressed someone because a few months later — after Bernice had given birth to twin boys — I was asked to emcee another baby shower. This time it was for Sherwood, before the birth of Don, the first of the four Schwartzes who were to follow.

I tried to keep my remarks fairly wholesome until Sherwood's father-in-law spoke. Mr. Seidman said he was disappointed in the evening. "In New Jersey, where I come from," he scolded us, "we talk dirty at stag dinners. You should be ashamed of how you talk, like pussies, not like men."

"Mr Seidman," I said when he sat down, "I won't presume to speak for the others, but go fuck yourself."

He shouted over the roar, "Now you're talking!"

I've been talking like that ever since.

"My one goal is to communicate with the greatest number of people I can and make them laugh at themselves."—Erma Bombeck

17. My One Goal

Danny Kaye seldom made people laugh at themselves because he was usually laughing at them.

During the weeks we tried to make him funny, we wrote scripts for 20 guest stars. In the 1940s, anybody with a job and a press agent was a star, as opposed to '90s television, where anybody who isn't a star is a producer.

Shirley Booth, Orson Welles, Martha Raye, Edward Everett Horton and Georgia Gibbs were five of the artists we worked with that 1946 season. Her Nibs, Miss Gibbs, one of Danny's favorite vocalists, was a frequent guest whose musicianship was widely admired, yet she never attained stardom.

Martha Raye did. Rowdy as a lumberjack and bawdy as a Marine, Martha could out-cuss a pimp, out-shout a hog caller, then switch gears and sing a ballad as tender as warm butter.

Shirley Booth starred on Broadway before winning the Oscar for her devastating film debut in *Come Back, Little Sheba.* She had proved her artistry with comedy when she played Miss Duffy, "the daughter of the establishment" on radio's *Duffy's Tavern.* Shirley was married briefly to the star of that show, Ed Gardner, a rascal whose infidelity began on their honeymoon. On their first night at sea, Shirley caught Ed stealing out of another woman's stateroom.

"Now you know the truth," he said. "I'm an international jewel thief!"

The most pleasant of our guest artists was Edward Everett Horton, a constant joy. The least was Orson Welles, who was also the most versatile; thus, as an actor, director and producer, he could be thrice arrogant.

Before I knew who Welles was, I was impressed by his voice as much as his attitude when he was imperiously ordering a take-out feast from a Hollywood Boulevard delicatessen. I'd never heard anyone pronounce salami and pastrami with such disdainful hauteur.

Orson did, however, make room for some humor in his life, I later discovered when we shared a bungalow on the Universal lot. He was shoot-

Left to right: Hal Wallis, Shirley Booth, Hal Kanter in the spring of 1954 in New York City.

ing the final scenes for *Touch of Evil* in which he was co-starring with Charlton Heston. Orson invited me in for a drink with Chuck, who said they were celebrating the finish of the film.

"Finish?" Orson bellowed. "The real work now begins!"

His challenge was making sense out of the miles of film he had exposed, and nothing in that movie ever surpassed the meticulous choreography of his astonishing opening shot.

Edward Everett Horton was for years the honorary governor of the San Fernando Valley, and when we moved to Encino, we became his neighbors. Eddie owned a large estate with several guest cottages. One of them housed F. Scott Fitzgerald and the lady then in his life, Sheilah Graham, who subsequently became a syndicated columnist.

Eddie's brother, Winter Horton, raised chickens, which were free to range the fields. We had a Dalmatian Doris named Rover Cleveland who was also free to range the fields. We always thought he was a cowardly animal so I was surprised when Winter complained to us that our dog was killing his roosters. "Hens, maybe," I said, "but he'd be afraid of a rooster."

Winter did not appear to have Eddie's sense of humor. We bought a long leash for Rover.

The Horton acres were often used as a venue for charity events. Doris and I attended one flower show in the garden, then sent our name inside to ask if Mr. Horton was home. We had never seen the inside of his fabled house. In a minute, I heard a "pssst!" from a window and when I turned, Eddie himself was beckoning us to the entrance. A woman admitted us and quickly closed the door as Eddie came to greet us, apologizing for "this cloak and dagger deportment."

"But you see," he twittered, "they all want to come inside where they'll trample my tea cups as flat as my roses. Better they think I'm in Maine."

He was delighted to see us and took us on an extended tour of the house, to arrive finally in a large room on the second (or was it the third?) floor, which looked out over the valley and where, Eddie said, his mother had died. He had spent many hours in that room, sitting with her while he memorized his lines for the next day's work.

I could attest that he was a fast study. When we did a television show a few years later, he got the 35-page script a day before rehearsal and when he showed up the next morning, he had committed it entirely to memory.

In talking about his mother, Eddie told us that when he took her to Paris to celebrate her eightieth birthday, Hedda Hopper arranged for him to take the dear lady to the famous designer Balenciaga, to make a red dress.

"Of course, Mother was thrilled," he said as he opened a large chiffonier. "And here is that red dress!" He removed it with a flourish and held it up for us to admire. As we did, his eyes glistened.

Later, on our way home, Doris said, "Do you get the feeling that Eddie sneaks up to that room every so often and slips into that red dress?"

No, I don't. It was too small.

The last *Danny Kaye Show* was broadcast on Friday, May 31, 1946. I did double duty on that final show, appearing as an actor with our guest, Carmen Miranda. The last laugh I wrote for that swan song came after mentioning the names of those who helped put the show on the air all season: Danny thanked "the censor, whose name we had to cut because it sounds dirty."

Polan and Rosenberg, my agents, had a new job for me that was to begin in two months. But first I had to meet the producer, Carleton Alsop, and my writing partner, Jean Holloway, at a dinner in Miss Holloway's Beverly Hills home. Her name sounded familiar and when I arrived, she reminded me that we had met briefly when I did the Olsen and Johnson shows for Kate Smith. She also told me her husband, Fred Benson, who was still in the Navy, was a fan of mine.

Hal Kanter, Danny Kaye, Art Van Horne, circa 1948, rehearsing a radio show for Armed Forces Radio.

Fred returned to civilian life but, from what I gather, not to Jean, a talented writer who was a gregarious romantic with bleached cotton-candy hair, generous to a fault which, in her case, was overeating. Like Mark Twain, she wrote while lying in bed but, unlike Twain, instead of an ashtray at her side, she had peanut brittle and marshmallows.

Jean was a gracious hostess and over the years we spent many stimulating evenings with the accomplished guests she sat at her table, very few of whom stole her silverware, which she always counted after every party.

Carleton Alsop was a tall, lean, handsome gentleman Jean adored. She was not alone, for many women felt the same way about him. Heads did turn when he arrived anywhere. "Carleton," Ray Bolger said, "never makes an entrance. He is an entrance."

A waiter once handed him a note when we were lunching at the Brown Derby. It was from Eva Gabor, seated nearby. Carleton read it and sighed, "She wants my body." He was, at that time, recently married to Sylvia Sidney, the screen star he called "my black concubine," having been divorced from screen star Martha Scott.

Before starting on the new assignment, I had to find a home for my pregnant wife and infant daughter. I looked at properties in the Valley, where Bill Danch had moved with Margene and their two children, Betsy and Jeannie. Margene saw a small house on Columbus Avenue in Sherman Oaks that I was certain Doris would love.

George Rosenberg suggested I get someone to handle the $20,000 purchase. He offered his own business manager, Myrt Blum, who entered my life for a couple of years and five percent of my income.

Jerry Hausner scoffed; he handled his own business affairs and thought I should do the same. But I didn't have Jerry's thirst for deal-making; he drew pleasure in getting the best of the bargain whether buying a house, a car or a can of cat food.

The sublease we had at the Mayflower was running out and Doris, with the help of friends like Bert Gold, Esther and Ernie Kaufman and Carol Spielberg, looked for an apartment for us to rent for the summer in Long Beach.

I returned in time to pick one that would cost us $1200 a month. Doris felt that was much too expensive, even though my new job would pay me $1000 a week, starting in two months. I could have taken a summer job but I wanted to be with Doris and the baby while we waited for the new one.

Among the many visitors we had that summer was Harold "Ace" Hastings, retired from the Air Corps to fly overseas routes for United Air Lines. The handsome pilot had money he wanted to invest in show business. I discouraged him. But I tried to encourage him to date Doris' pretty cousin, Blanche. He was willing but Blanche wasn't. So Ace, who thought Lisa was the most precious baby girl he'd ever seen, said he'd wait for her to grow up. He's still waiting, half the year on his Greek island and the other half in Texas.

Irving Kahn, a press agent at heart, booked me on several shows where I plugged *Classic Comics* and my upcoming *Don Ameche Show*.

On July 11, Doris informed me that it was time to get to the hospital for the birth of our second child. I immediately called for the car and driver I had engaged to stand by and, leaving Lisa with Katya, we raced to Women's Hospital in Manhattan, where my wife sweated through labor while I sweated bullets.

Doris' obstetrician, William Aldrich, who I hoped was an M.D., came out to tell me that my wife had had false labor pains and it might be some time before she was ready to deliver. When I demanded he do something to ease Doris' pain, he glared at me and said, "I didn't come here to ask your advice, young man; I'm here to tell you to go home."

I didn't. The pains stopped. In the waiting room, I dozed fitfully, expecting to be awakened any moment by the doctor or his nurse. Doris had gone to sleep. By early morning, I remembered that I had promised to be at CBS to be interviewed by Bill Leonard on his popular morning show. I managed to get to the studio for the broadcast, about which I remember nothing except my anxiety to race back to Doris as soon as possible.

When I returned, the floor nurse informed me that while I was on the air, I became the father of eight pounds of beautiful girl. Doris was glowing with pride as she showed me our hour-old daughter. The name she fancied was Dana, but I thought it should have a traditional spelling, so Doris, in her weakened condition, settled for Donna.

It was my job to spread the good news of Donna's arrival to our families. When I told my father-in-law, he said, "Another girl? You couldn't make a boy?"

I refused passage on his guilt trip.

"While researching, found this line of dialogue: '"Shit," he said briefly.' Bad. Poorly done. The way I would write it: '"Shit," he said at some length.'" — Will Fowler

18. "Shit," He Said Briefly

Fastidious Carleton Alsop thought that I should meet the people I would be writing for so he arranged for me to go out to Encino, where Don Ameche lived with his wife Honey, several children, a housekeeper and her family, a group large enough evidently to be considered a parish by the Catholic church, because the Ameches had their own resident priest.

Ameche at the time was one of the world's busiest actors. Between his films, radio shows, recordings and racing stables, it was a wonder he found time to father his brood. He did find time to show me around his estate, which he had bought from Al Jolson, who built it when he was married to Ruby Keeler. A few years later, Jolson repossessed it and moved back in with his new and younger wife, Erle.

Ameche was a no-nonsense gentleman, pleasant but businesslike, who allotted half an hour to get acquainted over a glass of wine. I later learned that he allotted the next two hours to drinking his parish priest under the altar.

It was said about him that Ameche would be a victim of dehydration if ever his corkscrew got straightened out.

The man was the envy of every actor with a thirst because Don could gulp the grape until four in the morning, be in makeup at seven and on the set by eight, fresh as a morning glory.

Ameche's co-star on the Drene Shampoo show was a jackass of a different color.

Pincus Leff was a short, sibilant, boastful burlesque comic who was known professionally as Pinky Lee. I was obliged to meet him at length before writing a line because I had never heard of the man much less seen him perform. When I arrived promptly at his address, I was met at the door by a seven-year-old boy who told me his father would be right out. He showed me a model airplane. I said it was nice. He said it cost $4.28. I said I didn't want to buy it. He said no, that's what it cost him.

He showed me a toy truck and said, "This cost $3.59." A framed picture of his father cost over $20 and a stuffed baby alligator cost $15, according to the kid's inventory. By the time Pinky came in, his son had revealed the price of every item in the room.

"Morgan's such a smart boy," Pinky said to me, then pushed the kid out of the room and closed the door, which, I estimated, cost $48.

During the time I spent with my new star on that hot summer afternoon, I became increasingly uncomfortable as I watched the glue on his forehead melt and the widow's peak of his toupee curl up. Adding to the discomfort were his examples of humor the clown expected me to provide: "I just had a terrible accident. I was coming here lickety split, lickety split, when all of a sudden, I split my lickety."

I found writing for him so distasteful I created another character I could have some little pride in writing, Byron Swinbourne, the Passionate Page Boy, played by Jim Backus. When Jim got bigger laughs than Lee, Pinky objected, so I amused myself by writing sound cues like ASSORTED SCREAMS FROM FAT WOMEN.

Our radio show was doomed from its debut, although I did not know it at the time. Nor, I suspect, did Carleton Alsop, who held advertising executives in contempt. He was particularly unimpressed with a gentleman from Procter & Gamble who looked more like a gaunt Baptist preacher than the influential time buyer that he was. His name was Halverstadt and he spent millions of P&G's advertising dollars every year. He came out from Cincinnati and summoned Alsop to discuss their new program for Drene Shampoo. Carleton was a producer who preferred to summon rather than to be summoned.

At a lunch meeting in the Hollywood Brown Derby, Jean Holloway and I were invited to join him, Halverstadt and several of his ad agency representatives.

After a few minutes of Carleton's charming small talk and large martinis, Mr. Halverstadt got down to business and told us what the show would be.

"My dear fellow," Alsop cut in acidly, "do you have a crystal ball in your navel that reveals to you alone what my show will be?"

While the advertising people held their collective breath, Alsop continued, "Your company bought my show. I make the show. My advice to you, sir, is slither back to your soap kettles in Cincinnati and boil your fats!"

If I knew then what I know now, I could tell the look in Halverstadt's eyes read "Cancel!"

On September 8, 1946, NBC announcer Truman Bradley read: "From Hollywood! Don Ameche presents—*The Drene Show*! ... And now, here's *Don Ameche*!"

Jean wrote that. She also wrote this, when Don signed off December 8:

"Next week, the Drene Show will be full of surprises. It'll be a brand new variety program featuring the songs of lovely Frances Langford and the hilarious new comedy star, Danny Thomas. And of course, I'll be here, too."

Don did not mention that he would have a new producer who employed different writers. One of them was Sherwood Schwartz, who helped make Danny Thomas hilarious.

After our final broadcast, I had dinner with Carleton and our guest star, his bride, Sylvia Sidney, in the Mocambo, a posh supper club on the Sunset Strip. There was a boisterous trio of men at a booth across the crowded room. Alsop identified them as the artist John Decker, the actor John Carradine and the writer Gene Fowler.

Gene Fowler wrote some of my favorite books. I wanted to meet him. "Do you know him?" I asked Alsop.

"Unfortunately," he said, "I know the lot of them and I will not expose you to that sordid nest of vipers."

What did Carleton hold against Decker and Carradine? They were Fowler's playmates. Sylvia explained to me later that Alsop and John Barrymore were staunch friends but when Gene Fowler wrote his Barrymore memoir *Good Night, Sweet Prince*, he completely ignored Alsop and Carleton never forgave him. Although Sylvia chided him for that, I never did meet my hero.

In October, two months before that last *Drene Show*, my wife and children arrived from New York to become provisional Californians. Doris felt she was a big city girl who would eventually return to the East. To help her make the move west, her cousin Blanche flew with her, holding infant Donna on her lap while Doris held Lisa, who was beginning to talk, an activity she now abandons only when she sleeps.

One of the most exciting days of my life was when I pulled into the driveway of the first house I ever owned, and was choked with emotion when I brought my wife and daughters into the six rooms where we would make a home. I had furnished it with a cradle for Donna, a crib for Lisa, my typewriter desk, a radio, a few kitchen utensils, dish towels, toilet paper and a refrigerator stocked with eggs, bacon, milk and cereal.

I had neglected a few things such as linens, lamps, curtains, carpets, pictures, cleaning supplies and several other necessities. But I was proud of what I had accumulated and expected Doris to express her joy.

She cried.

Not from joy. Not from relief.

We didn't have a bed.

Christ, a man can't think of everything; that's why he gets married.

"My sister, Lisa, can get along with anyone, even inanimate objects."—Abigail Kanter Jaye

19. Even Inanimate Objects

When a newspaper columnist accused me of stealing from my children, honesty compelled me to admit my habit of recording amusing things I overheard. My girls provided amusement for millions with lines selected from their conversations.

After *The Drene Show*, I had time to spend with them and Doris. Blanche continued to live with us as we gradually furnished the house, but once she decided to remain in California, she found a job in Hollywood and moved into an apartment there. Doris was tempted to move with her because she felt isolated so far from town in Sherman Oaks, but decided to stay with me and the girls for a little while longer. Until they got married.

Meanwhile, I became her chauffeur because she refused to learn how to drive. "To quote my friend, Maxine Fiel," she said, "mechanically, I'm not inclined."

All machines frightened her. I even had to do the vacuuming until we hired a housekeeper, which we did when my agents got me my next job. It was a week's trial with Ozzie Nelson on his successful *Ozzie and Harriet* show.

Ozzie's staff congregated in the den of his tasteful Hollywood home once a week, where they handed in their scripts, discussed the story line for the next show, then had generous dishes of ice cream that Harriet served.

As pleasant as the Nelsons were, I was not a fan of their low-key domestic comedy and asked my agents to find me something else.

I recall nothing of what I wrote for Ozzie and remember only two of the several writers I sat with in their den, Selma Diamond and Ben Gershman. Selma was one of the very few women comedy writers in the '40s and was very funny. Ben was the "story man" who submitted several ideas for a week, from which Ozzie would select the one that the genetically gloomy Gershman invariably considered the worst.

Ben's wife Frances, a former gym teacher from Chicago, often told people, "You don't like us because we're not attractive," which was only partially true. The Gershmans were the ones who didn't like the Gershmans. When Frances was given a cosmetic makeover at a party, all of the guests praised her new look. "What do you think, Ben?" somebody asked him and he replied, "It fans the embers of my indifference."

Ben felt comfortable with Selma Diamond because she was not the prettiest girl in town, either. When I met her, the first question she asked me was, "Are you married?"

"Extremely," I said. Selma wanted to meet my wife. "Whenever a married guy comes on the show," she explained, "he goes home and tells his wife he's working with a broad. I want her to get a look at me, she shouldn't worry."

One afternoon, I took her arm to escort her across a street. She looked at me with admiration and said, "God, Kanter, you make me feel like a tall, blonde *shiksa*!"

When she went into television, Selma moved to the other side of the camera and enjoyed a new career as a character actress.

After my second week with the Nelsons, I was happy to move on to my next assignment. I might have lasted longer with Ozzie but that was before I began enlisting my kids as collaborators.

The next year, Lisa was having a tea party with Donna in front of our little house on Columbus Avenue. I watched them from indoors. Lisa kept up a running line of conversation, providing answers to her own questions because Donna had not yet begun to talk. Or maybe Donna could but was just waiting a few months for Lisa to let her get in a word. Lisa did stop when a saleswoman approached and said, "Hello, young lady."

Lisa said, "Are you a stranger?"

"No," the woman smiled. "Why?"

"We're not s'posed to talk to strangers," Lisa said.

"My name's Marion," the woman said. "What's yours?"

"Lisa Kanter." She indicated Donna and said, "This is my sister, Mrs. O'Dell."

When Bob Hope appeared as the *Bachelor in Paradise*, he exchanged a similar dialogue in the film with a child actor who got two laughs. Bob got three by reacting.

There was another line in that same script that came from watching Doris apply polish to her nails. Our baby daughter, Abbe, held her hands out and said, "Kin I have some *poll nailish*?" I wrote that spoonerism into a scene but Jack Arnold, our director, changed *poll nailish* to *nail polish* because, he said, nobody would understand what *poll nailish* means.

Differences of opinion about coining words for comic effect contribute to the angrification of writers.

Donna provided me with another spoonerism that I put into a scene where Diana Dors played a drunk who asked for *another todka and vonic.*

At supper one evening, Donna held up a bare wishbone and said, "Mommy, put some more chicken on this."

Her description of a girl was, "She's old. She in her seventeens," and she once asked her mother, "Can you tell if a fish is a Republican or a gentile or Jewish?"

My precocious daughters admired a new suit I was showing Doris, and Donna said, "Boy, Daddy, you look handsomer than you are in that!"

And Lisa said, "Take off your ring and some other lady will grab you!"

When my parents visited California for the first time, Donna said to me, "You look like Grandpa, but you're just a daddy."

Showing a photograph of Donna to them, Lisa said, "In this picture, Daddy went to work and Mommy left home."

When the exterminators came to fumigate our house, we had to leave for several hours. Lisa, our pint-size philosopher, said gravely, "All the time the 'sterminator is 'sterminating, God is busy making more bugs!"

Donna insisted on watching me shave one morning and asked, "Can you shave off your mustass?" I said sure and when I did, Donna's lips quivered and almost in tears she asked, "Are you still going to be our daddy?"

I have worn a mustache ever since.

Most of our friends in those days were writers. Among the girls' favorites was Jack Douglas, who lived on a ranch with a large dog they used to ride on, along with Doug's kids.

One Saturday I was working with Sid Silvers in the backyard where Sid lay in a hammock, trying to think of a punchline for a scene. Lisa and Donna came out to remind me that it was time I took them to the pony rides at Playland.

"We'll go as soon as we finish this scene," I promised.

Two minutes later, they came back out and Lisa asked, "Are you finished yet?"

"No," Sid said. "We need a joke and your daddy can't think of one and I can't think of one and your mommy can't think of one so you'll have to wait unless *you* can think of one."

I was about to tell Sid that he was being a bit harsh on a four year old but he fell out of the hammock when Lisa said, "Why don't you call Jack Douglas?"

On January 2, 1947, I reported to my new job in the Bank of America Building in Beverly Hills. That was where Freeman Gosden and Charles Correll occupied a sprawling suite of offices where they conducted the business of *Amos 'n' Andy.*

That landmark radio comedy is one of the few examples of genuine American folklore radio has ever produced.

For years, Gosden and Correll wrote all of their 15-minute scripts themselves, five days a week. Freeman, the more sophisticated of the two, played Amos, the Kingfish and assorted other characters. Correll, a former bricklayer, did the typing and played Andy, Henry Van Porter and other smaller parts. Now that they were doing half-hour shows once a week, they engaged help to prepare drafts of their scripts. Their writers came in for four-week trials before being hired for a season. They felt it took four shows for a new writer to understand their show, even though most of us had been listening to them all our lives.

My first week was an auspicious beginning. I reported to work to meet their head writer, an amiable fellow named Bob Ross. He introduced me to the current team, a very young, skinny boy named Bob Fischer and a veteran humorist named John P. Medbury.

When a buzzer sounded, we entered the inner sanctum. It was a corner office where Gosden and Correll sat at a common desk made for them to face each other. A standard typewriter and stack of typing paper sat on Correll's side.

He was cordial, Freeman reserved, but both expressed their pleasure to have me join their team. I expressed my pleasure in working with two stars I had admired since I was a boy in Georgia. Freeman brightened when he detected a tinge of Rebel in my speech. I knew he was a Virginian so I encouraged the drawl.

The show was broken down into three acts. Each writer—or team—was responsible for writing two of the acts, which were assigned by Bob Ross. Then all of us would discuss the next week's story and break it down into three acts. Charlie typed the pages and their secretary retyped them and distributed copies to us to take home, where we would write our drafts.

First thing Thursday was the reading of the new scenes. Bob read them, doing all the voices in what I thought was a remarkably good imitation of Amos, Andy, the Kingfish and even his wife Sapphire, who was played on the air by the talented black actress, Ernestine Wade.

Neither Freeman nor Charlie criticized any of what they heard. Charlie chuckled a few times and smiled often. Freeman kept a poker face. It was time for lunch. We had our choice of going out or eating with our employers. I opted to stay. When the lunch they served was apple juice, wheat germ and alfalfa sprouts, I understood why Medbury and Fisher went downstairs and Ross retired to his office with a pastrami-stained brown bag.

After lunch, we all worked on a new storyline in Bob's office while

Freeman and Charlie put together the script from the pages Bob read earlier. Now and then, he was called into their office for a brief conference. When they came to a spot they weren't able to rewrite to their own satisfaction, they called all of us and we pitched lines back and forth until they heard — or said — one that pleased them.

At the end of the day, we were assembled again to go over the new storyline their secretary had retyped. Ross told me to write the first two acts and by 5:00, I was on my way home, feeling great. Unlike the way I felt about *Ozzie and Harriet*, I knew I could write for *Amos 'n' Andy*.

I enjoyed writing what I supposed were the first two acts. What I had written were the first two scenes! Freeman paid me the ultimate compliment: He laughed at this joke I gave the Kingfish:

> SAPPHIRE: Did you go down an' git dat job I told you 'bout this mornin'?
>
> KINGFISH: I phoned de place an' invited de man out here to interview me but he wouldn't come.

Charlie couldn't get over the fact that I was dumb enough to think the scenes were acts but smart enough to write two acts worth of dialogue.

The writers' presence was not demanded at the broadcast Tuesday nights, but we were required to attend the rehearsal Monday evening in the CBS studios at Sunset and Gower. There we heard Freeman and Charlie and the rest of the cast read the script for the first time. To me, a miracle was happening; Gosden and Correll disappeared to be replaced by Amos and Andy, alive and real and in that room.

After the second week, Rosie called me to say Gosden and Correll were picking up my option and giving me a raise.

It was time for me to join the Radio Writers Guild, where my colleagues eventually honored me by electing me to the presidency of the West Coast branch. And in that office, I won another badge of honor — an ulcer.

"Hollywood's lesson: It's easier to be famous than to be excellent."—John Lahr

20. *Hollywood's Lesson*

John P. Medbury was famous for his humor long before he came to Hollywood. He had been employed by William Randolph Hearst as a newspaper columnist and his daily output was eagerly devoured by readers from San Francisco to Boston.

He reminded me of another celebrated Hearst alumnus, Arthur "Bugs" Baer. I once toiled with Bugs on a gag edition of the *Journal* that King Features put out to welcome the *Hellzapoppin'* comic strip to their syndicate. He was an amusing cohort for the week I spent in his company.

Like John, Bugs was a short, compact gentleman who dressed soberly and looked more like a clergyman than a cynical dealer in wit. But behind their innocent facades lurked the mischief that endeared both men to their readers but often alienated strangers.

One night, Bugs and I were leaving the stage door of the Winter Garden when he was accosted by the infamous harridan shunned as Broadway Rose. She thrust a pad and pencil into his hands and demanded his autograph. "Whose name should I sign?" Bugs asked with a twinkle, sensing that she had no idea who he was. The slovenly woman ignored the twinkle and said, "Yours, stupid!"

So Bugs signed "Myrna Loy."

Medbury's mischief was more outlandish. He invited me to join him for lunch my second day with Amos 'n' Andy to escape their wheat germ diet and, as we started to cross the street, a timid man carrying a huge package stopped John and said, "Excuse me, sir, but can I get to Camden Drive this way?"

Medbury glared at the man and said, "You may this time, but never again!"

John was a practical joker who sometimes went to enormous extremes to amuse himself. He and his wife gave frequent parties and for one New Year's gala, he engaged an actor to torment their women guests. He sat nude behind a shower curtain in a bathroom designated "ladies only" and as soon as a woman settled on the porcelain, he pushed the curtain aside and said to the horrified guest, "Aw, jeezas, lady, I'm trying to take a bath in here!"

Hearing stories like that are more fun than living through them. When the Medburys invited us to their home, Doris declined. I was obliged to confine my association with John to the office, where he filled the air with smoke from his exotic Murad cigarettes.

Charles Correll, who had recently become a father again, objected to the smoke and during one writing session said, "John, a man of your age should stop smoking." John blew a puff of smoke at him and said, "A man of your age should stop fucking." Charlie turned mauve with embarrassment. He never brought up the subject again.

John continued to smoke his Murads and cough. "They're going to kill me," he said. "This time next year, you and Freeman'll be coming out to Forest Lawn and yelling, 'Get up, John, we need a blackout!'"

He wasn't far wrong. John died in his seventies, before the year was up.

We were sitting around trying to come up with an opening line for the Kingfish and wishing out loud that Medbury were here to give it to us. When we all realized that we were stuck, I asked Freeman, "If the Kingfish could actually come into this room right now and we explained what the situation is, what do you think he'd say?" Freeman immediately shifted into blackface and threw a line that made us all laugh. I don't recall what it was but I learned a valuable lesson from the incident: The actor knew his characters so intimately they could speak for themselves.

If a writer knows his characters as well as Gosden and Correll knew theirs, the characters will dictate their own dialogue when he writes.

Several years later, I ran into Correll at a party in Jack Haley's house where he proved that he still had Andy's unsophistication when he said he just returned from a tour of Europe. "What a great trip that was," he boasted. "Twenty-five countries in fourteen days!"

When I completed my assignment with him and Freeman, Doris and I took the girls out of nursery school for a winter vacation. We drove the Olds up the coast to San Francisco, across to Yosemite, then down through Nevada and back home in time to celebrate the holidays.

While we were out of town, Dorothy River tried to get me on the phone. She had been calling me for a week. I had neglected to tell her we'd be out of town.

"Always let us know where you are," she said. "Rosie and Barron want to know if you're ready to go back to work." I was, I said, if they needed the money. Dorothy said Rosie had a job for me and would call me back as soon as one of them returned to the office.

The job Rosie had for me turned into a career. It took me from radio to motion pictures to television.

It began the week after New Year's Day, 1947, when I went to work for one of the nation's favorite movie stars, the most popular vocalist in the world and a man I came to respect, enjoy and sometimes even like, Bing Crosby.

When I went to work for him and his producer, fellow AFRS veteran Bill Morrow, Rosie felt it was time for me to buy a new car.

Autos were still scarce in 1947. Customers were placed on waiting lists. Rosie said I might get lucky on a short list if I went to see Phil Hall, a Buick dealer in Beverly Hills. I pulled my ancient Oldsmobile into his service garage where it expired in a cloud of hissing steam.

"Wow!" some guy in a nifty sports coat said. "You just made it!"

I went into the showroom to meet Hall. He had a gorgeous pale blue convertible sitting in the window. I admired it, even though the price was more than I wanted to pay. I was not comfortable spending for something my family couldn't eat, drink or wear. In that regard, I still live in the past tense.

The man in the nifty sports coat came in and said, "My mechanic says you won't be able to drive that old coffee grinder out of here, so you want to let us fix it or have it towed?"

"Who's us?" I asked. Hall introduced Lindsay Howard, who owned the agency, among other things, and said to him, "This is the gentleman George Rosenberg sent in. He writes for Bing."

"Well," Howard said, "we can't let a Crosby writer prowl the streets in that rattletrap. Who's that convertible for?"

"Gene Raymond," Hall said. "He ordered it three months ago. And he's coming in tomorrow."

"Gene can wait," Howard said and turned to me. "Say hello to Bing for me."

I began a lifelong love affair with new cars as I drove home in that beautiful blue Buick.

When I met Crosby a week later, I told him Lin Howard said hello and how I'd met him the day my Oldsmobile died.

Bing smiled and said, "Lin and I owned a race horse who serviced a mare, then dropped dead. We named the foal *Last Bang*."

Bing and Dixie named the youngest of their four sons for their friend. Lindsay Crosby was a handsome youngster who tried manfully to keep up with his older brothers, Gary and twins Dennis and Philip. One afternoon, when Linny was about five years old, he asked me and Morrow to tell him some dirty words.

"If I do," Bill said, "your old man'll kill me."

Linny appealed to me. "I know one dirty word already. Tell me some more."

"Tell me yours first," I said.

Linny hesitated, then looked at Bill. "I won't say it, but I'll spell it." He then whispered, "D-A-M!"

Bill said, "Whew! Linny, do you know what that spells?"

"Sure," the boy said. "Shit!"

On our show, Lindsay used other words we wrote for him and his brothers.

Every performer had enormous respect and affection for our star. Bing could be an engaging conversationalist, the consummate gentleman, tactful, witty, easygoing and thoroughly professional in his work. He expected the same from his employees.

My first year with him was broadcast over ABC because it was the only network that would put recorded programs on the air. All the others aired theirs live exclusively, which is why network shows emanating from California were repeated for West Coast listeners. Some stars, like Bob Hope, enjoyed doing two performances. They could rewrite jokes that fizzled on the first show and had the satisfaction of hearing more laughs.

Crosby was different.

For the years Bing did his popular *Kraft Music Hall* on NBC, he disliked repeating his hour-long shows. When he became a business partner in the struggling new industry of tape recording, he added more to his personal comfort than he anticipated. We were able to record Bing's *Philco Radio Time* whenever and wherever he wanted. As tape became popular, Bing found he had another source of revenue that added a few dollars to his bank account. Several few.

The other networks soon capitulated and Crosby's former boss, William Paley, lured him back to CBS for the glory of a larger audience and a greater pot of gold. The increasing use of tape added to Bing's reputation as an astute investor, and when he went into the frozen orange juice business, Bill Morrow advised me to buy stock in Minute Maid.

Instead, I bought a few shares of Irving B. Kahn's Teleprompter company, where Kahn also made millions. I made 40. Dollars, that is.

"There are no small parts; only small salaries."—Jerry Hausner

21. No Small Parts

Working conditions with the Crosby show from the very beginning became the yardstick by which I was to measure all subsequent assignments, most of which were no match for the pleasant model Crosby and Morrow set with Bill's co-producer, Murdo MacKenzie.

Murdo was an audio engineer who helped develop the tape recorder after serving many years in the broadcast booth. The quiet, handsome Murdo, who married one of Bing's favorite singers, Trudy Erwin, always wore a jacket, shirt and tie to work. Bing never did. His casual wardrobe inspired many remarks like Clifton Webb's putdown of Bing's Hawaiian shirt: "It looks like a tattoo I once had removed from a maiden aunt of mine."

It was great fun writing for Bing, who seldom questioned our material, even when we poked fun at his baseball team, his family, his race horses, real estate, oil wells, movies or his rapidly receding hairline. One time he did balk at a joke was when Fred Astaire was our guest.

Both men were bald. Fred wore a toupee. Bing wore a hat. For Fred's appearance, I wrote an exchange in which he said he used to be taller and Bing said, "Yes, I used to brush mine up, too."

After the first reading, Fred whispered something to Bing, who later said, "Let's go easy on the hair jests, boys. Don't make me a professional darning egg."

Bill and I worked in his bachelor pad where we discussed the rough outlines of our script and divided the spots we were to write. I wrote my drafts at home, then returned with my pages to put together with his. But he seldom had more than a joke or two scribbled on a cocktail napkin, so we sat in his breakfast nook overlooking Sunset Boulevard and dictated the script to his first secretary, Jane Reidel, while his Creole cook prepared exotic lunches.

For the next five years that was our m.o. through the series of secretaries who followed Jane when she left for marriage. We were interrupted often by Bill's friends dropping in. One was his new neighbor Ronald Reagan, just separated from Jane Wyman and looking for dates.

Some of Bill's callers stayed for a while. One was a spirited beauty named Pat Dane, Tommy Dorsey's former wife who was once under contract to MGM.

Pat was always late and her producer, Harry Rapf, shouted at her before the entire company, "Young lady, do you realize how much you cost this studio by coming in late every day?"

"No, I don't, Harry," Pat shouted back, "but do you realize how much you're costing them by coming in on time?"

It was a less flip Pat Dane who called me in 1950 the night before I was to fly to San Francisco to tape the show I'd written for our legendary guest, Al Jolson.

"Bill just called," she said. "Don't go up. Jolson died this evening, so they canceled the show."

That did seem the logical thing to do.

One of Bill's secretaries was a pretty Texan named Betty. She was typing a letter in another room while Bill and I were talking with Larry Clemmons, a Disney animator who was helping us with an extra script. We were discussing the un–Disney subject of teenage sex. When Betty came in with the letter for Bill, he said, "Betty, did you ever get laid when you were in high school?"

Betty thought for a moment and asked, "You mean — in the school itself?"

Betty left Bill to go to work with Steve Allen in New York, where Steve met Jayne Meadows and Betty became Steveless.

Morrow was a gregarious wit who was one of Bing's closest friends and confidants. Every winter he played host to Salvatore DeLorenzo, an ex-prizefighter from Chicago known as Society Kid Hogan, who amused us all.

Reading the morning paper one afternoon soon after waking, S.K. said, "The government's sending some more of Lucky Luciano's guys back to Sicily. If this keeps up, our churches will fold."

When the Musician's Union threatened to strike all recording studios, we worked around the clock to stockpile several shows. In addition to Clemmons, Bill called in Izzy Elinson and Bobby O'Brien, who wrote guest spots for Burns and Allen, Walter O'Keefe and Bing's old sidekick, Bob Burns.

Bobby and Izzy went out to see Burns, who was proud of the San Fernando Valley acreage he owned and insisted on showing the two city boys around. After touring the outbuildings, Burns took them into a large room which held his pride and joy.

"What is it?" Bobby asked.

"A loom!" Burns said. "I made it myself! And I'll tell you something else about this loom. Until I made this one, I'd never even seen a loom before!"

"Hmm," Izzy said. "Then how do you know it *is* a loom?"

Working on a script for a recently married guest star, Al Lewis dropped by as we wrestled with Bing's introduction and made this suggestion: "From under the belly of Vincente Minnelli, we bring you Judy Garland!"

We encouraged Al to go back to writing his *Our Miss Brooks*.

Always a welcome visitor was Abe Burrows, who came in with lines for his frequent appearances as a guest. "I'm also bald," he pointed out to Bing, "but I don't have a mustache, either. It's a set."

Abe was the Olympic champion name-dropper. When the phone rang for him, he told his listener, "I'm over here working with Bing, Bill Morrow and Hal Kanter." John Scott Trotter, our jovial music director, arrived to go over cues for the operetta Abe had written, and when the phone rang again, Abe said, "I'm working with Bing, John Scott Trotter and Morrow." I didn't make the cut.

Later, Crosby himself dropped in and when a third call came for Burrows, he said, "Can't talk. Busy with Bing."

One week, I was in the studio control room while Murdo was on the stage, Trotter was going over an arrangement with Bing and Bill was in our dressing room. I was alone when the phone rang. A woman's voice demanded, "Who is this?"

"Who are you?" I asked.

"I am Dixie Lee Crosby and I want to talk to my *hushband* now!" She was obviously not at an AA meeting.

"I'm sorry," I said, "but he's on stage right now, rehearsing."

"Who the hell are you?" she asked.

"I'm Hal Kanter," I said because I was too nervous to lie. "I'm one of his writers."

Her voice changed abruptly. "Oh, I know you. I heard you on the show with the boys." She sounded close to tears as she asked, "Why won't they let me come play with you, too? Why can't I come see you?"

"Just a minute, Mrs. Crosby," I said. "I'll go get Bing."

I raced out to the stage and beckoned to him. "I think you might want to answer the phone," I confided. "It's Dixie."

Crosby turned to ice. He dropped his script, whirled into the control room and closed the door. He was gone no more than three minutes, then returned, picked up his script and frigidly said, "Take it from the top."

If he ever mentioned a word about that incident to anyone, it was not to me.

As we continued to tape *Philco Radio Time* on ABC, the other networks soon capitulated and Bing's former network boss, William Paley, lured him back to CBS. By then I had added "actor" to my résumé, having shared the microphone with Bing in several small parts. I played a network executive, a sponsor's representative, a janitor, an Italian waiter and a Japanese soldier. The four Crosby boys were also on that show and for the rest of their lives, whenever Linny or Gary saw me, they reminded me of "your Japanese lawyer, *Sosumi*!"

All this time, Bing was the king of cool. There is only one instance I recall him losing it.

We were taping the show in New York where our guest was Beatrice Lillie, one of Bing's favorite Brits. My first trip east with Morrow, I fell victim to his work habit, which was always to delay writing a script until the last hours. Bing was never happy about that. He felt that actors should have a chance to read the entire script, not just part of it, before performing it.

While Bing, Bea and Ken Carpenter were onstage in front of an audience, I was backstage in the star's dressing room, typing the "good night" spot — three pages of dialogue — and making five carbon copies. We didn't have the luxury of Xerox in the late '40s.

While Ken was reading the last commercial, Morrow snatched the pages from my typewriter and rushed onstage to distribute them to Bing, Bea and Ken.

In the script was a reference to England's Sir Stafford Cripps. When Bea — Lady Peel offstage — came to the name, shaken by the unnerving adventure of a cold reading to millions of listeners, she called him *Sir Stifford Crapps.*

Through the roar that greeted that spoonerism, Murdo barked "Music!" into Trotter's microphone, but the entire orchestra was so broken up they couldn't respond to the cue.

So he stopped the tape for the ten minutes it took to settle down before they could redo the "good nights." Later, backstage, Crosby said to me, "Never do that again. *Never*!"

The look in his blue eyes was the father of the laser beam. There may still be a hole in the wall behind where I stood.

When I mentioned Bing's anger to Bill, he laughed it off. Evidently, Bing forgave us both because the next week we enlisted his sense of humor to tape this brief exchange with Carpenter in exaggerated British dialects:

> KEN: I say, old chap, did you hear what Lady Peel said on the American wireless last week?
>
> BING: Don't believe I did.

KEN: Said Sir Stifford Crapps.
BING: Amazing! How does he manage on this austerity diet?

He sent it to Miss Lillie, who, she later told us, wore out the tape playing it in England.

But I never got over the look in that dressing room hallway, an ice stiletto that Crosby employed on another trip to New York. He had been golfing at White Sulphur Springs the week before and he came to Morrow's hotel where we were working to take us to the Paramount film exchange to look at newsreel footage of his golf tournament before we went to the theater.

The word spread quickly when we arrived to see the film, and by the time we came out of the projection room, the halls were crowded with fans. Bing was cordial enough as we pushed toward the elevator but when we got to the ground floor, it was almost impossible to get out. The building was jammed with noisy New Yorkers wanting to catch a glimpse of the man.

There was a solid mass of animals between Bing's limousine, waiting at the curb, and at the entrance to the building. It was impossible to get to that car. But then a remarkable thing happened.

The jovial Bing we had just seen turned instantly into Crosby, the ice-maker, whose frozen stiletto pierced the crowd. A sudden silence descended as he moved forward and a path opened for us to make our getaway to the theater.

When we arrived, there was a crew from *Life* magazine waiting. Nobody had bothered to tell Crosby and when the first bulb flashed, Bing ordered them out of the theater. As a result, his face didn't appear in the pages of *Life* for years.

Morrow could be equally high-handed. When Fred Allen was our guest in New York, he sat with us in the empty theater after rehearsal, sharpening a sketch he had helped us write earlier, when the head usher came in.

"There's a big crowd waiting outside, Mr. Morrow," he said, "and it's starting to rain, so can we bring them in earlier?"

"To hell with 'em!" Morrow snarled. "Let 'em stand there until we're ready."

Fred was pained.

"For God's sake, Bill," he cajoled in his nasal whine, "let them come inside. They're ugly enough when they're dry!"

Both Morrow and Crosby could also be sweet when one least expected it. The week before, Bing drove in from his Long Island hideaway just as we were finishing the last pages of that week's script. He was in a buoyant mood and as we walked to the elevator, he began singing, which he seldom did for free.

A registered nurse popped out of a nearby suite and said, "I thought I recognized your voice, Mr. Crosby. I have a sick old woman in here."

"I'm sorry," Bing apologized. "I hope I didn't disturb her."

"No," the nurse said, "quite the opposite, in point of fact. She's a devoted fan of yours. Could you take just a moment to say hello to her?"

Bing left us in the hall where we waited for five minutes, impatiently. Ethel Merman was our guest and she was always prompt. Another few minutes passed. Bill was about to knock on the door when we heard from inside the words to "Too-ra Loo-ra Loo-ra" as Bing sang the Irish lullaby to the woman.

He crooned a couple of other songs before he returned to us. Before Bill could say anything, Bing said, "We got stuck in traffic."

In Hollywood, a frequent guest was Judy Garland, one of our best-loved stars. As an actress, singer and comedienne, Judy was unsurpassed. Nobody ever delivered a comedy line better than she, with a more sure instinct for timing. Moreover, she could invest a quality of pathos into the silliest of lines, giving it a dimension of humanity it lacked on paper. Judy was an inspiration to write for, a delight to work with.

She had some widely publicized problems. When she made headlines with a reported suicide attempt, she hid from public view for a period and there was some speculation that Judy Garland was through, that she might never work again.

She was far from through.

Judy fought her way back to stability and chose the Crosby radio show as the vehicle to return to entertainment. She arrived in the studio with suave Carleton Alsop, who had taken Judy into protective custody against the curious. She was much thinner than the last time I had seen her, more agitated, but still a charming and cooperative woman whose luminous eyes could melt a man's pacemaker.

Music rehearsals under Trotter's amiable direction went as smoothly (as always) when he held the baton. Judy was in fine voice and giggled at the jokes, accepting without protest whatever changes we made and was prepared by Bing himself for any he might make during the performance. He often scribbled notes on his script, surprising us with changes he fancied.

As show time approached, Murdo sent Carpenter onstage to face the packed house, all of them eager to share the return of Judy Garland, in the flesh. Ken began his audience "warm-up." It was his custom to welcome them to the studio, introduce John Scott, his orchestra and our guests.

Backstage, Carleton Alsop urged me to get word out to Ken that Judy did not wish to be introduced before the show began.

She had grown fearful that the audience would be hostile, as some of the press had been. She didn't have the courage to walk out and face strangers who'd be checking her wrists for scars! Without dialogue to read or lyrics to sing, until the show began she wouldn't subject herself to their merciless scrutiny.

Bing happened by as Alsop was explaining all this to me. Without a word to us, he turned to Judy's dressing room and knocked for admittance. We heard the tears in her voice when she asked who was there.

"Old Dad," Bing said in his unmistakable lower register. As he went in, I found an excuse to go onstage and get the word to Ken. Then, as Bing wandered on, I wandered off. It always took a few beats for an audience to recognize our star. He could have been a stagehand — if he were better dressed.

"Why, it's Bing!" Ken said in mock surprise. The house thundered with applause.

"We've got a guest this evening," Bing told them when they stopped clapping. "Good kid, old pal of ours around here. I'm pretty confident you like her, too, so what say you let her know it?"

He turned to the wings, where a trembling Judy stood with Alsop's comforting arms around her.

"Some folks'd like to say hello, Judy."

That's all.

"Yeah! Yeah!" they cheered. The entire audience leaped up to greet her even before she set foot onstage. By the time she joined Bing at the center stage microphone to give him a kiss of gratitude, Judy Garland was back, clear-eyed and bushy-tailed, brilliant as ever.

She was magnificent in performance and remains in my mind as one of the three women I most enjoyed writing for.

"Some people are so sensitive, they feel snubbed if an epidemic overlooks them."
— Kin Hubbard

22. *Some People Are So Sensitive*

Of all the celebrated wits who were Crosby guests over my years with him, none was more amusing than Bill Morrow.

When flamboyant actor Monty Woolley was too ill to appear with us, Bill explained, "He got hold of a sour choir boy."

When Tyrone Power married Linda Christian, Bill said he didn't know the lady, but "her mother runs a crotch ranch in Mexico."

Talking about a city he loved, he remarked, "Any town is Paris when you're young." That line was too good to toss away so I built a routine with Claudette Colbert around it and John Scott Trotter used it as a title for a song that did not quite stir Cole Porter to gnash his teeth.

One of Bill's favorite playmates was also Bing's, Phil Harris, an original companion at golf, fishing and making music or mischief. After one round of golf at Lakeside Country Club, the trio refreshed themselves for several hours at the club's densely populated bar, then started to the Mocambo for a late supper. But Phil, who was married to Alice Faye, said, "You better drop me off, because if I'm not home by midnight, Alice rents out my room."

Another time, Phil said, "Alice and I have reached the stage where we took the mirror off our bedroom ceiling and put it over the dinner table so we can watch what we eat."

When he appeared at a Writers Guild awards evening, he was scheduled to follow a newcomer from Canada, Giselle MacKenzie. Because they liked her, Giselle did several encores. After the third one, Phil stuck his head out of the wings and yelled, "When are you getting off? I've had to shave twice already!"

Giselle had an infinite capacity for taking applause.

Louis Armstrong was another guest who was always good for a chuckle. His nickname was Satchmo, an abbreviated form of Satchel Mouth, because his mouth was so big it looked like he could blow a trumpet from either end. When Bing greeted his friend at one rehearsal, Satchmo said, "I'm pleasurated, Pops."

"How've things been going, Satch?" Bing asked him. "Well," he answered in his gravel voice, "the white folks are still in the lead."

"You've been tootin' a trumpet for over 30 years now, Satch. How long you figure it'll be before you retire?"

"Retire! That word is out of bounds in my vocabulary. I'm not gonna stop blowing a horn until they declare lungs illegal."

The two old pals spoke about other friends like the waggish one-armed trumpet player Wingy Manone, who drove jewelry sales people to distraction buying only one cuff link.

When the jazzman played Los Angeles, Wingy's only advertisement was a banner hung in front of the club that read "COME IN AND HEAR THE TRUTH."

Joe Venuti was another musician we enjoyed as much for his humor as for his artistry. He stroked hot jazz out of a violin long before Tevye fiddled on the roof.

Venuti had worked with Crosby in the Paul Whiteman orchestra and when Joe came on the show, there was always an exchange about those days. Bing did not regard the maestro with enormous affection, an attitude which found expression in the jokes we did about the King of Jazz.

Bill Morrow's attitude toward other guests was reflected in what we wrote as, I suppose, mine was also. I know that it was always easier for me to write for stars like Jimmy Stewart, Jimmy Durante, Jack Benny and Groucho Marx because I liked them. I also liked Bob Hope but Bill didn't and I found myself defending him often.

One year, when we taped a show with Bob in San Francisco, Bill wrote an opening wherein Bing told Ken Carpenter that they had come up from Los Angeles by train but Hope rode in the baggage car … in a cage. He'd broken out and come howling into the club car.

I thought that was too harsh but Bill said it would get laughs and that's all Hope ever wanted. We worked on another spot, where Bing accused Bob of being so greedy, he dressed in a skimpy woman's costume to work as a nightclub cigarette girl. There were other jokes about trying to get a date for Bob and when they struck out, they went to the Fleishacker zoo and shaved an ape.

Bob arrived for rehearsal at the Marine Memorial theater and picked up his script for the first reading. Evidently it was Bing's first look, too, because he chuckled as he read the opening spot with Ken. Bob shrugged off the first couple of digs at him, but when they got to the line about his breaking out of his cage, Bob said, "Hold it. What're you guys doing to me?"

"Gettin' even, Lard Bucket," Bing said, "for the things you said about me last week."

"What's the matter, Tin Tonsils," Bob sneered, "your sense of humor under arrest?" Some of us donated a laugh to placate him and we went on with the reading. But when we came to the shaving of the ape, Bob threw his script on the table and jumped to his feet. "Now you've gone too far!" he said. He was genuinely hurt and Bill didn't assuage his pain when he said, "Sounds like your sense of humor is in the brig."

Bing sided with Hope. He said he had too much regard for his bosom buddy to allow such disrespect just for the sake of a few cheap laughs. He winked at me, then suggested I do some dialogue repair while they rehearsed the musical numbers.

Another comedian who was a joy to write for was Jimmy Durante, a sweet fellow who appeared to have as much formal education as a fire hydrant. He consented to do a show for the benefit of the Cancer Society. I had agreed to write it and went to consult Jimmy at his Beverly Hills home.

"Listen," he said, "why should we knock ourself out doin' new stuff. Last month, I did a great spot with Bing. Let's do it again."

"What spot was it?" I asked.

"Something about me running the Panama Canal," he said. "I'll call them up and ask the guy who wrote it." He began dialing the phone, then abruptly hung up. "Hey!" he said. "You're the guy!"

It was on the Crosby show that I met an actor with whom I spent considerable time, the screen's menacing Peter Lorre. Even people who knew the little round man forgot that when he played the psychopathic child murderer in Fritz Lang's stark German film, *M*, Peter was starring on a Berlin stage every night in a comedy. When he wasn't chilling audiences to their bones, he was a most amusing companion.

One of our frequent watering holes was the Key Club across the street from the old NBC studios on Vine Street. Sitting at the curve of its horseshoe bar where we could see the other drinkers, Peter indicated one man seated behind him but facing me. "That man," he purred, "wants to challenge me to a stare-down. Ever since *The Maltese Falcon*, there's always been somebody who thinks he can outstare me. Like old Western gunslingers, they want to take on the top gun in town. Now you watch this eyeslinger. I'm going to turn around and in 20 seconds he's going to give up."

With that, Peter swiveled his head and locked eyes with the challenger. It did not take 20 seconds. In ten, the man nervously turned away to gulp his drink and retreat from the premises.

His secret, Peter explained, is that to stare down somebody, you have to engage both his eyes, but Pete's eyes were so far apart in his broad face, very few people could look into both eyes at once. When he worked with actors he admired, like Humphrey Bogart, he tipped them off how to act in two-shots with him. "Pick one of my eyes to look at and the camera won't tell our little secret."

Peter had another little secret that became his downfall. He was, by his own admission, a drug addict. My pharmacist, Ted Greenfield, once had Peter as his customer back in the days when drugs were dispensed over the counter. Peter came into Ted's apothecary several days a week for a supply and when he signed the register, he told Ted, "I really don't need this. I come here because you're the only one left who asks for my autograph."

At the height of his celebrity, when everyone wanted his autograph, Peter made a series of personal appearances. At the Capitol Theater in New York, he played for a week to SRO audiences four shows a day, reciting a monologue based on Poe's *Tell-Tale Heart.* At the end, the theater went dark save for a single spotlight for the star to return for a bow — which he never did. As his audience applauded, the stage sank slowly into the pit, with the spot following it down.

Peter's friend Milton Berle came backstage several times to use Pete's dressing room for assignations. Berle timed his visits to the actor's appearances but he had never seen his performance. One matinee, Milton's woman was late so he watched Peter's last few minutes from the wings. Peter came off stage to enormous applause and Milton urged him to go back for a bow. Peter merely smiled and started for his dressing room. Milton was frantic. "You've got to take a bow!" he insisted. "Listen to them! Get out there!"

"You go," Peter said. Milton did, even though at that very moment, his date showed up.

To this day, some people who were in that audience are still mystified how Peter Lorre turned into Milton Berle and gradually disappeared, screaming, "Don't touch that girl!"

"I'm O.K.— and neither are you."—Ed Simmons

23. *I'm O.K.*

It's been said that inside every writer, there's a shy actor. I know because I said it.

It's also been said that inside most actors is a caged writer straining to escape. I ran into one of them in 1947. We'll call him Jack Paar.

When vacation time arrived that first season with Crosby, I planned to spend a month traveling with my family, but my agents had other plans. So, after two weeks, I went back to work on Jack Benny's summer replacement, *The Jack Paar Show.*

Paar was a new comedian whose first few shows had gotten enthusiastic reviews, thanks to his brilliant writers. There were five of them: Larry Marks, Arthur Stander, Larry Gelbart, Sid Dorfman and Seaman ("Si") Jacobs. Marks and Stander, who shared the head writer responsibility, were the Mutt and Jeff of neurotics. Artie was small, lean, pugnacious; Larry was huge, grossly overweight and narcoleptic.

When Paar began tampering with their scripts because he felt he knew what was best for him, the writers thought otherwise and resented his input. Paranoid Marks spread the rumor that Jack Paar was an anti–Semite, which both Si Jacobs and Paar's Jewish announcer, Hy Averback, firmly denied.

After three or four weeks of bickering and blaspheme over the show, four of the writers resigned in a body. Only Si remained while the new, smaller staff was assembled.

I joined him, veteran jokesmith Mac Benoff, a swarthy astigmatic whose vision was not his only imperfection, and another writer whose bizarre work I had admired since he performed on a show he wrote for the NBC network. That was Jack Douglas.

The Paar show had offices on the second floor of a house in Hollywood where I met our star, a thin, balding blonde who appeared gracious and respectful of the fact that he and I had shared the less-than-idyllic life in the Pacific during the recent unpleasantness with the Japanese. That summer, Douglas became another friend who remained close to my family for the rest of his life, while Mac Benoff became an object of revulsion

Left to right: Hal Kanter, Jack Douglas, Jack Paar, and Si Jacobs writing Jack Paar's first radio series.

the moment he slithered down the stairs behind me after our first day on the job.

"How well do you know Douglas?" he asked when we got to our parked cars.

"I just met him today," I said. "Why?"

"You know how much he gets a week?" Benoff asked. I said I didn't and it wasn't any of my business, but Benoff said we should make it our business, because "he gets a grand."

"He deserves at least that," I said, and was appalled when he said, "We don't need him! If Jacobs writes the monologue, you and I can handle the rest of it and split Jack's grand between us."

"Are you serious?" I asked. The man was as serious as strangulation.

I had the uneasy feeling that the next day he would suggest to Douglas that the two of them didn't need me. But that didn't happen because "Doug" didn't come in the next day. He worked alone, at home. I went back to working at home myself.

Friday we had a reading with only Hy Averback and Paar's musical director, Jerry Fielding, to make adjustments the script needed.

During one of those sessions, when Paar tried to change a line in a spot Douglas had written, Doug slapped the pencil out of his hand and said, "Don't tamper with perfection!"

Paar nervously withdrew in deference to the writer he most respected and Doug's order became the battle cry for many writers since.

Jack Paar was easy to work for and with. He was only occasionally surly until he was told that his show would be renewed for the fall. Jack asked me to stay on with him, even though I still had my job with Crosby. As an added inducement, Jack promised to cast me in small parts, which I enjoyed doing.

When Rosie talked to Paar's agents about a contract, they balked at the salary he was asking. I suggested Rosie accept what they were offering with the stipulation that I would also get billing as a member of the cast.

"What do you want to be," Rosie asked, "the Jewish Orson Welles?"

No. What I wanted to become was the next Preston Sturges.

When Paar denied my demand for billing, Rosie told him to go on without me. He also told me to forget about acting, but as long as I thought I could write two shows a week, he had another job.

An advertising man named Adrian Samish wanted me to be the head writer for *Beulah*, a 15-minute show starring Hattie McDaniel. It was to be on the air five times a week and while I would be responsible for it every other week, I would be paid weekly. That appealed to me.

Rosie had an apprentice agent working for him, Mike Meshekoff, who had been a furrier before he became our First Sergeant at Armed Forces Radio. A quick student of the agency business, Mike was already handling Howard Duff and a promising young man named Jack Webb.

When Mike accompanied me to the agency offices in Hollywood, Mac Benoff was sitting in the waiting room. I had not seen him since he was replaced by Leo Solomon on the Paar show when Benoff handed in a sketch Paar had heard several months earlier.

Benoff asked what I was doing in the agency office. I told him I was collecting money for the Red Cross.

I followed Mike into Adrian Samish's inner office. Our meeting with the slick advertising man, who had come west from his New York headquarters, was brief. I agreed to take on the *Beulah* challenge and find two writers to assist me. We shook hands and I left Meshekoff to settle the details. Mac Benoff was still in the outer office when I left.

"Red Cross!" he sneered.

When I got home, Doris told me to call Mike at Rosie's office. He said it was urgent.

"Did you tell Mac Benoff," Mike asked me, "that you wanted him to be your partner on *The Beulah Show*?"

"Certainly not," I said. "Where'd that come from?"

"Where else?" Mike said. "After you left, he came in and told Samish that you two were partners on the Paar show and wanted to work together from now on, but before Abe made a deal, he wanted to check with you."

"Thank him," I said, "and tell him I wouldn't work with Benoff if we were Siamese twins."

I engaged two young writers I felt deserved the break I had been given by Wedlock and Snyder, the team of Julian and Leeds. Howard Leeds, the handsome one of the pair, had been an actor when he was a child. Arthur Julian had never been a child. Both were very funny. Howie's humor was sweet, Artie's was sour. Howard wrote lines like, "Beulah, you've washed my tie so often, I can hardly read the dry-clean-only label on it."

Artie said things like, "He was a premature baby; he was born three months before his mother got married."

Our star, Hattie McDaniel, the Oscar winner for her role in *Gone with the Wind*, was a lovely woman with a smile as wide and warm as it was genuine. She had a large home in Los Angeles where she invited us to a party that impressed us by the quality — and quantity — of her food. There were also buckets of iced French wines, Milwaukee beer and Atlanta colas. We were served by pretty women and an imposing chef presided over the steaks he carved with surgical skill. Later, he handed out cards that listed only his name, phone number and this simple legend: "Sharp knives a specialty."

The Beulah Show was produced and directed by Tom McKnight, a tall, sharp-featured, dour man who could find gloom in an armistice. Tom was a product of the theater who ten years earlier helped prepare *Hellzapoppin'* for Broadway. He also had been Will Rogers' producer, "One of the meanest bastards I ever encountered," he confided.

McKnight's bitterness stemmed from Rogers' attempts to destroy the timing of the radio show Tom produced. The cowboy humorist was contracted by a gasoline sponsor to talk for five minutes, alternating weeks with George M. Cohan.

A showmanly device McKnight instituted was an alarm clock, set to ring when the performers' time was up, whereupon the stars were to end their routines. Cohan did; Rogers kept talking. When the network complained, Rogers promised to honor the clock. He didn't. When McKnight was otherwise occupied, Rogers readjusted the alarm to give himself an extra minute and a half.

If Rogers never met a man he didn't like, as he would have the world believe, he must have overlooked Tom McKnight.

While Leeds, Julian and I were writing five *Beulah* scripts every other week, my opposite number for a while was Arthur Philips, who employed my jolly buddy Si Jacobs and a pompous man named Lee Karson. Artie himself was a wag who made a contest of every conversation.

"Hello, Artie," one might say. "How are you?"

"Soon as I hear from my liver, I'll get back to you," he might answer.

We both had to submit our storylines to Samish in New York before we wrote the scripts, a step Artie made fun of because he hated the extra work it entailed. "Showing a story to Adrian is like showing a recipe to an egg," he grumbled.

Samish failed to appreciate his humor and Artie was replaced by Sherwood Schwartz, my diligent friend who was easier to work with and astute enough to retain Si.

During this time, I continued to work at home in Sherman Oaks. With Lisa and Donna at the Happy Day Nursery School, Doris had time to do some decorating. Margene Danch and Margie Jacobs helped her visit wallpaper shops, paint stores and fabric houses. When her friends weren't available, she had two choices for transportation — the public bus or the private me.

Whenever I urged Doris to learn how to drive, she resisted and also expressed her unhappiness at being stuck so far from what she considered civilization. Doris was clearly homesick so that winter, we bundled up the girls and I drove them and Betty Neilsen, our Danish part-time maid, to Union Station, where they boarded the Super Chief to New York.

Doris soon discovered that apartment living was more complex than she had remembered; exasperated by the demands of two small children and a mother's helper who didn't help, she returned earlier than planned. The homecoming gift that awaited her was a sleek new Hudson coupe and the ultimatum that she learn to drive it or stay home.

I failed two nerve-wracking attempts to teach her myself, so we engaged a brave instructor to prepare my wife for her driver's license test, which she passed with flying colors. She has been flying ever since and has the speeding tickets to prove it.

In the next two years, during which the girls learned some of their mother's choicest epithets for drivers who got in her way, we rented our little house to actor Robert Paige and his wife, Elizabeth Peacock, while we built a new one in the hills of Encino.

During that time, I continued to write both the *Crosby* and *Beulah* shows, one of the few writers doing two prime time programs on a regular basis. I became involved in the Radio Writers Guild, our children's nursery school, entered television as writer and a performer, earned my first screen credit, joined a studio softball team and covered myself with ignominy on the playing fields.

Other than my pathetic lack of prowess with bat and glove, I enjoyed a productive period in which the most significant and joyous event was the birth of a daughter we named Abigail.

Just before midnight on January 27, 1951, when Doris said, "It's time," I leaped out of bed to start for the hospital. Before I got out the front door, I remembered something. So I went back to get Doris' overnight bag. And Doris.

We raced to Cedars of Lebanon in Hollywood where Doris' doctor met us in the maternity ward to take her one way and send me another. As the hours crawled by, I fell asleep in the waiting room among several other men waiting for the flapping of the stork's wings. It was dawn when I was awakened by her doctor.

"Congratulations," he said. "It's a beautiful, healthy girl and you've got a beautiful, healthy wife."

I stumbled into the lavatory to wake up my face enough to welcome my daughter and thank my wife when one of the other expectant fathers asked me if the stork had landed.

"Yes," I said. "It's a girl."

"Your first?" he asked.

"Third," I said. "Three girls!"

With that, another man who had dozed off in his chair, jerked up in alarm. "Three girls!" he screamed. "What'm I gonna do with three? We got just a one-room bungalow!"

Donna was thrilled to have another sister she called "Abbadaba." While Lisa accepted Abigail, she told me she'd rather have a pony.

One day, after urging Rosie to get me a job writing a screenplay, he told me to meet him at Universal Studio in Leonard Goldstein's office. Goldstein was one of the town's busiest producers who made no pretensions about the Art of Film. He made movies, a product that critics demeaned as "corn," to which Goldstein's stock reply was "the color of corn is gold."

The producer owned the movie rights to Bill Mauldin's cartoon characters *Willie and Joe*, the front line G.I.s of World War II. He did not have a story but he knew what he wanted to put on the screen.

"Did you see *Mister Roberts*?" he asked me. "It's a play."

I had seen it and also read the book. "That's the one about the Navy."

"Yeah," he said. "What I wanna do is split Mister Roberts into Willie and Joe, put 'em in the Army and work up to that great scene where"—Goldstein leaped to his feet to act it out—"they've got these binoculars, watching this nurse take a shower and one of them says, 'She's got a mole on her ass!'"

He laughed heartily and asked how long did I think it would take me to come up with a story that funny. I looked at Rosie, who turned away to light a cigarette, then told Goldstein I'd like to have a day to think about that.

That meeting was too laughable to be real. What kind of a joke is Goldstein? I asked Rosie.

"He gets movies made," Rosie said.

"Not with me," I said. If a mole on a naked woman's butt is all he took away from *Mister Roberts,* he was not the producer I wanted to put me in the movies.

Rosie nodded and said, "You've got two good jobs in radio; you can afford to wait. Meanwhile, try television."

So I bought a set.

"Television? The word is half Latin and half Greek and no good can come of it."
—C. P. Snow

24. No Good Can Come of It

"Television," Fred Allen said, "is called a medium because it's not well done."

The Columbia Broadcasting System was anxious to prove that it could be done better and convinced an American comedy legend to help do so.

He was Isaiah Edwin Leopold, a man who could be as stubborn as cypress or tender as willow, born in Philadelphia in 1886, and he made the world laugh until he died in Hollywood in 1966 as Ed Wynn.

He was my idol long before that. As *The Texaco Fire Chief*, his outrageous puns, delivered in a voice that cracked like dried bark, his "opera" librettos and the laughter they elicited left an indelible impression on me.

When I discovered he was starring on Broadway in *Hooray for What*, I sneaked away from school in Long Beach, hitch-hiked to Manhattan, then walked to the Winter Garden theater and bought a balcony ticket for the matinee with my last 50 cents.

I fell in love with Ed Wynn that afternoon when he came on the stage wearing a huge yellow overcoat with a pattern of large green checks.

"My, it's hot today!" he giggled, unbuttoning the coat. Instead of shedding it entirely, he removed a flimsy lattice overlay of the green checks, tossed it aside and grinned his relief. I almost fell out of the balcony laughing.

Twenty-five years later, an elated Mr. Wynn remembered not only that coat but its colors, the name of the tailor who constructed it to his specifications and every other laugh he had gotten in the show. We were meeting for the first time in the Hollywood office of Harry Ackerman, Vice-President in Charge of Programming, Columbia Broadcasting System, West Coast. He had a long business card.

The prospect of working with Ed Wynn made me giddy but the gentleman couldn't have been more charming, receptive or democratic, probably because I immediately let him know that I had worshiped him for 20-odd years, so we had something in common.

I was invited to work as the head writer for the first network television show to emanate from California. The network offered me what was said to be the largest fee ever paid a television comedy writer to that year of 1948. But the CBS offer was a salary cut to $750 a week. Despite the loss of revenue, I keenly wanted the opportunity to work with Ed, so Rosie negotiated a non-exclusive deal with the network which allowed me to continue writing for Bing. It meant giving up *Beulah*, which was more demanding but not as satisfying.

The producer already selected for the Wynn show as Harlan Thompson, a veteran filmmaker who worked on Mae West features. Ralph Levy, the tasteful young man with a ballet background and a million dollar smile (later adjusted for inflation), was brought from New York to direct Wynn.

Ralph had done variety shows for CBS and was the only one of us with experience in the new medium. He would learn enough about comedy from Ed to go on later and design the TV debuts of Groucho Marx, Burns and Allen, Jack Benny and *The Beverly Hillbillies*. We didn't realize it then but we were all pioneers.

I was allowed to select my writing staff, which the budget had limited to two associates. I chose friends I knew to be inventive, industrious and inimical to sobriety, Seaman Jacobs and Leo Solomon. Si had worked for Wynn in radio and shared my enthusiasm for him. Leo, an outspoken wit of omnivorous appetite, shared Si's enthusiasm for money.

For our first show, we wrote a joke that was widely repeated: "A television star had a baby last week, but she doesn't know if it's a boy or a girl because it's still out of focus."

That was a line Wynn loved because it so aptly reflected the primitive state of the medium.

Our star also professed to love Harlan Thompson's selection of Gertrude Niesen as our first guest artist. Niesen was an acclaimed "saloon singer" who could melt the wax in your ear when she set the torch of her sensuous contralto to a blues lyric.

I regarded our first rehearsals, conducted by a deferential Ralph Levy, as a classroom in which Ed was the instructor. Even before we began to write for him, he emphasized the need to give a comedy star "an entrance." A comedian should get a laugh immediately, Ed insisted, and an example he extemporized remains as a lesson:

A man enters eating peanuts and tossing shells on the stage. The enraged manager rushes out, carrying a shotgun and threatens, "The next man who dumps shells on my stage is going to get a load of buckshot in

Left to right: Hal Kanter, Arthur Stander, Frank Fox, Ed Wynn, Si Jacobs. Si worked with the author on every show he produced from then on and has remained his dear friend ever since, through four marriages and five collaborators.

his caboose!" Now the star enters, and what is he doing? Of course, he's blithely opening peanuts.

During dress rehearsal for our first show, with the orchestra in the pit and a sprinkling of friends in the house seats, Gertrude tried a piece of business Ralph had given her in the scene with Ed. It got a laugh that Ed did not expect. Pleasure emigrated from his face to accommodate a scowl that could turn fresh cabbage into instant sauerkraut.

"If that bitch goes for that laugh tonight," our chivalrous star hissed to us in pent-up anger, "I'll *fart* her off that stage!"

We learned that any production over which he had control, nobody but Ed Wynn got laughs in an Ed Wynn show.

Years later, at a party in our home, a beaming Ed escorted a genteel widow he was spending time with after his last divorce. While Ed was engrossed in a shouted conversation with the nearly deaf Jack Oakie, Jack's wife Vicki asked Leo if he knew anything about Ed's attractive lady friend. "Only one thing I can be sure of," Leo said. "She doesn't get laughs."

Following the broadcast of our first live half-hour, the audience gave our star a standing ovation, which he hated like a bear hates honey. Ed made a curtain speech that lasted longer than the show.

Meanwhile, the telephone in his dressing room was answered by Ed's dresser, and when Ed returned to the room, soaking in perspiration and ego gratification, he looked at the message.

"Fanny Brice!" he cried. "I'll bet she saw the show!"

A group of us crowded around as Ed spoke to Fanny. She had indeed watched the show in her Beverly Hills home and pronounced it superb.

Following some gracious and endearing chat with the comedienne who was then riding high in radio as *Baby Snooks*, Ed thanked her again and hung up, his eyes glowing.

"Fanny Brice!" he crowed. "The greatest lady in our theater! Funniest woman who ever drew breath! She said I was a triumph! Tonight, we have made theatrical history! That's from *Fanny Brice*!" His tone was her coronation.

Everyone present clamorously agreed with Queen Fanny's evaluation. It took half an hour for the crowd to thin and Harlan could ask Ed who he'd like as a guest star for the next show. Several names mentioned were vetoed for one reason or another.

Phil Weltman, the William Morris Agency representative for both Wynn and Brice, asked, "How about your friend, Fanny?"

"Fanny Brice?" Ed snarled. "What the fuck can *she* do?"

The comedian may well have been afraid of her. Despite 40 years of stardom and his confidence onstage, Ed needed chemically augmented courage before he ventured out there. When he was five minutes away from his television bow that night in 1948, I was alone with him in his dressing room and watched in awe as he pulled a bottle of bourbon from the valise in which he kept his precious 50-year-old stage shoes. He filled a water tumbler and drank the whiskey as if it were a glass of skim milk.

He patted his belly and confided, "It drowns the butterflies."

He then doused a handkerchief with SeaBreeze after-shave lotion and daubed his lips with it, explaining, "I don't want anyone onstage to know I've had a nip."

A nip? His breath bleached the stripes out of my necktie.

The reaction to our first show ranged from cheers to qualified approval except for one review by the critic of *Daily Variety*, Jack Hellman. The day it appeared, we were having lunch in the Brown Derby. Ed was bitter about the Hellman notice.

"It was a personal attack," he moaned, "and why, I don't know. I've never even met the man, wouldn't know him if—"

As if on cue, Jack Hellman entered the crowded restaurant. He was not an attractive man: lean, lank, crumpled, long-jawed, a soggy cigar clamped between stained teeth, hawk-beaked, he had enough nose for a family of three.

Si nudged Ed and whispered, "That's Hellman."

A beatific smile invaded Ed's face; he clasped his hands in ecstasy and said, "Oh, I'm so *glad*!"

Early television lighting and camerawork were erratic and many performers refused to hazard appearances, so it was difficult booking stars on our early shows. Only the more adventurous chanced being seen to disadvantage by most of the nation's viewers in our grainy black-and-white kinescopes, film photographed from the TV tube, rebroadcast to the East and often distorted in the process.

A television set, some wag said, was "smog with knobs."

Bob Hope sneered on radio that when vaudeville died, television was the box they buried it in.

Among those willing to appear with Ed were performers astute enough to sense television was the future of entertainment, people like Carmen Miranda, who was our second guest, Dinah Shore, Charles Laughton, Mel Torme, Eve Arden and my Army buddy, Howard Duff.

Lucille Ball agreed to a guest shot for a different reason. She wanted only to get a job for her husband, Desi Arnaz.

"Asking any working writer what he thinks of critics is like asking a lamp post what it thinks of dogs."—John Osborne

25. *What a Lamp Post Thinks of Dogs*

With some stars, you know where you stand; with others, you know where to kneel. I could never be knighted because I have difficulty kneeling. That may be one of my problems with more than one of my stars.

I once received a gift wristwatch with this inscription engraved on the back: LOVE LUCY. No punctuation. I don't know if it was an expression of affection, a suggestion or a command.

The fact that it was handed to me by Lucy's second husband, a man who knew where to buy jewelry wholesale, further obfuscates the message.

Don't misunderstand. I liked Lucy. I never loved Lucy but I liked her ... although I often felt she would have made a more cherished stranger. That feeling came long after her television debut.

Before TV became the Russian roulette game it now is, some actors accepted roles only because they had car payments or their dentist threatened to repossess their prettiest teeth. Some others who had worked in every other form of theater wanted to experience the new one. William Frawley was one of those.

Bill asked to appear on our show, a job that led eventually to his longest-running role, the rasp-voiced Fred Mertz, who continues to amuse the world in never-ending reruns of *I Love Lucy*.

Lucille Ball and Desi Arnaz made their first television appearance on *The Ed Wynn Show*. Desi, as personable as he was handsome, had made a few films, but while his wife continued her steady orbit in stardom as a versatile leading lady, Desi's career was in decline.

When we gingerly approached Lucy for a guest shot, she agreed only if we gave Desi a co-starring role. It was a fateful decision on her part.

Weeks earlier, we had managed to break Ed's ban of other comedians. That happened when Victor Moore appeared with Milton Berle. Ed's longstanding dislike of Berle was aggravated by the way Milton upstaged his venerable friend, Victor.

Ed's primary resentment of Milton was based on his claim that he, Wynn, was the first star to work with other acts on a vaudeville bill, a strategy brash Berle adopted. Ed dismissed Milton as a thieving upstart comic and, in doing so, defined the difference between a comic and a comedian.

"A comic says funny things. A comedian says things funny."

Wanting to write for other than novelty acts, Leo, Si and I goaded Ed into inviting Victor Moore to play with us by suggesting Ed show Berle the treatment a star of Moore's caliber deserved. In a moment of vanity, Ed agreed.

When Victor, then in his 70s, waddled into our offices on Sunset Boulevard a few days later, he and Ed embraced warmly.

"Victor," Ed cried, "you're wearing makeup!"

"Always," Victor cackled. "In case I drop dead, they won't have to touch me."

"I saw what Berle did to you last month in New York," Ed said. "Shameful!"

"I'm surprised you recognized me," Moore said. "The son of a bitch stood in front of me the entire hour."

He asked for the men's room and hoped it wasn't a long walk. "When I come home from the race track every day, I sometimes can't make it into the house. I pee in the bushes. I've killed all the ivy around our garage."

It was impossible not to adore that cherubic man. Working with an artist he respected, Ed found an obvious truth he had overlooked for years: The more stature your actors have, the larger the laughs you get.

Thus the ban was broken and we enjoyed the talents of such comedy stars as Joe E. Brown, Ben Blue, Andy Devine, Frank Fontaine, Garry Moore, the Three Stooges and the few surviving original Keystone Kops.

We also worked with the brilliant Buster Keaton. Few people could ever approximate Buster, whose silent movie comedies are constantly being rediscovered as masterpieces of invention and execution that still have never been excelled.

Another funny guest, the now almost forgotten Leon Errol, deserves to be rediscovered by today's audiences. The rubber-legged Australian's frantic film farces with Lupe Velez were among the most frenetic of all time. On our show, Leon did a four-minute pantomime of a drunk trying to mail a letter. It was his own routine and there is not a comedian alive today who can approach it in hilarious agility.

One who could was James Barton, another artist for whom Ed—and I—had profound respect. Barton was the star of *Tobacco Road*, one of the first plays I saw on Broadway. As Jeeter Lester, he had fascinated me and I hung around the stage door after the matinee, hoping to meet him. Instead,

I met Sam Byrd, who played Jeeter's idiot son. He told me Barton had already left. I had not recognized him.

Following his run in *Tobacco Road*, Barton played vaudeville and I sat through three of his shows at Loew's State Theater. I had gone out of admiration for the actor, not realizing what a versatile song and dance man he was. Nor did I know that Barton was one of the toughest men in the theater. Offstage, he was unrecognizable. He had no nose. It was said to have been eaten away by the disease named for the Greek shepherd, Syphilius, which one does not contract by wearing wool.

Before he went on stage, Barton applied a putty nose. Close observers could detect that it changed shape from one performance to another.

On our show he did a monologue I had the temerity to update and which he approved with enthusiasm. He also sang "You Made Me Love You," the song he had introduced 30 years earlier but was made popular by Al Jolson.

Our musical director lived in Europe during Barton's Broadway stardom. He was Lud Gluskin, a name that sounds like oil being poured into a tub. He was thickset, bald, grumpy, overweight and walked rapidly with his long arms extended in front of his belly. He was instantly recognizable if you were told to find a man who looks like he's trying to catch a chicken.

Lud's concert master rehearsed the orchestra; Lud was the director of all music affairs for CBS in Hollywood and was busy elsewhere until the dress rehearsal. For Barton's number, he chased a chicken in and thumbed quickly through his cue sheets. I sat in the audience with Mrs. Barton.

Barton himself, battered hat in hand, his wiry, unkempt hair sticking out of his tough old head, leaned against the proscenium in an unpressed suit, waiting for his music. He looked like a derelict who had wandered in from Skid Row to cadge a sip of sauterne. For the show, all he'd do was brush his hair and shape his nose.

Lud squealed when he came to the lead sheet of "You Made Me Love You."

"Is Jolson on the show?" he asked anybody.

"No, Lud," Ralph Levy's voice boomed from his control room. "Let's get on with it, please."

"But this is Jolson's song!" Lud protested.

"It's James Barton's. Just get on with it!"

I was squirming in the audience, realizing Ralph's discomfort was equal to mine.

"Barton?" Lud persisted, looking around at his sideman. "Who the hell is James Barton?"

Left to right: Leo Solomon (writer), Hal Kanter, Harry Ackerman (CBS vice president), Ralph Levy (director) and Ed Wynn.

I left my seat so fast, my shadow still sat. I growled in Lud's ear, "Shut up and play. *That's* Barton." I nodded toward the proscenium, where the actor was glaring at Gluskin. Whatever Barton was thinking could have gotten him ten to twenty years, with a good lawyer.

Lud gave the downbeat. Barton moved to center stage and began the lyric. He sang every word of it staring at the conductor. Never once did his eyes leave Gluskin, never once did his voice falter. The lyric took on nuances never heard before.

"You made me love you ... you dog, you! ... I didn't wanna do it..."

Nobody ever delivered the song so well, so meaningfully. It was a moment of magic. As obtuse as Gluskin was, he did appreciate talent. I watched the flush of embarrassment climb the back of his neck, like cherry soda in a thirsty kid's straw.

The song ended. There was a hush in the house for a fraction of a second. Barton's eyes were still riveted to Gluskin, who looked up sheepishly.

"That," Barton growled in measured cadence, "is who James Barton is, you skin-domed cock sucker!"

The musicians led the applause that followed.

As memorable as Barton is, he had nothing to do with Lucille Ball's first television triumph. Buster Keaton did.

Keaton was arguably the greatest, most ingenious silent movie clown in film history. When we met to discuss his television debut, Buster, then 60 years old, offered a pantomime that involved his getting stuck in a pool of molasses and taking several hazardous falls. He brushed aside our fears for his safety, got to his feet and showed us that he was still as flexible as a Slinky. Men half his age did not have his dexterity, grace or humor.

Buster suggested the scene be done as a silent movie with titles and a 1920s wardrobe. Ed's wardrobe was always timeless, so that was no problem. The titles were. We solved that by having the actors hold up their own dialogue, lettered on large placards. It was cumbersome, but it added to the satire we introduced as "silent TV." It proved to be one of our funniest shows.

So now we were to entertain and be entertained by another talented performer, Miss Ball.

Leo and I were dispatched to the Arnaz ranch for script discussions. Lucy and Desi then lived in Northridge, deep in the San Fernando Valley. During the drive from Hollywood, we decided to play Lucy as a Theda Bara–like vamp in a '20s costume and do another "silent TV" sketch. We had several gags worked out by the time we found their house.

We presented the notion to Lucy. The lady with the tangerine-colored hair had seen the Keaton show and realized the merit of our proposal.

"But what about Desi?" she asked. He was not present at our meeting.

The three of us ping-ponged ideas and learned quickly that Lucy was a resourceful, clever woman who knew the difference between amusing and funny. We agreed on enough for us to go back and begin writing with Si, who had been occupied with another section of the script.

The resultant half-hour was a triumph. Ed was brilliant. Ralph Levy's direction was inspired. Lucy was hilarious and fun to work with. Desi was pliable and helpful, a skilled musician who knew what he was doing, yet there was no hint that he would soon become television's first tycoon.

It was also obvious that he and Lucy were very much in love.

They requested permission to repeat our scene later on a special telecast from New York. Shortly thereafter, they began *I Love Lucy*, wherewith Desi innovated the three-camera technique of shooting in front of an audience. That marriage of film and radio comedy changed television for all time and led to the medium's sweetest reward — residuals.

What went wrong in their domestic marriage is something of which I

Top: **A favorite photo of the author: Buster Keaton (left), the author, and Ed Wynn, circa 1949. *Bottom:* Ed is in his usual rehearsal sweater and hat. Lucille Ball was trying out the wig she wore for this "silent TV" sketch.**

had no intimate knowledge until Lucy confided that when she took over the Desilu Studios, her first executive act was to fire a producer she accused of being a pimp for Desi.

From our first show, Ralph Levy thought it would help Ed rehearse if his cues were lettered on cards he could read. Our art director, Ken MacClellan, furnished a stack of them and a felt marking pen and asked if any of us could letter quickly. A young network page, Barney McNulty, volunteered. Rehearsals continued as Barney began rapidly lettering the script on the stage apron. His felt pen squeaked so loud, Leo interrupted the proceedings to ask, "Barney, what are you writing with, a mouse?"

Barney got rid of the squeaks and his page's uniform and made a career providing cue cards for enough stars to put several children through college. Many of them are his.

Gloria Swanson was another old friend of Ed's who surprised us with her comedic gifts. Two years before the silent movie queen made her stunning return to the screen in *Sunset Blvd.*, Miss Swanson played a puppet in an ingenious sketch on our show. She and Ed were attached to long elastic cords in a set designed as a marionette theater to play a love scene. We established that the puppeteer was in love with Swanson and every time Ed took a step toward her, or she towards him, they would be pulled back by the unseen puppeteer in the flies. They battled the puppeteer, their lines became tangled and the results proved again that the bigger the star, the bigger the laughs.

Years later, Doris and I attended a picnic at Ty and Sylvie Jurras' farm in Encino where their friend Gloria Swanson was a guest of honor. If she didn't remember me, she certainly remembered Ed and the jealous puppeteer.

Lucille Ball did remember me. And 30 years after her Wynn show debut, when Lucy had dropped out of television for a time, I got a call from her second husband, Gary Morton, the strapping former standup comic with a voice lower than his golf handicap.

"You know Gary's motto," Milton Berle said. "Show business is my wife!"

Gary invited me to his office at the Goldwyn Studio to confide that Fred Silverman had coaxed Lucy into returning to TV for NBC. He offered me a job to develop new series concepts. I was available so I went to work for Lucille Ball Productions.

That's not the only mistake I've made.

"Man does not live by words alone, despite the fact that sometimes he has to eat them."
— Adlai Stevenson

26. *By Words Alone*

September 30, 1963, Ed Wynn typed this note to me himself on his engraved stationery:

> Dear Hal: My 77th. birthday is Sat. Nov. 9th/63. The testimonial dinner is Sunday, Nov. 10th. Johnny Carson will be the toastmaster of the dinner!
>
> Now, Hal, this is strictly a business deal ... I would like to deliver a wonderful speech ... I know you are busy, but please send me to New York with a whopper.

I found time to write what Ed reported to be the *whopper* he wanted and when he returned, he insisted he pay me for my services.

When I demurred, he said, "Nonsense! I would not expect to go into a butcher shop and ask him for a free lamb chop. This is your livelihood and I insist on paying. How much do you want?"

"Three thousand dollars," I said.

There was silence on the phone for a moment, then he said, "The price of lamb chops has certainly risen."

I laughed and told Ed to forget the payment. But he persisted. "Get your tailor to make a nice suit for you," he said, "and send me the bill."

"Will you pay it?"

"Yes," he giggled. "If it's less than a lamb chop."

By coincidence, I was wearing that suit the last time I saw Ed. I was then employed at 20th Century–Fox and the comedian came to the studio to have lunch with me.

Edward G. Robinson stopped at our table to greet and chat with his friend before joining another group. When he left us, Ed said, "He looks wonderful for a man his age."

"You look wonderful, too, for a man your age."

Ed put on a mock frown that only his face could make so amusing and said, "I was downtown last week and saw a building as old as I am. It looked terrible!"

I reminded him of the time we were walking on Vine Street when a man greeted him with a cry of delight, saying, "Ed Wynn! I'd know you anywhere. You haven't change in 40 years!"

"Really?" Ed said. "I must've been the oldest looking 30 year old you ever saw."

This day, Ed had come to lunch because he wanted another speech he was going to make in Washington.

"It may be my last, you know," he chided gently. "If God spares me, I'll be 80 this year and every appearance I make has to be memorable, because it may be my last.

"If God spares me..."

He repeated the phrase several times, although he was never one to speak of ailment and frequently demonstrated his boast that he could still touch his toes without bending his knees, a feat I myself never found to be necessary.

Our conversation turned back to Ed's date in Washington where he was to be honored and his need for something to say. He also supposed I could use another suit.

"How much longer are you going to keep this up?" I needled him.

"Until," he said, "you're the best-dressed writer in town."

Sunday, June 19, 1966, I got a call from *Daily Variety*'s Army Archerd, who told me that Ed Wynn had died at 7:45 that morning.

Twelve years later, the Texaco company co-hosted a memorial evening with Milt Larsen at his Society for the Preservation of Variety Arts.

Doris and I shared a table with Si and his second wife, June Jacobs. Si was also June's second husband and he said, "It's tough to shop for June because she exchanges everything. That's how I got to be her second husband."

At the same table were Ralph Levy and Buddy Ebsen, another old colleague of Ed's who appeared on our show long before Ralph cast him in *The Beverly Hillbillies.* That evening, Buddy recalled a time in Texas when Ed got in a hotel elevator that was crowded with cowboys. One of them said, "Actors and cockroaches — that's all there is in this hotel — actors and cockroaches!" Then he looked at Wynn and sneered, "Are you an actor?" And Ed said, "No; I'm a cockroach."

Milt Larsen had asked me to be one of the speakers at the memorial, and my remarks evoked an appreciative response from Ed's only son, Keenan. He asked me for the copy, which he had duplicated and returned with this note:

> Dear Hal: Here are five copies of what I feel is the finest observation of Dad I have ever read. Needless to say, I have kept ten copies for myself. I

> think what affected me the most was the fact that it was not "kiss ass." It was Ed Wynn.
>
> All my love, Keenan.

Keenan's handwriting was so bad, he could have become a doctor instead of the fine actor he was.

He almost didn't become either one when we built our red barn in Encino. Keenan was the leader of a band of motorcycle riders who used our hills for their private playground Sunday mornings. They were loud and came perilously close to our house on High Valley Place. We had a neighbor who told me he was going to arm himself with a shotgun and fire at them if they persisted in ignoring his shouts to stay away. He asked me to join him as an assistant vigilante. I declined that request and another to help string barbed wire across our hills.

Instead, I warned Keenan that there were enemies in them thar hills. The 'cycle gang moved elsewhere. So did my neighbors.

Here's what I wrote for the night at Larsen's:

> Offstage, he was a man of grace; courtly, charming, well-informed, a witty conversationalist, a gracious host—but quick to anger when he was displeased.
>
> Onstage, he was, physically, a classic clown. His body seemed to contain no bones, his hands fluttered like disoriented butterflies; his face was made of Silly Putty long before that product was on the market and his voice often broke on high notes even before it reached them. His bizarre wardrobe was in sharp contrast to his offstage elegance in clothing.
>
> Intellectually, he was a shrewd observer of the foibles of his fellows, a scholar of comedy, a teacher and a patron of silliness in all things—and a jealous guardian of his own talent for making us laugh.
>
> Emotionally, he was a romantic, stuffed with stubborn pride and the often erroneous notion that he was an astute businessman. He had instant recall of names, dates, places, events—and jokes ... and he seldom forgave those he felt had wronged him—until, in his later years, he grew mellow and realized he had wasted a lot of energy disliking those he considered his enemies.
>
> The older he grew, the more astonished he was to discover the range of his talents and I think that at the end of his life, he was more contented, happier and, inevitably, more lovable than he had ever been.

I learned more about the art of making people laugh from Ed than from any other single person with whom I worked.

That still obtains.

"If writers were good businessmen, they'd have too much sense to be writers."— Irvin S. Cobb

27. *If Writers Were Good Businessmen*

A sip of compliment stimulates me; a few gulps and I'm intoxicated. Once I recognized that, I began to disregard compliments I don't deserve. But as I grow older, I find that I deserve all I get.

I was still young when someone from Armed Forces Radio paid me a compliment. He told me that when they asked Danny Kaye to record a *Command Performance*, Danny agreed to do it only if I wrote it. I gulped the compliment and wrote a show that went so well, we were asked to do another. Soon after we taped that, Danny went to England.

At that time, my parents were traveling abroad to exploit Dad's *Classics Illustrated.* Mother was indisposed in London and when Dad had to be in Paris on business, she remained at the Savoy an extra day before joining him.

While waiting to board the plane to France, Danny Kaye arrived for the same flight. Mama remembered they had met at a broadcast of his show in New York and re-introduced herself as "Hal Kanter's mother."

"He sure got fat," Danny said, turned abruptly and walked away.

"I was so upset by the man's unmitigated and unwarranted rudeness," Mama wrote me, "that during the entire flight to Paris, I ignored him completely."

Many months later, Doris and I attended a play at the Huntington Hartford Theater in Hollywood. During one intermission, I went outside to smoke a cigarette. In the crowded lobby, I heard a familiar voice.

"Hal Camphor!" It was Danny's usual greeting to me. He considered it amusing. I stopped anyway to shake hands with him and Sylvia, who whispered her hello. Sylvia always whispered. If she were drowning, she'd whisper, "Help."

"I've got a bone to pick with you," I told Danny, described the airport incident with Mother and asked, "Why'd you do that?"

"You are fat," he snapped and as he walked away from me, Sylvia whispered a giggle.

March 18, 1950, Hollywood, CBS: Hal Kanter (left), Ilona Massey and Joe E. Brown.

We didn't see each other until he needed me, several chapters later.

Bing Crosby never did need me, but he did continue to rely on me to help keep him clever on the radio. Among the best of our Crosby shows were the ones we did with Al Jolson, who was indeed the world's greatest entertainer. And if any people doubted it, all they had to do was ask Al.

Bill Morrow and I didn't ask. We wrote this for one of his appearances:

CROSBY: It's guest time now and all of us are tingling in anticipation of the approach of the world's greatest entertainer. Yes, folks, the auspicious moment has arrived when it is my pleasure to present the one and only—AL JOLSON!!

(APPLAUSE)

JOLSON: Bingy, boy, I loved that introduction. And I love you ... and you know why?

CROSBY: Why?

JOLSON: Because when a man's *good*, you're big enough to come out and say so!

CROSBY: It seemed the thing to do, Al ... I figured it would sound better if *I* said it.

On another show—we taped three in a row in December of 1949—they continued in the same vein with this exchange:

> JOLSON: I tried being modest once but it didn't work out.
> CROSBY: Maybe you didn't try hard enough…
> JOLSON: I tried with all my heart, but somehow, when I started thinking of myself as being only *good*—I felt like a phony.

Jolson got away with that audacious attitude because the audience thought he was kidding. He was not. Bill and I wrote the lines, but his attitude was his own.

At the time, I was still doing the *Ed Wynn Show* and one day Ed called me to say he had shared a dais with Jolson the night before at a charity affair. He was excited and said, "Al wants to do my show! I told him you'd go out and talk to him about the script, so call him right away!"

When I did, Jolson's young wife Erle told me to come over. The Jolsons were back in the house Don Ameche occupied when I had called on him. The house on Encino Avenue was five minutes from our new home. Erle met me at the door and walked me to the side of the house, where Al was lying nude beside his pool, basking in the bright winter sunshine. He was surprisingly well built for such a little guy.

"Take off your clothes," Al greeted me, "and have some rays."

I took off my tie and Erle went back inside because that's all I took off.

"About the *Wynn Show*—" I began, and he said, "What *Wynn Show*?"

"Ed told me you'll do our show next week."

"What show? What are you talkin' about?"

"Al," I said, "did you talk to Ed last night at the Ambassador Hotel?"

"Oh," Jolson said, "Ed Wynn, yeah. His television show?"

"Right. He said you told him you'd be his guest next week."

"Next *week*?"

"That's what he said you said."

"I lied," Jolson smiled. "I didn't want to hurt the old man's feelings!" Jolson was six years older than Wynn.

"What can I tell him?" I asked.

"Tell him I gotta think about it," he said. "And just between us, when Jolson goes on the TV, it ain't gonna be on somebody else's show. When Jolie goes on, it's gonna be as big as when I did the first talkie! It's gonna be an hour show. Maybe two hours. It's gonna be all the stations, all the networks at the same time. The whole world is gonna be watchin' and it's not gonna have no commercials. It'll open with somebody like General Eisenhower an' he'll say, 'Al Jolson is brought to you by General Motors' an' I come out singin'. Then I'll welcome the people an' sing some more, then sit on the stage, like I used to do on Broadway an' tell a couple of stories, then sing some more, do a few more gags and sing 'til it's time to say good night and Eisenhower will come back to say, 'Al Jolson was brought to you by General Motors.' That's my show!"

"Sounds great," I said, trying to conceal my amusement at his *chutzpah*, "but if you had all that already laid out, why'd you ask me to come over?"

"Whatta you mean, *why*?" he frowned. "Who do you think I want to write the jokes for me!"

Jolson never did that show but if he had, I doubt he'd agree to pay what my agent was asking. When Frank Sinatra asked me to write a special for him, Rosie quoted such a large fee Frank didn't talk to him for the next two years.

During one visit to the Crosby show, Jolson told us he was going to Hawaii and said, "I'm gonna bring you a present, Bingy." He boasted that he had a seamstress there who designed much nicer native shirts than the ones Bing wore. "I'm gonna have her make a couple for you."

"Mighty considerate of you," Bing said.

"I'm gonna bring shirts back for all of you," Al promised John Scott Trotter, Ken Carpenter, Murdo, Bill and me. He instructed his one-armed aide, a man he called Lew, to write down everybody's name and shirt sizes. When we finished reading the script around the table, they all went into the studio to rehearse the music and in a burst of largesse, Al instructed Lew to get the sizes of all the musicians in Trotter's orchestra. Hawaiian shirts for all!

I remained in the rehearsal studio, polishing some of the script that needed attention. Jolson returned to make a phone call. As I sat there, Lew came in and handed Al a slip of paper.

"What's this?"

"The names and sizes you want," Lew told him. "For the Hawaiian shirts."

Al looked at the list, crunched the paper into a ball and tossed it in the wastebasket.

Nobody got a shirt from the world's greatest entertainer.

I vividly recall my last visit with him. In 1950, Bill was in San Francisco with Bing and I went to see Al about his next appearance with Crosby. Al had recently returned from a triumphant USO tour of Korea and he had several stories he wanted me to include in the script.

Our appointment was for the evening and Al was sitting in his den with a new gadget he proudly exhibited. It was the first remote control television device, a long wire connecting the receiver to the viewer.

"Watch this!" he said, turning down the volume of the show he was watching. "Arthur Godfrey! The only thing that sonnova bitch proves is that all you have to do to be a success in show business today is show up!" Then he added, fiendishly, "But not in my house is he gonna!"

He twisted a knob and Godfrey's image was replaced by Morton Downey, in full voice.

"Listen to that Irish shit!" Jolson snarled about the popular tenor. "I can *fart* better than he sings!"

He turned off the set and regaled me with amusing stories of cowardice and bravery in Korea. Al tickled me, as usual, because he was so full of himself. And he had a few things to say about Bob Hope, who had followed him overseas, such as, "Why can't he stay out of my war?"

He also had amusing anecdotes about all of his USO tours and I was able to fashion from them what I felt sure was a surefire comedy spot for him and Bing. I sent it to Morrow and told him I'd be up early the day before taping the show to help with any rewrites and do a bit part Bill had written.

Four night later, I got a telephone call from Pat Dane, who was still sharing Morrow's Sunset Plaza apartment. Bill had just called her from San Francisco to tell me not to come up the next day.

"The show's been canceled," she said. "Al Jolson died an hour ago."

Every time I drive to and from the Los Angeles Airport, I see the statuary that rises over the tomb of the man who was the world's greatest entertainer and, if I have no reason to drive that way for a few months, I make one up. The memory of Jolson is a reminder of what excellence in entertainment can be.

"I set out to write with a clean sheet of paper and a dirty mind."— Patrick Dennis

28. A Clean Sheet of Paper

The last time I saw Eddie Davis, he was compiling a book of jokes about hospitals, where he had a lot of unfortunate experience but was still able to laugh. Then he moved to Arizona, without saying good-bye, and when I learned that Eddie had stopped laughing, I grieved over the loss of a mentor I regarded with affection.

I thought about him often when Rosie told me to report to producers Jerry Wald and Norman Krasna about half past 1950. They were at RKO, the Gower Street studio where I once typed scripts for Davis.

On the basis of my work with Crosby and Wynn, the producers engaged me to write a screenplay of a Howard Hughes production called *Two Tickets to Broadway*. I was to work with comedian/writer Sid Silvers, my refreshing friend who had already started toiling on the screenplay. The story was based on an idea songwriter Sammy Cahn sold Jerry Wald and it would be directed by James V. Kern.

Sid and I worked quickly, trying to keep up with Howard Hughes' casting demands. Hughes, who had recently bought the studio, kept adding people to the cast. Where or when he saw the people Wald and Krasna were instructed to hire, nobody seemed to know.

When our script was ready, Krasna and Wald explained why production could not begin on *Two Tickets to Broadway*, even though Busby Berkeley was ready to choreograph the dances and the cast of Janet Leigh, Tony Martin, Gloria DeHaven, Eddie Bracken and Ann Miller were standing by, already on the payroll.

"So what's holding us up?" Jimmy Kern asked.

"The okay from Hughes," Krasna said. "Can't get to the man."

"We have to wait for him to get back to us," Wald said.

At that moment, an airplane flew over the building. Sid raced to the open window, stuck his head out and yelled, "Howard! For God's sake, *say* something!"

One afternoon, I was leaving the lot to meet a friend for lunch when Norman Krasna was coming in with two bulging briefcases.

"Good morning," I said with a smile. "Is this what time the bosses come to work?"

"You son of a bitch!" Krasna screamed and threw his briefcases to the ground. "How dare you!"

Before I could apologize, he threw down the hat from his bald head, ripped off his glasses and waved them under my nose. "Do you know how long I was up last night, reading the shit you guys are writing? You have any idea how long I stay here at night after you go home?"

I was terrified by his outburst. The veins on his skinny neck stood out like sausages. His whole head turned as red as St. Nick's knickers. I was afraid he would have a heart attack before he could fire me.

"Please, Norman," I said, "calm down. I didn't mean to offend you. I was joking. I'm sorry." I picked up his hat and returned it to him. He picked up one briefcase and a studio guard who had watched the moment of drama, handed him the other.

"Thank you," Norman said to him in his most pleasant tone of voice, then turned to me and grinned, "Scared you, didn't I?"

I soon learned from his agent, Irving "Swifty" Lazar, that alarming people was one of Norman's gambits. He was the film colony's most effective salesman who pitched his ideas with passions bordering on melodrama. I would inherit one of them eventually at Fox.

But it was RKO where Jack Oakie and Milton Berle made *Radio City Revels*, so the first chance I got, I went to look for the stage where I had watched them work with Bob Burns. I was with Tom Gries, Wald's assistant, who indicated a handsome man approaching us and said, "There's the funniest guy in town. Do you know him?"

No, but I always wanted to meet the funniest guy in town. In fact, I once planned to do a show with Fred Allen called *The Funniest Guy in Town* when he completed *Much Ado About Me*, the autobiography that he never did complete himself.

The funniest guy Gries introduced me to was Don McGuire. He was a well-dressed, personable former military policeman who had some acting experience before embarking on a writing career. As he stood there talking to Tom, I anticipated he would soon say something funny. He didn't. When I decided Gries had no ear for funny, a red light on a nearby sound stage went on to signify the company was going for a take, accompanied by the sound of a bell that demanded silence.

McGuire looked at his watch in alarm and said, "Yikes! I'm late for algebra!" and ran off. I knew that we had to become friends.

There were two comedians I became friendly with too late to work with beyond their roles in *Two Tickets*. They were the veteran vaudeville team of Smith and Dale, who were headliners longer than I had been alive. Their relationship was said to be the inspiration for Neil Simon's classic *The Sunshine Boys*.

Among others in that cast were my buddies Bob Crosby, who played a pivotal role as himself, and Jerry Hausner, who played a small role as a struggling theatrical agent who rents desk space in another agent's shabby office and sublets drawer space in the desk to the second lead, who was played by marvelous Eddie Bracken.

When Howard Hughes gave the yellow light to proceed, Wald and Krasna put our show into production. Sid and I remained to make additional changes in the script that were requested by the director, ordered by the producers or demanded by Hughes. I was able to spend a lot of time on the set, learning how to make movies. I also spent some time in the cutting room, absorbing lore from film editor Harry Marker that would someday benefit my work.

Late one afternoon I slipped onto the stage just as the bell rang for a take. I found myself in the back of the set where Layne "Shotgun" Britton put a warning finger to his lips. "Shot" was a football star in Alabama who had become one of Hollywood's favorite makeup artists, actors' outspoken pals and town clowns.

"Take nine!" a voice called from the set, and then Jimmy Kern said "Action!"

The scene was one where our leading ladies each had one line apiece, which they delivered on cue. But when it was Ann Miller's speech, she garbled it.

"Cut!" Kern called.

"I'm sorry," Ann said.

"Sorry don't feed the bulldog, baby!" "Shotgun" yelled.

"Take ten!"

Ann blew the line again. "Shot" began packing his makeup case and said to me, "If that broad blows that line again, I'm taking my nose off her and going home!"

To explain what that meant, he told me that he glued a tiny piece of sculptured plastic on Miller's nose every morning he made her up.

By the time *Two Tickets to Broadway* was completed, producer Paul Jones was preparing a Bob Hope film at Paramount, *My Favorite Spy*. Jones had a script that was written by Edmund Hartmann and my fellow Guam veteran, Jack Sher. But Jones felt the screenplay needed another polish, so he drew up a list of comedy writers and presented it to Hope to select one. Bob glanced down the list, pointed to my name and said, "Get him."

I moved to Paramount and stayed there through the next few chapters.

"If Abraham Lincoln were alive today, he'd be turning in his grave."—Gerald R. Ford

29. *If Lincoln Were Alive Today*

Paramount was an exciting studio in 1950, when Billy Wilder characterized it as an institution where the inmates had taken over the asylum.

It was a privilege to be one of those inmates who shared the asylum with such megatalents as Wilder, his estimable partner Charles Brackett and an awesome list of writers who made the lunch hour a 90-minute daily adventure. It was there we were treated to many of Billy's observations like, "France is a country where the money falls apart in your hands and you can't tear the toilet paper."

To a wannabe opera singer who insisted on auditioning for him, Wilder said, "You have Van Gogh's ear for music."

Somebody asked him what he thought of Erich Segal's film adaptation of Segal's own *Love Story*, and Billy said, "I tip my hat to him, not so much as a writer but as an alchemist; he certainly turned chickenshit into chocolate."

One of the other attractions of lunch on the lot was the "word game," a contest wherein each player gave a letter from which we constructed words on a grid of 25 squares. Scores were given for five-, four- and three-letter words and each player's ante was 25 cents a game, winner take all. We played anywhere from eight to ten games a day and Billy Wilder was usually the winner, rivaled only by Charlie Brackett, producer Joe Sistrom or designer Edith Head.

Lesser Samuels, a heavy-set fellow who wrote *Ace in the Hole* (also known as *The Big Carnival*) with Billy, refused to play the word game. When I said, "He prefers to just sit there in his own lap," Lesser donated a chuckle to the laughter but later told me he had no desire to contribute to Wilder's wealth. He believed that in the years Billy spent at Paramount, the word game had financed half of his art collection and all of his wardrobe.

During one game, Jack Sher was *kvetching* about Billy's German accent. "What'd you say?" he snarled, "Dammit, can't you speak our language?"

Billy peered over his glasses and asked, "I suppose your mother was Pocahontas?"

Sher had barely enough blood left to blush.

My friend from Guam had signed a contract with Paramount and when I completed work on *My Favorite Spy*, the studio put me under contract and assigned me to collaborate with Sher on an original for Hope. When we turned in the first draft, called *Military Policeman*, we were called to a meeting with Don Hartman (who was head of production), his story editor Bernie Smith and several other production people. Both Hartman and Smith had voluminous notes on changes they deemed our script needed. As Bernie lectured us on screenwriting, I was amused by his pedantry but Jack grew furious.

"Jesus Christ!" he exploded. "The girls in mimeo said this is the best comedy they've typed in ten years and you're trying to fuck it up!"

Hartman and Smith exchanged looks and I tried to disappear.

"Maybe," Don said, "we ought to let the girls in mimeo decide what pictures we should make."

Of course, we made changes in the script. Don Hartman also made a change in Jack's relationship with Paramount and I completed the script with the input of veteran screenwriter Frank Butler. It was a major hit when it was released as *Off Limits*.

I was assigned to work with another Hartmann—with two *n*s—Edmund, a soft-spoken, literate gentleman and one of the wittiest it has been my good fortune to know. We were asked by story editor D. A. Doran ("A man," Charles Brackett once described, "of instant indecision") to write another original for Bob Hope, released as *Here Come the Girls*. It was an 1800s musical comedy in which Bob played a hapless chorus boy forced to substitute for Tony Martin when the star's life was threatened by a madman.

The typical Hope-genre farce was directed by Claude Binyon, a skilled screenwriter making one of his rare forays from the typewriter. The songs were provided by two accommodating young men who were started on their lustrous career by Olsen and Johnson, Jay Livingston and Ray Evans.

The musical director was Joe Lilly, an energetic, silver-haired, funny fellow who arrived late for a meeting and announced that he had just come from a check-up after which his doctor told him, "Don't buy any long-playing records!"

The doctor proved to be accurate.

The producer of *Here Come the Girls* was Paul Jones, an amply constructed, wide-chested, gimlet-eyed, self-styled "hillbilly from Tin-a-see" who boasted he could walk away from Hollywood any time "because I

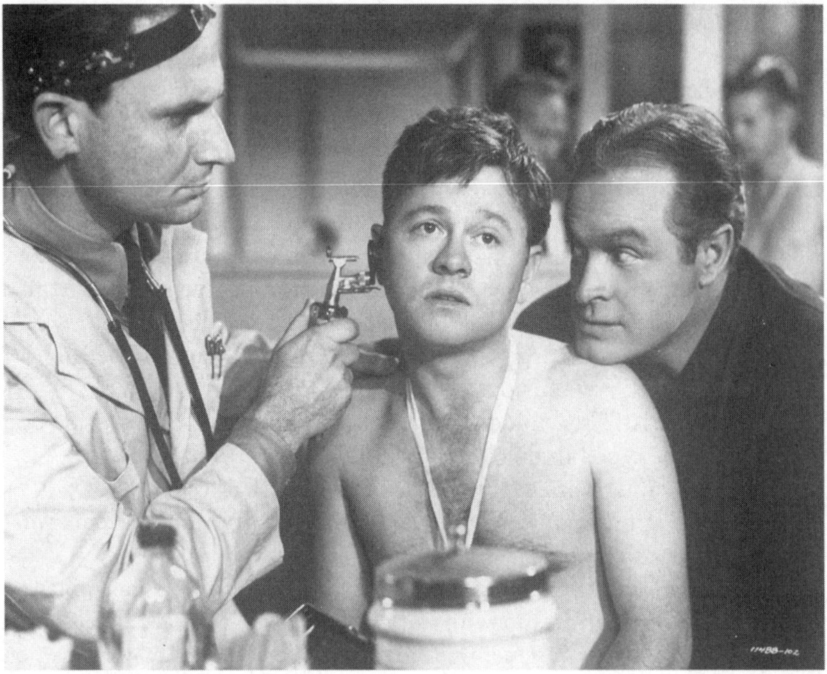

When the doctor's light went through Mickey Rooney's head in *Off Limits*, Bob Hope's reaction was such a big laugh that audiences didn't hear what he said: "This man is officer material!" The original title of this Paramount comedy was *Military Policemen.*

married a good woman who had $500 in the bank and she hasn't touched a penny of it."

Paul was an inflated elf who started as an assistant property manager and became an able, sensitive producer of comedy and drama. He preferred comedy, which was endemic to his nature, and was devoted to his writers and actors, generous in his praise of both. Ed Hartmann had worked for him before.

One of Paul's early chores was unique. W. C. Fields, then under contract to Paramount, would not come to work unless he was given $1000 in cash every morning before leaving his house. Jones rose at dawn each day, went to the studio where a paymaster counted out ten $100 bills, was then driven in a studio car to Fields' home, where he would hand the money to the crotchety comedian in his bedroom. Fields would count it, then rise, shower, dress and accompany Paul back to the studio, drinking his breakfast en route.

I don't know if Paul was himself a drinker but he always seemed to have a mint in his mouth. He was also invariably dressed in a suit with a necktie securely knotted at his collar and an expensive hat always on his head. If he was pleased with the pages Ed and I sent to him, he responded with a phone call expressing his enthusiasm or send us a box of candy. Sometimes he did both. Either was a rare gesture from a producer.

One of our scenes did not please him. We were summoned by Marie, his spinsterish secretary, to report to his office immediately. When we did, his door was closed. Marie announced our arrival and told us to wait until he buzzed. A minute passed before the buzzer sounded and the door latch clicked. We entered to stare in disbelief at an astonishing sight.

Paul Jones had lowered his pants, dropped his drawers and bent over, holding up the hem of his jacket and shirttail to expose his broad, fleshy backside and dangling scrotum.

"You boys want to fuck me?" he growled. "Go ahead! Do it for real, not on paper!"

We glanced back in embarrassment at Marie, who was closing the door — but very slowly.

"Paul," Ed said when the producer pulled his drawers up, "an empty candy box signifying your displeasure would've sufficed."

"Just for this, young man," Paul said, stabbing our pages with his finger, "no race track for you this afternoon!"

Later I asked Ed how Paul knew he took off for the races several afternoons a week.

"He goes with me," Ed explained.

While we were writing, Paul had a production on the stage, an item that starred the enormously successful Dean Martin and Jerry Lewis. He had gone to the set one morning and fun-loving Jerry, a junior grade sadist, grabbed a pair of shears and sliced off a generous portion of Paul's hat brim.

"Fun-nee?" Jerry cried. Paul did not reply. He simply stood, staring morosely, as Lewis sliced another portion of the brim.

"Fun-nee?" he shrieked. "Fun-nee, Paulee?"

Paul refused to react. The manic clown kept snipping away until Paul's fashionable hat was reduced to a fez. He walked off the stage with dignity, disguising his disgust.

Three days later, Ed and I were back in Paul's office. We had to force ourselves in because the outer office was jampacked with boxes filled with hats, from floor to ceiling. Somewhere behind them, Paul's voice implored us to help ourselves to a few dozen. He had all sizes, all models.

Jerry Lewis had suffered remorse at his prank. The delivery of the truckload of hats was his way of asking forgiveness. Paul forgave but never forgot.

When we completed our screenplay, Ed was assigned to another while I stayed to do the final polish with the director, Claude Binyon, whose work I admired for its brittle sophistication. I had met him briefly on Guam, where Capt. Binyon was filming a documentary for Col. Frank Capra.

Claude was a physically strong man who worked the cattle on his California ranch between writing and directing movies but was painfully shy and hesitant in his speech.

One long morning we sat facing each other in his office, going over a scene in which his ideas disagreed with what Ed and I had written. For over an hour, we discussed it until we reached an impasse Binyon could have avoided simply by reminding me that he was the director and it would be done his way. Instead, he stared at me in silence before he managed to stammer, "I h-h-have an idea."

"Yes?"

"L-let's stop talking."

Dear Claude; he shot the scene our way, but never blamed us for it.

Bob Hope's first scene for him was played with a newcomer to films, Rosemary Clooney. "By the time Claude would say 'C-c-c-ut,'" Bob told me, "Rosie was back in her dressing room."

One morning I sat on the stage with Hope's quondam gag man, Monte Brice. I was wearing a red tie, my jacket buttoned at the waist, and red socks, which were prominent as I crossed my legs. Hope emerged from his portable dressing room, glanced my way and said, "That's the longest red tie I've ever seen!"

Twenty years later, Bob's adopted son Tony was working in the legal department at 20th Century–Fox where I still wore red socks and that day had on a red sweater. As I passed Tony in the hall, he smiled and said, "that's the longest red sweater I've ever seen."

I whirled around so suddenly Tony was alarmed. "Just kidding," he said. I explained why I was startled.

"Dad never told me that, honest," Tony swore. I was sure he didn't. Bob Hope must throw away dozens of lines like that every day and wouldn't remember, much less repeat, a fifth of them.

Hope's remark remains indelible because it was my first realization that he could be witty without cue cards. I remembered Tony's because the night before I had been in a discussion about heredity versus environment in establishing one's sense of humor. Tony Hope confirmed my vote for environment.

The offspring of amusing people do not always inherit their talent; comedians cannot be bred, although several I know tried regularly. If the sperm bank to which Nobel Prize winners have contributed does eventually produce a corps of brilliant scientists and artists (an unlikely prospect from this time and personal perspective), the future may develop an even larger crop of comedians. The current fraternity of funny men contains more than a few who would not hesitate to fill a test tube if they thought they could get laughs from the attending nurse, or these days, an audience.

Comedy has not changed but comedians have.

"Pictures have changed a lot in recent years ... but why should I depress you?"—I. A. L. Diamond

30. *But Why Should I Depress You?*

If you were paying attention in 1952, you may recall that Adlai Stevenson was the Democrats' candidate for president that year.

Many writers supported him. Some of us worked for him, writing speeches and sketches for actors to perform at political rallies, and we were invited to Dore Schary's home to meet the candidate.

The event was held in a tent beside the film executive's swimming pool that was so large it contained a rowboat christened *Schary's Dory*.

I wrote a sketch that made Stevenson laugh. I continued to support Adlai, who did not blame my contribution to his campaign for its ultimate failure.

Bob Hope told me I was wasting my time working for Stevenson. "He hasn't got a chance," Bob said. "Eisenhower is a shoo-in."

I doubted the comedian's political wisdom. My friends were Democrats and I had the impression that most astute voters were Stevenson supporters, so when Hope scoffed at me, I made him a bet.

All I have to show for my loyalty to Adlai is a canceled check for $50 endorsed by Bob Hope. Also the knowledge that Bob could read the public pulse more accurately than I.

I spent some time working with Billy Wilder on the Stevenson campaign and he asked me if I'd like to work with him on a screenplay. Of course I would, as soon as I finished my current project.

"Come see me this afternoon," Billy said.

I mentioned that to Lesser Samuels and he cautioned me to beware of Billy.

"He's going to test you," Lesser predicted, "to see how compliant you are. Don't let him bully you if you want his respect."

When I sat down in Billy's office, he asked me to take another chair, one with my back to the window. I did so. Then he sat behind his desk and said he wanted to know more about me. But before I could tell him anything, he asked me to lower the Venetian blinds on the window because the sun was in his eyes.

"I'll move so you won't face the sun."

"No," he said. "Lower the blinds."

"Show me how to lower them."

"I don't know how, either," he said, "so we'll get together later, after the sun goes down."

The next day, Billy called me to say, "I knew you were good, but I didn't know how good. I talked to Doran and he told me how much your salary is. I can't afford you." Billy hired a magazine writer from New York to write with him and playwright Sam Taylor on the film that became *Sabrina.* I never did work for Billy. But Ernest Lehman, the writer who did, learned how to write screenplays from the master.

One contributor to my education was the distinguished gentleman Frank Butler, with whom Bill Morrow and I shared screenplay credit on *Road to Bali.* Frank, who was born in England in 1890, served the British Army in India and, en route back home, interrupted his journey with a stop in California. The tall, handsome officer was offered a job in a silent movie which he took for the adventure. But when the director learned Frank had his own authentic army uniforms and paid him extra for wearing one, he decided to stick around and pick up some more easy money.

Frank's wit and elegance established him as one of the community's popular contributors as he went from acting in two-reel comedies to writing them. By the time we met at Paramount, Butler was the dean of comedy screenwriters. It was he who helped us to do a rewrite of *Off Limits* before Jack Sher was taken off the script.

Now I was working on *Road to Bali* when Butler arrived from his turkey ranch in Bakersfield to spend a few days working with me on the script. He read the pages I had already done, told me that my sight gag—Bing and Bob escaping a gorilla, dive into opposite ends of a hollow log and emerge from it on opposite ends—was one of the best he ever read. I was so proud of that, Frank easily sold me a few Thanksgiving turkeys.

A month after we finished the script, I asked Harry Tugend, our producer, when the film would go into production. He said he was waiting for Bing to approve the script.

"He's had it for two weeks," Harry said, "but he hasn't said a word about it."

"Then let's ask him," I said. Harry said, "We don't do that. We wait for Bing to tell us."

I thought that was nonsense. The next day, I was on my way to lunch when Bing stood in front of his dressing room, getting some sun.

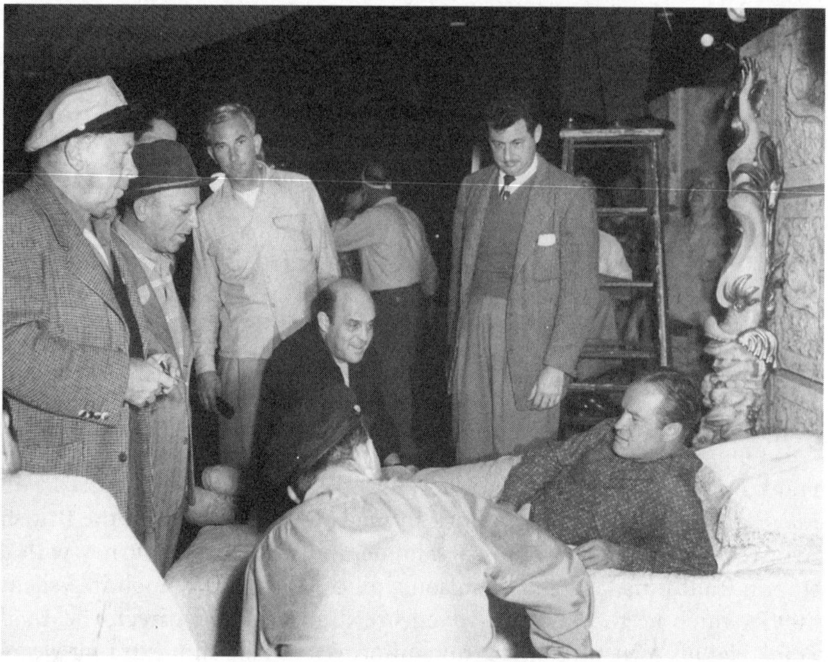

On the set of *Road to Bali*: Left to right: Monte Brice, Barney Dean, a technician, Bill Morrow, Hal Kanter, Bob Hope; the man with his back to the camera is Bing Crosby.

"Hey, Bing."
"Hi."
"You read the *Bali* script yet?"
"Yeah."
"Well?"
"Funny, but a little chase-y, no?"
"We can fix that."
"Let's do it."

I went directly to Tugend's office to report my conversation with the Groaner. A week later, *Bali* went into production. Morrow and I had taken some of the "chase" out of the script and we were in a meeting in Don Hartman's office with Harry Tugend, director Hal Walker and the songwriters, Johnny Burke and Jimmy Van Heusen, to listen to their score.

Bill and I sat facing Hartman across the long room, while Jimmy sat at the piano and Johnny stood to sing the lyrics. "We've written two ballads," he said, "and we'll do them both for you to take your pick because you probably don't want two ballads in the same show, do you, Don?"

"Oh, no," Hartman said. "You can't have two ballads in one show!"

Morrow leaned toward me and whispered, "He's right. That's what killed *South Pacific*, you know."

I had to laugh.

"What'd he say?" Hartman asked. Bill repeated it and Don had to laugh, too. But not sincerely.

During this time, I joined Jack Douglas and Sid Dorfman in a weekly half-hour TV show called *Scoop the Writers*. Gale Robbins was the first emcee of the comedy quiz but was replaced with Rose Marie by our producer, Rolly Langley, a man who wrote a syndicated gardening column, and who lived in a Hollywood home where the lawn was a forsaken tangle of dead weeds. Rolly had a brown thumb.

The audience reacted favorably to our first show but we anxiously awaited the verdict of our critics. Sid Dorfman made the first call from our dressing room to his mother. Their conversation was brief.

"She told me," Sid said, "I should have worn my gray suit."

We were pleasantly surprised with good reviews from the local press but after 13 weeks, we were canceled because we were too "raunchy" (according to the management of Channel 5) in 1953.

One of Jack Douglas' pet targets was Liberace. The station was inundated with protests from his fans, so, at the end of our third show, Doug said, "A lot of you people object to my remarks about Liberace because you say he's the world's greatest piano player … and others say he's the world's greatest singer … so, good night, Liberace, whatever you are."

When we were dropped by Channel 5, Rolly sold us to Channel 11 where we had a small but loyal audience for another 13 weeks. Our jokes were purloined by dozens of comics, who traded them with others throughout the country.

One week, I talked about my cat, who liked candy: "He was a Persian cat. He wore a fez. He was either a cat or the quietest Shriner you ever saw. But he kept us up at night, crunching on peanut brittle. I stopped buying candy for him so he started catching sweet mice."

I watched an amateur hour from New York in which the winner used my lines. A lot of losers also helped themselves to our material. We had a cult following, if not a cultured one.

One evening I told a joke about a man who gave his sweetheart an unusual gift: He had Leonardo da Vinci's *Last Supper* tattooed on her back. Many years after they had lost touch, he was at the opera and saw a woman in a backless gown he recognized as his old flame. But she had gained so much weight, all of the apostles were smiling. The following day I got an irate phone call at Paramount from a Father Driscoll to register the church's displeasure at my sacrilege. He was firm in his demand that I apologize.

"I'm sorry if I offended anyone, Father," I said, "and I do apologize."

"Indeed?" he said in a brogue as suspiciously Irish as Paddy's Chayefsky. "Your apologizing to me is not sufficient!"

"What would you consider sufficient?"

"Put me on your television show next week so I can drop my drawers and have you kiss my hairy Irish ass!"

I was so outraged I failed to recognize my caller's voice until he began laughing. It was Jack Sher, indulging in my least favorite form of humor, the practical joke, which I find sadistic, even when I'm not the goat.

At a large party in Steve and Jayne Allen's home, I stood in a group that Alan King approached. King is a forceful, take-charge dynamo with a wicked sense of humor. "Look" he said, "Carter's over there..." We looked across the crowded room where Jack Carter was listening to effusive Eydie Gorme. "Now," King instructed us, "let's all laugh out loud and watch what Jack does."

Phil Silvers, Red Buttons, Jack Albertson and I joined King on cue. Immediately, Jack left Eydie in mid-sentence to confront us.

"What, what's the gag?" he begged. "Tell me!"

"You wouldn't get it," King said and walked away chuckling.

"Red!" Carter pleaded with Buttons, "Tell me!"

"Hah, Jack, forget it," Red frowned and also walked away. Jack Albertson followed him. Carter turned to me and desperately whined, "Hal?"

I like Jack and feel kinship with his need for approval, although not as acutely as he does, so I told him he was being put on. He didn't believe me. He said I was a prick.

An hour later, King sidled up to me at the buffet table and growled, "You told him. You prick."

A few years later, producer Frank Glicksman, who was a talented painter and sculptor, invited me to pose for him. For several nights, over a few weeks, I went to the Glicksmans' house on Lloyd Place, where his wife, Pearl, served elegant dinners. While she helped their daughter Susan with her homework, I accompanied Frank to his atelier (a converted garage), to sit while he worked his clay. We laughed a lot during those sessions and the night he unveiled the finished piece, I was impressed, flattered and gratified.

He had two copies made — one for me, which I brought home. Doris admired it but asked me where I was going to put it.

"Not here," she said. "One of you is enough."

I took it to my office at 20th Century–Fox to use as a prop. If Hitchcock managed to put himself in every movie he made, I thought I'd get in my television shows. In the series *Valentine's Day*, Tony Franciosa played

Frank Glicksman, the sculptor and practical joker.

an editor, his boss was played by old friend Jerry Hausner and his silent partner was played by my bust. Smart directors always made certain it was featured in close shots.

One day my secretary, Myra Stuté, called my attention to a piece of fan mail from Denver. The writer identified herself as a woman who had once slept with a soldier from Lowry Field—and wanted to know if that piece of statuary was of the same soldier. I dismissed the letter. The soldier I was in Denver was a skinny whelp who resembled nobody like the distinguished gentleman Frank sculpted.

But more letters arrived from the same woman, who said she'd checked records in Washington and learned I was the same Hal Kanter. She demanded I come marry her, make our child legitimate and bring them to Hollywood!

That does get a man to thinking. And by the time I got a letter from her son, threatening legal action if I failed to provide the support his mother was seeking for them, I was in a panic.

In desperation, I confided in Frank, blaming him for my sudden insomnia. He began to giggle. As I slowly began to recognize a hoax, Frank's giggles erupted into howling, foot-stomping, floor-pounding laughter. Finally, he admitted all the detailed planning that had gone into his elaborate practical joke.

While that bust now sits safely in my home, there is another copy of it that keeps popping up on other shows. When it was first called to my attention after it appeared on an early *Murphy Brown* episode, I made some inquiries and learned from art director Roy Christopher that a Hollywood property rental house owns it — so now anybody can rent me.

"No matter how accomplished you are as a writer, you're always a beginner when you sit down to do the next thing."—Elaine Equi

31. Always a Beginner

Writers complain about the loneliness of our profession. But when my writing is going well, I'm in the company of my characters, putting on paper the words they dictate. When they stop, I know that the story is wrong or the scene doesn't fit and that's when it gets lonely.

One of the better things about writing in a studio is that when you hit a block, you can walk down the hall to find a friend who's happy to help you with your problem because it procrastinates having to solve his own.

Jess Oppenheimer, the father of *I Love Lucy*, was working with Norman Paul and me on a script for the Television Academy's awards show. Norman was a prodigal pacer and as we worked in Jesse's den, Norman wandered out to the patio, then scurried back to the den and said, "A great line came up while you guys were out of the room."

When I collaborated with Lesser Samuels, that sweet man of Buddha-like proportions, I entered his office one afternoon and discovered him staring out the window into the middle distance, his hands clasped over his belly, slowly shaking his head.

"What's wrong, Lesser?" I asked.

He said, "I was just contemplating the fact that my life is slowly Kraft-Ebbing away."

We were working on a biography of the Duncan Sisters, *Topsy and Eva*, for producer Harry Tugend. When we completed a scene, we always brought it down to his office and sat there while he read it. And always, Harry—who began his long career writing for Fred Allen—would reach for a pencil before he picked up the script. That habit annoyed Lesser.

"It tells us that he had no confidence in our work," he said. "He presupposes it needs correcting even before he's read a line."

The next time we handed him some pages, Harry reached for his pencil and Lesser startled him—and me—by slapping it out of Harry's hand.

"Read it first, damn you!" he snarled.

Harry apologized. "I know how you feel, Lesser. Forgive me." Then he picked up the pencil. As we returned to our fourth floor offices, Lesser said, "That's going to cost Paramount one half a day's work from me."

We completed the first draft of *Topsy and Eva* and were told that the next draft would be written by another writer. I was disappointed until I learned he was one of my literary heroes, Ben Hecht. I made it a point to meet him. He could not have been less interested. Maybe he didn't have time. He rewrote our entire script in a week.

The following week, I was called to D.A. Doran's office.

"As you know, Hal," D.A. smiled, "Ben Hecht did a polish job on your Duncan Sisters scenario. But Hecht is *persona non grata* to our friends in Great Britain due to his militant stand on the Palestine question, so it would be inconvenient for us to give him screen credit on your picture."

"*My* picture, D.A.? He rewrote it."

"Oh, there's enough of your work in it to justify your getting credit," he said as he flicked a sheet of legal paper toward me. "If you'll just sign this."

"Let me read the screenplay first," I said. "I can't take credit for something I didn't write."

"Why not?" he smiled. "Credit's been given to a lot of people who never wrote a word."

"So I've heard," I said. "And that's why the Screen Writers Guild was created."

Nobody got credit on *Topsy and Eva* because it was never made.

For too many years, screenwriters seldom got respect from producers. One embittered author summed up their attitude when he told us that Cecil B. De Mille, displeased with a scene he turned in, fixed him with a piercing glare that could melt a Crusader's armor and snarled, "In the bowels of the Earth there are worms and in the bowels of those worms there are writers!"

That was the same C. B. De Mille who told me to contact him after the war and, when I did so, he did not respond. What a narrow escape I had!

As the West Coast vice-president of the Radio Writers Guild, I attended a meeting in New York with my East Coast counterpart and representatives of the Screen Writers Guild, Dramatists Guild, John Hershey of the Authors League and Rex Stout of the Mystery Writers of America. Our purpose was to amalgamate our organizations under one umbrella as the Writers Guild(s) of America, East and West.

During a break, our Hollywood contingent went to Rockefeller Center to have lunch. (That was before Californians *did* lunch.) Our waiter hovered over us as we ordered and, in an accent as American as his mother's apple strudel, asked if we were "gentlemens from Hollywood." Karl Tunberg said yes.

"Do you know a man named Joe Pasternak?" he asked.

Yes, everybody knew Joe.

"He's famous, no?" the waiter asked.

Very famous. Now, where are our drinks?

The waiter returned to serve us and ask if Pasternak was really a successful movie producer.

Oh, yes, Pasternak was most successful.

"When I was a boy in Hungary," the waiter announced, "Pasternak was a janitor in my father's synagogue, saving his pennies he should come to America. He was a janitor because he could not read. I have not seen him in 30 years and now he's a big shot!"

He walked away, bitterly murmuring to himself, "Pasternak, Pasternak, Yussel Pasternak."

We finished our lunch and signaled our waiter for the check. He was waiting to pounce, slapped the check down and shouted to all of us, "Believe me! I'm much happier than Pasternak!"

Much later, I told that anecdote to Joe. It amused him and he said, "He's probably right."

Joe made a lot of people happier.

Charles Marquis ("Bill") Warren was another colleague at Paramount. He wrote and directed *Little Big Horn*, a modest film that received such excellent reviews, *Time* did a feature on it. In those days, moviemakers had confidence that our audiences were literate and often began films with a foreword. Warren opened his picture with a quote from Abraham Lincoln and got a call from a *Time* editor who asked where Bill got it because their researchers could not find it anywhere.

"In my grandmother's attic," Bill said. "It was from a letter President Lincoln wrote to her."

"I hope you saved that letter," I said when Bill told me about it. "It's probably worth more than your picture."

"My grandmother didn't have an attic," Bill grinned and extended his arm. "Shake hands with Dishonest Abe."

Carroll O'Connor was honored by the Masquers Club in Hollywood and among those who paid tribute to him — beside himself — was the legendary Mary Pickford. She was not there in person, but her praise was read by her husband Buddy Rogers, who extolled O'Connor's artistry. Mary Pickford never knew she had written such a glowing tribute to a man she never met.

Unless O'Connor reads this confession, he will not know Buddy

Hal Kanter addressing a Masquers Club affair honoring Carroll O'Connor (circa **1988**).

appealed to me to give him those words to read that night because Mary had never heard of Carroll.

Years before, at that same Masquers Club, I shared the dais with Miss Pickford herself when the honored guest was Harold Lloyd. I did not have to write for anyone but myself that night. I told him that when my parents took me and my siblings to the Lucas Theater in Savannah every Saturday afternoon to watch a Harold Lloyd comedy while they went off to do Mommy and Daddy things, I never dared dream that some day I would have this honor of thanking my old baby sitter in person.

Harold enjoyed that and luckily, I did not have to follow Miss Pickford, who showed us all what a star really is when she ad libbed a warm, gracious and very funny speech. And that night, she was almost as drunk as Louella Parsons.

At another social event, I met a long-haired intense male musician who called himself Alice Cooper. He was enthusiastic and admiring when we were introduced but I could not return either the enthusiasm or admiration because I was unaware of his contribution to our culture.

"Oh, Daddy!" my daughter Abbe wailed when I told her that the next day. "Get *with* it!"

Alice had been anxious to meet me because he idolized Olsen and Johnson's *Hellzapoppin'*. Someone at the party had mentioned my former relationship with the team.

"My God," I told Cooper, "you must have been an infant. That show was before the war."

"Oh, not the show," he said. "The movie. I'm trying to buy a print of my own."

I explained that I had nothing to do with the movie. That was written and produced later, when I was in uniform.

"Oh," Alice said and abruptly moved on to accost Groucho Marx, who hadn't the slightest idea who Alice Cooper was, fortunately for the bizarre musician. Groucho could be merciless and his sarcasm could maim. He once invited my secretary to lunch and promised her, "You'll be as safe with me as in your own whorehouse."

During the war, when he contributed to the morale of our armed forces, Groucho visited Lowry Field where he was approached by a hearty officer who shook Groucho's hand and said, "Mr. Marx, let me thank you for the laughter you've given us all these years. I'm Col. Jack Johnson."

"Not the great colored heavyweight?" Groucho asked.

When a telephone rang in a camp service club, Groucho grabbed it and said, "World War Two!" a line that the occasionally amusing Mort Sahl took credit for in his first movie.

Mort was cast in that film by Jerry Wald after Sahl replaced Zsa Zsa and Eva Gabor on an Academy Awards presentation. The Gabor sisters were just beginning their movie careers when Wald invited them to appear on the thirty-first Oscar show he produced in 1959. They were limited to a cameo appearance and when they arrived for rehearsal at the Pantages Theater, Zsa Zsa objected to the brevity of their script. Jerry handled the controversy that followed in his usual manner — he called in somebody else to deal with the irate lady.

Unfortunately, he called me. I listened to Zsa Zsa's shrill complaints and turned to Jerry to make an observation.

"Miss Gabor's correct when she says she and her sister are such big stars, it's an insult to ask them to do this simple joke, Jerry, so let's get somebody else to do it and they can go home."

Zsa Zsa stalked out. Eva apologized for her sister's behavior, but loyally followed her out. And that's when Mort Sahl was chosen to replace the Gabors and, as a bonus, was given more to do on the show than gave him his 15 minutes of stardom.

The next time I saw the garrulous Gabor was at a party in London. Zsa Zsa thought she remembered me and said, "I wish you could give me something for my headache, doctor."

"You've got me confused, Miss Gabor," I said. "I'm a writer."

"Oh," she said with a coquettish laugh, "of course, darling! I'm going to be interviewed by the BBC tomorrow. Can you give me some jokes for that?"

"Tell them about your new book," I said.

"What new book, darling?"

"*I Never Married a Man I Didn't Meet.*"

If she didn't use that herself, I did. Several times.

"My agent gets ten percent of everything I get, except my blinding headaches." — Fred Allen

32. *Ten Percent of Everything*

> If Diogenes was still seeking an honest man at the gates of Eternity—on May 10, 1969, Diogenes found him.

That's how I began the most difficult talk I was ever asked to deliver—my first eulogy—and those pages were stained with tears as I continued:

> It was then, last Saturday morning, George Rosenberg's lungs labored their last—and that honest man moved from here to Eternity.

Among the many who mourned his passing was Robert Coryell, a former banker who brought dignity to the much maligned agency business when he became Rosie's partner. Rosenberg & Coryell, successors to Polan & Rosenberg, eventually took in others and grew to become one of the world's largest. I remained their client even after Coryell retired, until one day when I called the office and asked to speak to the agent who was purportedly handling me.

Some clod whose name my mind refuses to recall got on the line and told me there was nothing he could do for me. I hung up and called his boss in New York, Marvin Josephson, who was distressed to hear that one of his underlings had treated me so cavalierly. Marvin assured me that he had big plans for me; as the only survivor of Rosie's first client list, there was nothing he would not do for me. And, by God, true to his word, there was nothing he ever *did* do for me.

I turned to Marvin Moss, one of Rosie's employees who left their agency to open his own office when Bob Coryell retired. Marvin represented me for the rest of his life, even though I had some doubts about him when Rosie first assigned him to handle me for films.

Marvin brought me an offer from Universal. When I drove out to the studio to discuss it, Marvin convinced me that it would be a good career move for me to accept but I wanted to think about it overnight. Driving off the lot, I looked back at the billboards the studio had at the entrance in those days, boasting their current releases. I called Moss the moment I got home to announce my decision.

"I'm sorry," I said. "I cannot indenture myself to a studio that thinks Jill St. John and Douglas McClure are stars!"

Marvin lost that commission but won my esteem when he chuckled and said he understood.

Among the clients Rosie brought to Hollywood were two men he discovered when he heard a radio program while he was in Carmel for Crosby's golf tournament. The show, produced in San Francisco, called *Yours Truly, Johnny Dollar*, contained such original dialogue Rosie called the station to ask who had written it. The author was the station's staff writer, Richard Breen.

Dick was a graduate of Fordham University who wound up in San Francisco because it was the only place he could find work after getting out of the Navy. He did not have an agent and would be pleased to allow Rosie to find him a better job than his present one, if he could. Rosie assured him he could and proved it within a week with an offer to write a film for Paramount.

Dick had one request: Could Rosie help the staff announcer who played *Johnny Dollar* find work in Hollywood?

"Bring him along," Rosie said. "We'll set him up in a show of his own that you can write."

So Jack Webb came down with Dick Breen to make names and fortunes for themselves, Rosenberg and Coryell and everyone connected with *Dragnet*, *Pete Kelly's Blues* and *Adam 12*.

While Dick was working with Brackett and Wilder at Paramount during the day, he was writing a new radio show, *Johnny Modero*, for Webb at night. His dry wit and colorful turns of phrase attracted me to him and I admired his ability to speak clearly in behalf of writers when he joined our guild and quickly rose in the ranks of its management.

By 1951, Breen was so established in the Hollywood community, the Academy assigned him the title of general director for the twenty-third annual awards, a chore we now call producer. But in '51 the Oscar show was only heard, not seen, because the film nabobs considered the family-watching machine the enemy that kept people from buying tickets to the movies.

Dick wrote and produced a smooth show with finicky Fred Astaire as the master of ceremonies. The following year, producer Arthur Freed took over the chore and engaged Danny Kaye as emcee and Dick as writer with Sylvia Fine. When Dick found the task of pleasing the neurotic Kayes more daunting than the fastidious Astaire, he asked me to put in a few lines to placate my old bosses. That favor began a collaboration with Breen that lasted, off and on, for the next 15 years.

March 19, 1953, Bob Hope was the emcee when the first Oscar show was televised. Again, the script was written by Richard L. Breen, but I was among the cluster of Hope writers who contributed to his monologue. And that started my relationship with the Academy of Motion Picture Arts and Sciences that would last longer than any other writer, producer, director or performer: 28 annual Academy Awards presentations. Only Bob Metzler, who handled the Oscar's business affairs, ever worked on more.

In addition to contributing to Hope's script for the twenty-fifth awards, producer Johnny Green asked me to write material for Claire Trevor to read as an audience warm-up. The Oscar-winning Miss Trevor made my words sound so good, the following year I was asked not only to write the entire show but also to do the audience warm-up myself.

Mitchell Leisen was the general director in 1954 and the NBC directors, Bill Bennington in Hollywood and Grey Lockwood in New York, cut between our co-emcees, Donald O'Connor in the West and Fredric March in the East. The show started in California, where the disembodied voice of Raymond Burr identified "Hollywood's glittering hour ... the night dreams come true for some of its citizens ... movietown's election night ... the final game of the World Series ... the running of the Derby ... the Rose Bowl. This is Academy Awards night!"

In the Pantages Theater, the orchestra rose from the pit and Andre Previn conducted the overture while the cameras explored the celebrities in the house.

Then we cut to the Center Theater in New York where Burr's voice identified other stars arriving from their performances in Broadway theaters. Cutting back to the West Coast, Burr introduced the president of the Academy, the distinguished Charles Brackett, who welcomed the audience in a charming speech of his own design and introduced the emcee as "a veteran player who for 17 years has creaked around in front of the cameras ... Donald O'Connor."

Young Donald got laughs with the material I prepared for him and Fredric March, whom he introduced in a split screen with New York. The audience was impressed with what was then big stuff for TV.

Donald ad-libbed a line that caused some embarrassment. Mitch Leisen made it a point to shoot Ann Blyth in closeups to avoid showing that she was in the last months of her pregnancy, but when Ann finished her song, O'Connor said, "That was Ann Blyth and family."

On that Oscar show, there were two other firsts. The nominees for

Best Actress were announced by Gary Cooper from Mexico, where he was on location. His participation was filmed there — and after reading the nominees (Leslie Caron in *Lili*, Ava Gardner in *Mogambo*, Audrey Hepburn in *Roman Holiday*, Deborah Kerr in *From Here to Eternity* and Maggie McNamara in *The Moon Is Blue*), he said, "And the winner is..."— then shrugged. It got one of the biggest laughs of the night.

He turned it back to Donald in Hollywood, who got his own laugh trying to imitate Coop as he opened the envelope. Incidentally, trivia freaks, do you remember who took the Oscar that year?

(Here's a hint: Audrey.)

The other first was the announcement of the Best Actor, which was made by the lady who won her Oscar the year before for her film debut in *Come Back, Little Sheba*. Now she was trying out a new play in Philadelphia and our camera went backstage to bring us Shirley Booth from her dressing room. Shirley wasted no time in reeling off the names of nominees Marlon Brando, Richard Burton, Montgomery Clift, William Holden and Burt Lancaster.

Then she prolonged the suspense as she asked Donald to open the envelope and whisper the name of the winner to her over the telephone line we had installed for this moment. The winner was clearly a surprise and Shirley shouted, "Congratulations" to William Holden.

Couldn't have happened to a nicer guy.

Twenty-three years later, Holden presented the Film Editing award. Before the show, he asked if the Ray Bradbury who wrote his script with me was the science fiction author. When I said yes, Bill asked to meet him because he "worshiped" his work.

"Wait in the Green Room," I said, "and I'll bring him in because our office backstage is too small for you to bend over to kiss his ring."

When I told Bradbury that Holden wanted to meet him, he asked, "William Holden, the actor?" He was as excited as a kid opening a birthday present. I introduced them and watched two fans, each of them impressed by the other, and left them knowing they were both sincere, unlike some others I recall from that same night.

Marty Feldman, the English comedian, was one who expressed pleasure with a sight bit I gave him. It required a special shirt which producer William Friedkin had wardrobe construct the night before. Feldman was to read the long list of nominees for short subjects, and adjust his cuffs while doing so. Each time he did, the sleeves got longer until they were both sweeping the floor. The effect was hilarious in rehearsal.

But Feldman lost his nerve at the last minute and relied on his bug-eyed face and deliberately broke a plastic replica of Oscar in a misguided

Rehearsing the sixty-ninth Oscar show—Shrine Auditorium in Los Angeles, March 1997. Associate producer Mike Seligman (left), producer Gil Cates (right), with Hal Kanter in between.

attempt to amuse; it did not break the way he anticipated, so he stomped on it. It was not funny and helped further Chevy Chase's earlier attempts to diminish Oscar's stature—and statue.

Another chore I'd been doing for several years was the audience warm-up. It always took a while to get their attention because people were still arriving when I began to speak, a frustrating situation I usually referred to with ambivalent good nature and bitterness.

Without any introduction other than a fanfare from the orchestra, I walked out onto the vast stage of the Dorothy Chandler and introduced myself to explain my role in the program.

> I face the challenge of diverting you from each other—to call a few facts to your collective attention. If I can collect it, I'll get on with that assignment.

I beseeched them

> to participate in the mounting excitement and give us frequent bursts of laughter, applause, cheers and other manifestations of mass insincerity when your favorite loses.
>
> As in all years, you are invited to make a speech of acceptance. But only if you win.

> You will be able to determine if you're a winner after the sealed envelope is opened and your name is read.
>
> When that moment of truth bursts upon you in a blinding flash of ecstasy, please try not to panic. A piercing shriek of delight is permissible, of course, but when you hear your name read aloud, do make an effort to get up from your seat.
>
> However the bulletin reaches your nervous system, we ask that you come onstage to accept your award. We suggest you use the stairs to get here. It's less messy that way...
>
> Winners — please exit stage right, where the press awaits to deify you.

Each year, the show seems to get longer and each year I was asked to instruct the winners to keep their acceptance speeches short. In 1958, when the show itself ran short, the NBC-TV director, Alan Handley, wrote an article in *TV Guide* accusing me of having frightened the nominees into cutting their speeches down to such a minimum, he ran out of show 20 minutes before its allocated time. In desperation, my erstwhile friend Handley coaxed Jerry Lewis back to conduct the entire cast — the world's highest priced glee club — in unrehearsed song. It was Oscar's most embarrassing 20 minutes. Placing the blame for that on me was nonsense. For years, winners ignored my appeals for brevity and there's no evidence that their acceptances were any shorter that year. Handley and Jerry Wald, the Academy producer, had simply misfigured the length of the show and cut a song number and several jokes while they were on the air.

"They timed this thing," Bob Hope said later, "with a sun dial."

Halfway into the thirtieth annual awards, David Niven appeared to say, "A moment ago, we received word backstage that Mr. and Mrs. Bartley Emerson of Silver Springs, Maryland, just returned from their neighborhood theater and turned on their television set. They want to know why they're not seeing Richard Dix in *The Ghost Ship*.

"Well, Mr. and Mrs. Emerson — tonight the motion picture industry is bringing you our annual Academy Awards program."

Immediately the Emersons' phone began ringing — and kept ringing for the next two days. My brother-in-law, Bart Emerson, called me from their home in Silver Spring and raised hell with me for allowing David Niven to use their names. To Bart, it seemed the entire world was watching and this world was populated by thousands of idiots who want to reach out and touch anyone connected with the movies.

My sister Saralea, who always had a better sense of humor, was amused, but she did extract a promise from me never to use their name again, except when writing checks. But when I wrote the part of a whimsical Southern lady to play Elvis Presley's mother in the movie *Blue Hawaii*, I named her Saralea. Elvis thought it was because I liked cake.

"Early in life I chose between honest arrogance and hypocritical humility. I chose honest arrogance and have no reason since to regret it."— Frank Lloyd Wright

33. *No Reason to Regret It*

The first time I saw a whale up close was in the Sea of Cortez. How small I felt, how helpless and afraid! I was in a tiny open boat with a barefoot Mexican *pescadero* and our proximity to that enormous mammal gave me a new perspective. I was not as important as I had felt a moment before.

I wonder if any of the people I deal with in Hollywood would feel the same. They comprise the largest collection of virulent egos west of the United States Senate.

At Oscar time, they're not all in front of the camera. Agents, personal managers, press agents and meddling friends all exercise their considerable influence on performers to make life uncomfortable for those of us trying to help Oscar shine. For the 28 shows in which I have been involved to date, my exposure to their virulence has been limited to a few tempestuous hours.

With Rex Harrison, a man of severely limited amenity, it lasted a few minutes at the end of a long day.

On April 18, 1966, we were still rehearsing the thirty-seventh Awards in Santa Monica when I decided to go home. As I started out, producer Joe Pasternak and Academy president Arthur Freed were engrossed in what seemed a spirited debate with Rex Harrison. Freed beckoned me over.

"You know Rex, of course," he said, and to Rex he said, "Our writer."

"He did not write the music," Harrison said, ignoring me. "And you cannot play "I Could Have Danced All Night" for Julie's entrance. That's to be played for Audrey!"

Pasternak said to me, "He's upset because Andrews wasn't in the movie; Hepburn was."

"But Andrews was *My Fair Lady* on Broadway," Freed said.

"We know that!" Harrison screeched. "But this isn't Broadway. This is bloody Hollywood!"

"Actually," I said, "this is Santa Monica."

Harrison looked at me for the first time and said, "*Wherever*! This must be corrected, so let us all put on our thinking caps!"

I considered this none of his business so I said, "Mr. Harrison, you brought up the question — so you put on your thinking cap. I'm going home to put on my sleeping cap."

As I walked out, I heard him screeching, "Who is that rude person?"

Rudeness can be contagious. I had restrained myself earlier when Harrison complained about the dialogue he was to exchange with Bob Hope. I waited for Bob to assure that their dialogue was amusing even if it wasn't written by George Bernard Shaw. Later, on the air, the sly Hope gave the scornful Harrison a lesson in charming an audience.

Another year, another rehearsal, I overheard an ego-swollen Peter Bogdanovich telling Cybill Shepherd he wanted to rewrite her lines. I was sitting in the second row of the hall and Miss Shepherd was sitting in the first row — in Bogdanovich's lap. The man was so full of himself, I was surprised there was room for the girl. Bogdanovich had no reason to be there other than his passionate pursuit of Shepherd. If he did rewrite whatever Mort Lachman and I had prepared for her, I cannot recall due to an abiding case of disinterest in both of them.

Raquel Welch was another who showed up with a skinny Frenchman with hair larger than hers who demanded changes in her script. After a tepid exchange with an amused Tom Selleck standing by, I suggested we lose the banter between Welch and him when they present the Editing award. Tom was willing, but the lady wasn't. She wanted to stay on camera as long as she could and knew a laugh would ensure that, so she finally accepted our material — then took it upon herself to change her line. Laugh? It never started.

She was only one of several over the years who rewrote scripts. Most of them fell on their faces; the rest fell on their asses. Some, like Richard Dreyfuss, an intelligent actor, did not try for laughs but rewrote serious speeches to make them what they considered better. They were seldom better, merely different.

My frequent Oscar collaborator, Buz Kohan, agreed those shows are never written as much as rewritten, too often by people who can't write.

In 1982, Mickey Rooney threw out the entire speech I gave him and accepted his honorary Oscar with clichés of his own, and got one laugh by saying he was so happy he could kiss Louis B. Mayer.

Robert Redford, a gentleman blessed with the three essential Ts — talent, tact and taste — considered what I had given him to present an honorary award to Henry Fonda as fine, but thought it could be improved. So we sat in a dressing room and did so like civilized collaborators.

The author with Paddy Chayefsky (left).

Jack Lemmon, one of my favorite people, was another keen editor who improved material by suggesting cuts. Jack can do more with a look than most actors can with an aria.

In 1978, Vanessa Redgrave used the forum of her Supporting Actress award to speak for her political beliefs and accuse those who protested them of being "militant Zionist hoodlums." Her remarks were resented by many, including writer Paddy Chayefsky, when I encountered him in the lobby while sneaking out for a smoke during the commercial.

Paddy was angrily talking to a tall fellow I did not know when he saw me and said, "Kanter! You've got to answer that woman!"

"I can't go out there," I said, "but in ten minutes, you'll be able to give the writing awards — and once you're out there — "

Chayefsky nodded and began immediately making notes on the back of his program.

The Oscar-winning writer had a few well-chosen words for Miss Redgrave which he prefaced by saying he was sick and tired of actors exploiting the Academy Awards for their personal propaganda. The audience showered Chayefsky with applause and shouts of "Bravo!"

In 1981, Norman Jewison produced the fifty-third Awards and asked me to write it with Buz Kohan and Rod Warren. My first assignment was to provide the opening speech for Norman's prize piece of casting — a welcome by Ronald Reagan, speaking from Washington, where he was playing his biggest role since leaving Warner Bros.

It had to be written far in advance for the White House staff to approve and arrange time for the president to stay awake long enough to film it.

A week or so later, Norman congratulated me. "The president is filming your opening tomorrow," he said, "and they changed only one sentence. Isn't that great?"

"What'd they change?"

Norman showed me the copy from the White House, a minor cut of my original and the change of "Mrs. Reagan" to "Nancy."

"You should be proud of this," he said. "You've written for the president of the United States!" Norman is a Canadian.

When the film came in, I had to admire how well Ronnie played the president.

March 30, 1981, the night the world was to see the president's welcome, he was in a hospital room, the victim of an assassination attempt by a crazed movie fan who thought his action would impress Jodie Foster.

Emcee Johnny Carson's first reaction upon hearing the news was, "This is awful. The first five minutes of my monologue are about Reagan!"

The Academy's Board of Governors met that afternoon to discuss postponing the show, which would cost us thousands of dollars, whereas if ABC did so, the network would be responsible for the costs.

John Hamlin, an ABC vice-president, convinced his superiors to pick up the bill once we were assured the president would recover and the show would be aired the following day.

Norman got an amazing call from some admiral in the White House.

"If you can get a crew here," the officer told Norman, "we can deliver the president to you live!"

"But doesn't he have tubes in his nose and arms?" the astonished Norman asked.

There was a pause as the admiral conferred with someone, then he said, "Yes, but we can pull them out for TV!"

Norman told the admiral he would get back to him, after another meeting in Santa Monica to decide whether to show the president's welcoming address at all. The White House's offer was dismissed immediately.

Johnny Carson, Academy president Fay Kanin, executive director Jim Roberts, ABC's Hamlin, TV director Marty Pasetta, Buz Kohan and I debated whether or not to include the film.

Fay wasn't sure; the network wanted to avoid controversy; Marty cautioned us not to take chances in case the president had a relapse; Buz said this was no time for pessimism and Johnny Carson insisted we could not avoid the president's state of health and must publicly express the industry's concern and prayers for his safety. Jim Roberts and Norman agreed, not only because he was loath to lose film he had labored to obtain.

I maintained that as long as we knew Reagan was out of danger, it would reassure the country to see him on the screen, in good health, good voice and good humor. Johnny agreed with this and said it would comfort the nation to see a vigorous president. So on March 31, a hearty, happy Ronald Reagan welcomed the world to share the Oscar derby with him and Nancy.

This was the third consecutive year Johnny Carson served as the program host and he was magnificent. Johnny's personality, intelligence and choice of material from his own writing staff augmented his quick wit and ability to handle any situation that arose during the show. In my book—which this is, come to think of it—Johnny was second only to Bob Hope as Oscar's best friend.

In 1992, director Gilbert Cates produced the Awards with Billy Crystal as host for their second time, the first year I worked with them. Billy had his own special material writers, Bruce Vilanch, Robert Wuhl and David Steinberg, while Buz and I got credit for writing the rest of the show.

In 1997, for the sixty-ninth Oscar, Billy worked again with Bruce, David and four new young writers to prepare what was the most brilliant opening any comedian ever had and established Crystal as the new heavyweight champion of Oscar hosts.

Going back to that sixty-third show, one of the assignments I drew was Best Foreign Film. Gil Cates' talent coordinator, crimson-haired Danette Herman, set Sylvester Stallone to present the award. I erroneously assumed he had a sense of humor and was willing to kid the public's perception of his mumbling Rocky Balboa character, so I wrote a brief, amusing introduction to the foreign films.

When Stallone received his copy, he called Gil to scream that he was insulted. Gil handled the complaint diplomatically. He took the onus off me by saying we all thought he has such a great comedy delivery, he'd enjoy employing his sense of humor.

The actor modestly admitted that he did have a "great comic delivery"—and suggested that he'd write something himself, an offer Gil politely turned down with the promise that I would rewrite the spot to reflect more accurately the artist's dignity as an international star. Stallone bought that. Gil is a greater salesman than Willy Loman in his prime.

When Stallone faced his audience, I sat with white knuckles as he grunted through the paragraph I provided.

But the following year, when Michael Caine had the same reaction to the words I wrote for him, he was not to be placated. Gil's Willy Loman struck out. Caine refused to appear on the show, so my introduction to the Foreign Language Oscar was read by the alert and cooperative Glenn Close, who is much prettier.

One of the secrets of the sixty-fourth Awards was the participation of NASA and the crew of the space shuttle *Atlantis* who were going to present a special award to George Lucas. In Cape Canaveral, the Associated Press correspondent discovered that the Oscar statuette was aboard the flight and the Los Angeles bureau was trying to verify that fact and find out why. They were going to break the story Sunday, the day before the telecast.

Chuck Warn, the adroit master of public relations for the Directors Guild on loan to the Academy, did not confirm to the journalist the reason Oscar was in space and struck a bargain with him. If he'd forget that "rumor," Chuck would give him another closely guarded secret they could put on the wire: Billy Crystal was not at the Sunday rehearsal, nor was he there the day before. He was quite ill and there was some question as to whether his doctor would sanction his appearance at all.

That mollified the questioner and Billy's health became another story that added to the suspense of the show. A lot of fingers were crossed and there were several covert meetings to draw up emergency plans in case Billy was prevented from performing.

Gil, Academy president Karl Malden and I were at least three who agreed that the one star who could step into the host spot in an emergency was Tom Hanks. He was nimble, funny, appealing and was willing to pinch hit for Billy, if need be.

The need was not to be; Billy recovered sufficiently to hit for himself. And he hit a grand slam that year. Tom would have to wait for his nights of glory when he won his Oscars for Best Peformances by an actor, not a host.

When it was announced Gil would produce the sixty-seventh Awards, a rumor I heard was confirmed: The host would be David Letterman, a man I never believed was in the same league with Hope, Carson or Crystal. Letterman's attitude had always been hostile, childish and mocking.

He was described by his producer Peter LaSalle as "a man of many moods, all of them bad." The comic remained in New York, where he housed a platoon of writers and was hard to pin down as to what he planned. The two or three ideas that came through to us suggested the worst of my fears.

"We're going to do two shows this year," I predicted. "Dave's and a Letterman show with some awards tossed in."

Among Letterman's ideas was to raffle off a car and preparations were under way to do so before Gil's good taste came to Oscar's rescue. But he could not talk Letterman out of a running gag of a spinning dog that chases his own tail whenever the audience applauded.

None of Letterman's attempts to amuse had the vaguest relationship to the theme Gil had chosen for that year's show, "comedy in the movies." To celebrate that, he had fallen under the spell of Academy Award winning film maker Chuck Workman. That billing was stipulated in the contract between the Academy and Academy Award winning film maker Chuck Workman, one of the few people I ever knew who could strut while sitting down.

He poured his sense of humor into an elaborate opening number of interactive video, a concept that Buz Kohan had successfully introduced years before. This time, Workman took longer, got into boisterous arguments with choreographer Debbie Allen and associate producer Mike Seligman — and the result was a shameful waste of prime time.

Recalling more than two dozen Academy shows I participated in, I prefer to remember the moments like Marlene Dietrich striding across the stage of the Pantages Theater, wearing a long black velvet dress with a thigh-high slash on its left side, exposing a famous leg with each step, bringing cheers from the audience.

Martha Raye and Jimmy Durante reading lines Milt Rosen and I wrote for them, and getting more laughs than we'd written by mangling the names of the Documentary Film nominees.

And Walter Matthau getting one of the decade's biggest laughs when he read properly, "This show is being sent live around the world and if my tailor is watching in Hong Kong — it still doesn't fit."

Shirley MacLaine and Peter Ustinov giving the Sound awards, providing their own sound effects.

Rock Hudson singing a duet with Mae West, looking voluptuous and naughty. Mae was discovered reclining on a divan and stayed there. Some considered that showmanship, but the truth was that Mae couldn't stand without assistance.

Howard W. Koch, who held the record for the number of Oscars he produced, always insisted that I remind the nominees in my warm-up to keep their acceptances short—but the year Howard won the Hersholt Award himself, he ignored his own plea for brevity.

But who am I to talk? I'm doing the same.

"I'm not very keen on Hollywood. I'd rather have a nice cup of cocoa, really."— Sir Noël Coward

34. I'd Rather Have Cocoa

Of all my Academy Award shows, two women, Barbra Streisand and Madonna, stand out for their dedication to their own talent.

On Streisand's first date with Oscar, she insisted TV director Marty Pasetta tape a full dress rehearsal of her number, then corrected his lighting, camera angles, sound balance, her own wardrobe, makeup and hair. Her perfectionism paid off; Streisand was perfect on the air.

Years later, Madonna worked even harder and longer on her Oscar debut. She was also the most troublesome, demanding everything from dressing rooms to rehearsal time. According to director Jeff Margolis, Madonna was also the most nervous.

She brought the dress and shoes she would wear for the show to the rehearsal and sat in the booth with Jeff to check his spotlights and ordered a shy stand-in with her coloring to hold up her dress for the camera. Not wear it. Just hold it up. Madonna kept the trembling girl under the lights so long, she broke into hives.

Madonna wanted her microphone to come up from the floor of the Shrine auditorium. For that to happen, an extra stagehand was employed to crawl through a small aperture high over the stage and take the cue from below to hit the proper switch. During the commercial before the star's entrance, the stage manager signaled him to check the mike but got no response. Thinking quickly, he rushed on stage with a standing mike, just in case.

There was pandemonium in the control room when the stagehand failed to respond to Jeff's cues. He sent the stage manager backstage to tell Madonna she would work to the standing mike. After all those hours of meticulous rehearsals, the lady's reaction was, "Don't you fuck with me!"

The stagehand who was engaged for that simple task had fallen asleep in the middle of the biggest show of the year. The irony of the slumberer's name was not lost on movie people. It was Gary Cooper.

If Madonna suffered any trauma at the sight of that microphone standing there, she must have gotten over it when her number was received with enthusiasm. Later, she joined the audience with her date for the evening, Michael Jackson, and seemed to enjoy herself enormously. Michael seemed not to. Madonna insisted he join her in the theater. A dominating woman, she demanded to know where he was going, even when he went to pee, accompanied to the restroom by two bodyguards.

Another memorable woman was Elizabeth Taylor. I have been in her company with several husbands, five of them her own. While the men changed, she never seemed to. She was always beautiful, from the first day I saw her, young and vulnerable, standing in the sunlight on the Paramount lot, where she was filming *A Place in the Sun*.

There are women like Taylor who attract our attention, others like Madonna who demand it and a scant minority you cannot ignore any more than a brushfire in your mustache.

There was Ingrid Bergman's elegant beauty, the animal magnetism of Sophia Loren and the blazing light of Tallulah Bankhead, the leading lady who described herself as "pure as the driven slush."

Once interviewed by Maurice Zolotow, who asked if the story was true that she had given birth to an illegitimate child, Tallulah emphatically denied it. "However," she said, "my abortions would fill this room."

Maurice was a gentleman; he did not reveal the dimensions of the room.

When she appeared in Las Vegas as a financially rewarding lark, Tallulah engaged the writing services of Hugh Wedlock and Howard Snyder, my old benefactors. The writers, ignorant of her unabashed proclivity for freedom, were stunned when she greeted them stark naked. Howard did not know where to allow his eyes to work. He removed his glasses, hoping Tallulah would become only a blur as she nonchalantly served drinks and chatted up her usual storm, nude as a fish.

"She was proud of her breasts," Hugh said, "especially at her age—and I was proud of my hard-on at mine!"

The closest to nudity Tallulah ever got in my presence was during a TV show I staged when she didn't wear any of her fabulous jewelry. That was years after our first meeting in Ole Olsen's dressing room, which she pretended to remember when I recalled it to her. I was producing the *Kraft Music Hall*, an NBC-TV half-hour that starred the boisterous Milton Berle, when Tallulah became available for a guest appearance.

Berle and Bankhead had appeared together earlier so both knew what they were in for. I expected fireworks during the five days we rehearsed the live show. They both surprised me. The first day, Milton's sophomoric attempt to amuse the lady was to unzip his fly, but Tallulah waved him off and said, "Put it back, Milton, I've seen bigger and better and thicker and slicker."

For the rest of the week, my usually meddlesome star was on his best behavior. He not only admired Tallulah, he was afraid of her. If he was more quiet than usual, it was not only because Tallulah monopolized all conversation.

Her talk was always rich, even if it was incessant. She asked me to have lunch with her every day. She also asked me to pay for it every day. It was worth it, even though it meant sharing her with anyone sitting nearby.

Among the performers engaged for that episode was the ubiquitous midget, Billy Curtis. Tallulah and Billy spent hours in serious discussion about the plight of little people, one of the few times I'd ever seen that mischievous little man engrossed in anything more meaningful than placing a bet or arguing for a larger salary. Tallulah was a woman of compelling compassion.

Showtime.

She stood behind the curtain as Berle and Jimmie Rodgers worked in front of it, singing a parody titled "I'll Take Tallulah," which led to her introduction. Camera director Ben Tompkins was in the control booth and I was on the floor, at Tallulah's request. She groaned and put her arms around me. Her small body quivered with stage fright.

"Come on," I whispered and lifted her chin. "You've accomplished every triumph in the English-speaking theater. There isn't anyone out there who doesn't know you, admire you, respect you. You're beautiful, talented, magnetic, magnificent. When Milton speaks your name, that house is going to explode with affection because, like Garbo and Chaplin, you're the only Tallulah there is!"

"Arrant bullshit!" she croaked.

The reception she got from Berle's audience immediately restored her considerable faith in herself. They enjoyed her parody of reading poetry to jazz — where the "poetry" was pulled from a bowl of fortune cookies.

The laughs were bigger when she engaged in the banter with Milton: "It's wonderful to have a Berle hour on TV again," Tallulah said, to which Berle responded, "My show's only a half-hour."

"Not when you're watching it, darling."

"Ah, Tallulah," Berle laughed, "you've got a great delivery. Where'd you park your truck?"

Their insults led into an entrancing musical duet in which they continued getting laughs as they sang "I Remember It Well" and then danced off to enthusiastic applause.

Tallulah fled to her dressing room to pack hastily even before the final credits rolled. When we were safely off the air, I ran down to thank her. She was racing to the airport but stopped to kiss me and introduce me to her friend and volunteer driver, Richard Deacon, with these words:

"This is Hal Kanter, who's more rabbi than cantor, our producer and writer and director and scoutmaster and the dearest, wittiest man I've known since my late, darling Robert Benchley." She then turned to smile at me and added, "Whom I hope you will soon join!"

A man remembers things like that.

I still love her a little bit.

"Years ago, I discovered the meaning of life, but I forgot to write it down."—Hugh Gallagher

35. I Forgot to Write It Down

Paramount owned a comedy by Sam and Bella Spewak that I wanted to adapt for the screen. When I expressed that desire to D. A. Doran, he asked me to relay my enthusiasm to William Wyler, whose most recent triumph was *Roman Holiday*.

"Speak up," Wyler said, cupping a hand to his ear when I came into his office. He was hard of hearing. He was also hard to convince that he should follow *Roman Holiday* with another comedy.

So I was assigned to a project for Dean Martin and Jerry Lewis. I was again writing with Ed Hartmann for Paul Jones, but there was an irritant added to that pleasant association.

His name was Danny Arnold.

A shrill, shrewd young comic, he was a perfect stooge for Jerry Lewis and presented the comedians an idea for a story about golf, the game he knew was a hobby for Jerry and a religion for Dean.

Jerry told Paramount they would do it as their next picture, so the studio bought the story from Arnold and gave it to Paul Jones to produce. He agreed to allow Danny to learn how to write a screenplay and assigned Ed and me to teach him.

I was still learning how myself, but I did know enough to listen to Ed. Danny already knew everything so he did not listen to anybody. From the first day we began work on *The Caddy*, he disagreed with every suggestion we made.

The second day, Danny discarded our ideas on the grounds that Jerry did not like them. The third day, he came in with a scene that we read and then dismissed. Danny stormed out of the office. I suspected he would complain to Martin and Lewis. Ed said Danny might talk to Jerry but not Dean.

"Dean doesn't give a shit. But Jerry, yes. He gives a lot of it!"

Danny did go to Jerry and reported everything we discussed: story, actors, our producer or what we ordered for lunch. He was Jerry's spy and while I enjoyed working with Ed, I could not abide Danny any longer. I walked out of Ed's office during a wrangle over a story point, went to Paul Jones and asked him to relieve me of the assignment. Paul was sympathetic and told me to take a week's vacation.

I needed that. I had been very involved with Writers Guild business, writing a TV special and a nightclub act for Ed Wynn, working on the Adlai Stevenson campaign and making frequent excursions to find a larger home. Doris encouraged me to spend a few days away from work with our girls.

On a Sunday morning in June, I drove Lisa and Donna from Sunday school to Las Vegas, where we spent the night. They were not impressed. The next day we drove to the Grand Canyon. We got out of the car and approached the rim to view that vast spectacle where Lisa glanced down and said, "Okay! Now let's go see the Painted Desert!"

When we arrived there, Donna announced she would not go on to the Petrified Forest. She wanted her mommy and her baby sister. Not that I can be pushed around by a sobbing five year old, but we immediately headed home.

Back at work, I was called to John Mok's office. John was Paramount's pleasant new story editor, having moved there after working for the legendary Hal Wallis. The move entailed leaving the Wallis suite on the second floor for Doran's old office on the first.

Mok had an assignment for me, a loan-out to Wallis himself, to write the screenplay of a Damon Runyon short story called *Money from Home.*

It meant I would be writing for the comedians Wallis introduced to movies and who were still under contract to him: Martin and Lewis. One appealing aspect of the job was the test to discover whether I could write for the movies' current hottest comedy team without the assistance of Danny Arnold.

Money from Home turned out to be my first solo screen credit and the first of seven screenplays I eventually wrote for the best producer I ever worked for in Hollywood.

Hal B. Wallis was a quiet man with a sweet smile which he wore infrequently. He was married to the silent screen comedienne Louise Fazenda, who was well aware of her husband's appetite for work, wealth and women.

He was an attractive man, always well groomed, who released his independently produced Wallis-Hazen films through Paramount, the studio where he maintained his offices. His partner, Joe Hazen, conducted their East Coast business in New York.

Unlike many executives who surround themselves with assistants, Wallis had very few. His two closest adjutants during my years in his employ seemed to be a boyhood pal, Jack Saper, and a perceptive young associate producer, Paul Nathan. The three of them often ate lunch together, and when one day I was invited to join them, I felt I had been voted membership in an elite club.

One hot summer afternoon, returning from the commissary, Paul and I were walking behind Wallis and Safer. The two men wore short-sleeved sports shirts; without a jacket, Wallis seemed to have no shoulders. I commented to Paul, "Now I know what to get him for Father's Day."

"What?" Paul asked cautiously.

"Shoulders," I said. "I get the feeling that every now and then, Hal might like to shrug."

A year later I was in his office, attempting to convince him to buy a story I liked. When I completed my pitch, Wallis looked at Paul and said, "If I had shoulders, I'd shrug."

Paul grew crimson. And I learned that if I ever wanted Hal Wallis to learn something, all I had to do was mention it to Paul.

While I was writing *Money from Home*, Bob Hope called me to have a chat in his dressing room. He wanted me to take over his television shows as producer and head writer for the new season. The next day, Rosie met with Bob's TV agent, Jimmy Saphier, to discuss terms.

Hope was unaware that I was under contract to Paramount at that time. When Saphier told him that, Bob backed off. He didn't want to obligate himself to the studio by asking their permission for me to do his TV shows. The matter was academic: When Rosie requested that permission from the studio, Paramount refused.

Bob continued to summon me to his dressing room to ask for jokes for his various appearances. And after the successful previews of *Road to Bali*, he asked me to reconsider coming to work for him full time. I promised him I would. But before I did, I had a lot of other living to do.

Wallis was pleased with my screenplay of *Money from Home* and engaged George Marshall to direct it. Marshall, who began making movies when they were silent, was an old hand with both action and comedy but I was distressed when I visited his set and heard him ask his script girl for "the titles"—and she handed him the script I had written.

I bitched to Wallis about having such an out-of-date old man working on a contemporary comedy. Wallis assured me that old man knew more about how to put comedy on the screen than any hip young modern and when I saw his dailies I became a believer.

I described one scene in a few words: "The heavies chase the jockey through the barn." Marshall invented so many sight gags to illustrate that simple sentence, it took him two days to shoot it.

Watching George work, I learned much about directing movies — my next goal, I confided to Paul Nathan. He was sympathetic because his own ambition was to advance from associate to producer. In one of our frequent conversations, he learned that I had written radio dramas and a few days later, he put a book on my desk and said, "Read this."

The next day, Paul gave me a screenplay based on the book and said, "This is going to be Shirley Booth's next picture. *About Mrs. Leslie.* Tell me what you think."

I thought it was a soap opera. A sudsy weeper and five Kleenex nose-blower, unrelieved by any trace of humor.

An hour later, Paul called. "Meet me in the boss' office."

Wallis sat at his enormous desk, frowning. He was an Olympic frowner. Across from him sat a thin, slightly balding, energetic young man with horn-rimmed glasses who jumped up when we entered. Paul said, "Danny Mann — Hal Kanter."

As we shook hands, Danny said, "I hear we agree."

"About what?"

"About *Mrs. Leslie,*" he grinned. And Wallis said, "Danny's going to direct it. But the script needs work."

That was no surprise. All producers say that about all scripts always.

"Paul tells us you've got some ideas," Danny said. "Let's hear 'em."

I ad libbed several. Danny pulled off his glasses and listened, nodding approval. "Good," he said. "Good. Some of that's good."

He put his glasses back on and turned to Paul. "There are writers who talk and there are writers who write," he said. "This one talks, but can he write?"

"He's written four pictures for Mr. Wallis," Paul said.

"But they were all comedies," Danny said to Wallis. "Right?"

Hal nodded and said to me, "Put aside the Runyon script for a day and write a scene for *Mrs. Leslie.*"

"One scene?"

"A love scene."

"I'd rather take it from the top," I said. "Why don't I start with Fade In and — "

"Just do the scene," Wallis said. "How do I know you can write romance?

I looked at Danny. He was smiling. Almost gloating. Was I going to have trouble with everyone named Danny? I started out of Wallis' office but when I got to the door, I turned and said, "It just occurred to me, Hal — the only scripts I've done for you were comedies. How do I know you can *produce* a love scene?"

Wallis' face went white. Paul almost choked. Wallis sputtered, speechless and pointed to his shelf of Oscars, to his Thalberg Award. I had one of those terrifying flashes when I sensed I'd gone too far; I'd never work for Wallis again. I'd never work at Paramount. I might never work in pictures again. Except maybe Columbia.

But Danny broke into laughter. "C'mon Hal," he said to Wallis, "let the man start at the top." He winked at me and I forgave the rascal.

Danny went back to New York and his beloved theater while I rewrote *Mrs. Leslie* to Wallis' satisfaction. It was still soap opera, but it had more of what Danny wanted: a little humor, a little more humanity. Wallis sent me to New York to fine tune the script with the director.

The day I arrived, Danny invited me to breakfast. He was living in an apartment across the street from Carnegie Hall and after breakfast he wanted to go for a stroll. To me, a stroll was from my Paramount office to Oblath's bar across the street but to Danny, a stroll was a field trip.

We strolled from 57th Street down to the Battery, then back up Broadway to the Russian Tea Room. And all the time we walked, Danny talked. The only time he stopped talking was when he had corned beef in his mouth.

He talked about his family, his school days, his saxophone playing, his philosophy of acting, of films and art and poetry, of politics and pussy—everything but my screenplay.

The next day we did talk about that, only this time in my room at the Plaza. Danny liked the script. He had suggestions we incorporated in the next draft that we took to Shirley Booth. She was appearing in *Time of the Cuckoo* in Central City, Colorado. On the trip west, Danny talked some more. Having nothing better to do, I listened.

I heard a lot of good sense and good jokes. Danny enjoyed stories that illustrated points he wanted to make and he kept both Shirley and me laughing for the days we spent together. Shirley, who won her Academy Award with his direction of *Come Back, Little Sheba*, obviously loved Danny—and so did I. He protected my work; Shirley accepted his assurance that the script had no problems.

When filming began in Hollywood, I spent time on the set watching Danny work. It was an education listening to him discuss a scene with his crew and cast. But for every minute he spent with his camera and sound men, he spent ten with his actors.

One afternoon, Robert Ryan, Shirley's leading man, told me what a pleasure it was for him to play a role where he didn't have to knock somebody down or shoot somebody up. He appreciated the script and working with a leading lady of such stature.

"And that director," I nodded toward Danny. Ryan looked across the stage to where Danny was talking passionately to a bit player.

"Danny Mann?" Bob said with a smile. "He's not a director. He's a fucking psychiatrist!"

About Mrs. Leslie remains one of my favorite pictures, with a lot of dialogue I'm proud to have written. One of the lines could have been Danny himself speaking when Mrs. Leslie, talking to the young lovers, says, "Get it all. Don't settle for half."

Danny wanted it all, too. He would not accept half from his actors, or from his writers.

Not even from Tennessee Williams. We did *The Rose Tattoo* together. Again for Wallis. I wrote the first draft in Hollywood and went to New York where Williams came up from Key West to meet me.

And do other things.

"I can never understand how two men can write together; to me, it's like three people getting together to have a baby."— Evelyn Waugh

36. *Three People Have a Baby*

Tennessee Williams was short, stocky, with a large head and an even larger appetite for whiskey and cigarettes, and went for a swim at the YMCA every afternoon he was in New York.

Before we met, Danny Mann—who had directed two of Williams' Broadway plays—warned me that he was shy, suspicious, zealously protective of his work and was intimidated by tall people. He suggested I remain seated when we were introduced. But I didn't want to show disrespect for my fellow Southerner so I thought when the moment came, I would leap to my knees.

That afternoon in Wallis' suite at the Plaza, Williams sat on a davenport between me and his agent, tiny Audrey Wood, who did most of the talking. Williams called me Mr. Kanter (which he pronounced *Kanna*) until I suggested that if we were to be working together, "Hal" would do. "Thank you, Hal," he said, leaned closer, batted his eyes and said, "My friends call me Tom."

Wallis was as pleased as a Hungarian matchmaker. He gave us both his blessings and left us to collaborate on the final draft of the film that later would win the Academy Award for Anna Magnani.

Tennessee was shy. Hal Wallis was also shy. But Danny persuaded them both to appear in *The Rose Tattoo*, on camera in the crowded club as drinkers at the bar. Tennessee needed no direction from Danny to do that with conviction.

The day we began working, I walked to his apartment on the East Side and up two flights over a restaurant where a handsome olive-skinned young man peered cautiously out of a door chained from the inside at ten o'clock in the morning. I introduced myself and the young man, who was wearing a bathrobe, admitted me to the small, crowded apartment that so reeked of cat urine, I could barely smell the whiskey in the beer stein he was holding.

"I'm Frank," he said. "Tom will be right out."

Williams was watching the Army-McCarthy hearings in the bedroom.

"Good morning, Hal," he called, then, "Frank, did you pour Mr. Kanter a drink?"

"Yes," Frank said of the stein he offered. "Bourbon."

I asked for a glass of water instead.

Tennessee came in holding another stein of bourbon. He wore a robe over his pajamas and asked if I'd prefer Scotch or rye instead.

"It's a little early for me," I said.

"Not for me," he said unnecessarily. "How can you work on an empty stomach?"

He beckoned me to follow him to the bedroom, chattering like a nervous magpie. "Have you been watching the hearings? That mendacious charlatan, Senator McCarthy? I'm fascinated that the people of Wisconsin can't see what a monster they've sent to our nation's capitol as their representative!"

The bed had not been made so he indicated a seat on a small upholstered divan that was stained with generations of cat piss. Between Williams' talking, the fumes of his whiskey and the suffocating stench of the upholstery, I had to get some fresh air and asked for the bathroom.

I did not find any there, either, so I stumbled out and said, "Tom, I forgot to bring some notes from the Breen office on the script. Why don't I go back to the hotel — and we can meet there after the hearings are over?"

I fled the premises, never to return. From then on, Tennessee wrote in his apartment while I worked at the Plaza and we met each afternoon at the hotel to exchange pages and discuss our progress. Our most intense discussions were over the demands of the Breen office censors who insisted we cut anti–Catholic dialogue. But Tennessee stubbornly insisted it would remain in his play and, in the end, much of it did.

One afternoon, Danny invited us to an advance screening of *About Mrs. Leslie*. Tennessee was anxious to see his work and also, I suspect, mine. We rode to the theater and, while in the cab, he began to rant about Joe McCarthy again. Tennessee was incensed about the way McCarthy had tortured his fellow playwright, Arthur Miller.

"So incensed," he said, "I sat down and wrote a scathing letter to that miserable mountebank, a long, incisive and I must say brilliant indictment of his methods and his morals. I sealed it in an envelope, addressed it, affixed a stamp and took it down to the corner. As I was about to drop it in the mailbox, I said to myself, 'Thomas Lanier Williams, why are you involving yourself in politics, which you have always avoided?' And when

I could not give myself a satisfactory answer to that, I withdrew the letter from the box and tore it up. Stamp and all."

He did say he enjoyed *About Mrs. Leslie.*

Another afternoon, he called to say he could not work. "My bulldog died this morning," he said. "I've got to go out and buy a new one."

It was the first I heard that he had a dog. Maybe that wasn't all cat piss on his sofa.

Two days later, Tom called to say he had some pages to bring to the hotel at six. At seven, I was entertaining three friends when he called from the lobby.

"Come up and have a drink, Tom," I said. "There's somebody here who'd like to meet you."

"Oh?" he asked cautiously. "Who?"

"An Army buddy of mine, who reviews plays for *Cue*— Jack Keating."

"He's the only New York reviewer who liked my *Camino Real*!" he said. "I'll be right up."

Keating was Jack Sher's commanding officer when we all met on Guam. He returned to establish himself as a respected critic and shared with Tennessee a healthy regard for Tennessee's work as well as his unhealthy regard for sour mash.

Tennessee was so pleased to meet Keating, he overcame the discomfort of meeting my other guests, Irving B. Kahn and publicist Leo Pillot. When Leo reminded us we had a reservation for dinner, Tom said he had to explain something about his new pages and asked if we could be alone.

"Use the bedroom," Leo suggested.

Tom coyly asked, "Whatever do you think we have in mind?"

What he had in mind was cutting half a scene I had written and restoring a scene of his own I had cut. My compromise was to let him have his way.

In time, our collaboration was completed and I returned to California to take another job, on loanout from Wallis, to add dialogue for the Western *Vera Cruz.* It starred Gary Cooper and Burt Lancaster and was produced by Hecht-Hill-Lancaster, Burt's independent company. I worked in Burt's office where every afternoon he met with Rodd Redwing, an Indian gunslinger who was teaching him how to handle six-shooters.

Burt walked around the lot wearing his guns, yanking them out of the holsters and twirling them back in until he became an expert. And while he professed mild interest in what I was writing for his movie, he was full of questions about his next, *The Rose Tattoo.*

I was disappointed when Wallis cast Lancaster as the leading man in that. I had hoped he would use Eli Wallach, the actor I saw play Mangiacavallo on stage. But Wallis said nobody knew Wallach and no Americans knew Anna Magnani, so he needed a name like Lancaster to bring people into the theater.

Wallis was right again. Burt delivered a fine performance but he, like everyone else in the cast, was outdazzled by the magnificent Magnani.

Tennessee fought me on the credit for the screenplay and, rather than taking it to the Writers Guild for arbitration, I accepted Wallis' plea to compromise with an "adapted by" credit. By that time, my credits were appearing prominently on one of television's most popular new shows, *The George Gobel Show.*

More people saw that in one night than all the plays Tennessee Williams ever wrote, Paul Nathan assured me.

A year later, Danny Mann said, "I've got a big compliment for you. I ran a rough cut of the picture for Tom and when the lights came up, he said, 'The best scene in the picture is with the Japanese tattoo artist — and it isn't mine!'"

"A compliment, Danny? The son of a bitch didn't even mention my name!"

April 10, 1972, was the last time I saw Williams. It was the night he presented the Oscar for screenwriting and the Academy honored Charlie Chaplin. After the ceremonies, Doris and I were seated with Tennessee at the Governor's Ball. We exchanged comments on the evening's festivities for several minutes before I realized Tom was so drunk, he didn't remember who I was.

Jackie Coogan came by our table to say hello. He had just talked with Chaplin for the first time since the great man had made Coogan the biggest child star of the century.

"What did you talk about?" I asked jack.

"Our favorite subjects," he grinned. "Each other!"

Then he added, "But he did give me some good advice. 'Stay warm,' he said."

Groucho Marx told me he also spoke with Charlie that evening and his only message to him was, "Stay warm."

Doris and I flew to Europe the day Mr. and Mrs. Chaplin returned to Switzerland. We shared the same flight to London and, although I did not speak to Charlie, I stayed warm.

"If you see my producer, give him my contempt."— Harry Warren

37. *If You See My Producer*

Saturday evening, October 2, 1954, a close-up of a sweet, gentle elf appeared abruptly on NBC television. He was a wistful, impeccably dressed boy tenor with an Army surplus haircut who ambushed and held hostage the attention of millions when he introduced himself.

"Good evening," he said. "I'm very glad to be back. I was here yesterday—for the rehearsal."

To his vast relief—and mine—the audience laughed. They continued laughing as he went on:

"My name is George Gobel. George *L* Gobel. The L doesn't stand for anything, really. It's just so that I can have GLG embroidered on my shirts ... so at the laundry, my stuff doesn't get mixed up with Greta Garbo's ... stuff."

By Monday morning, people across America were talking about us. I say *us* with pride of authorship because I created *The George Gobel Show.* It became TV's highest-rated half-hour of the '54-'55 season.

It began as a favor to a friend, but started earlier, when we wanted to see this new comedian we'd heard was "different." So Mildred Schwartz called the Hilton Hotel in Los Angeles, asked for the room in which George Gobel was playing and a man took her reservations for the Schwartzes and the Kanters. We were all proud of Mildred for obtaining such a choice table for us in a room filled to capacity that evening.

Everybody in the supper club enjoyed the little comedian. I relished him. For days, I repeated some of his lines to anybody who would listen. George Rosenberg was one who did.

Gobel had been signed by NBC, but the first attempts to create a television show for him were aborted. They finally turned to Rosie's client, Bill Morrow, to try his hand. Bill didn't know Gobel and was reluctant, so Rosie asked me to put in a good word about Gobel to my erstwhile collaborator.

Bill said he'd consider it if I wrote the show with him. I said I'd consider

George Gobel and Hal Kanter.

that and we made a date to meet Rosie and Gobel's agents on a Saturday morning at 9:30. When Bill had not arrived by ten, we decided to watch the failed pilots without him.

Bill never did show up but my enthusiasm for Gobel was reinforced and I was bursting with ideas about how to present him on television. They offered the job to me. I said I would take it if I could also direct the show.

Rosie obtained my release from Paramount and I went to Chicago to meet my star at the Palmer House, where he was doing two shows a night. His press agent, Sam Honigsberg, escorted me to the dinner show and told me that George was looking forward to meeting me because at the time he was playing Los Angeles, he had reserved a table for us when Mrs. Schwartz had been mistakenly connected to his room!

That told me a lot about the man and I learned more when, at our first meeting, George offered me a bottle of Scotch and said, "I don't trust people who don't drink."

I was proving that he could trust me when Sam reminded George he was due across town to address a convention of funeral directors between shows. En route, I suggested a joke about a cut rate funeral: They put your loved one in a plain brown envelope and mail it out of town.

"Did you just make that up?" George asked and I said, "Yes. That's what I do." Then I added to the joke, "For a dollar extra, the clerks at the dead letter office hum a hymn as you go through."

By the time we reached the convention, I had given him several more lines and to my amazement, George remembered every one of them and repeated them in the proper sequence. We were both rewarded when that routine got enormous laughs from the assembled funeral directors. George was paid in dollars, I was paid in the confidence he had in me from that evening on. I became his writer-director-producer and remained his friend long after we stopped working together. Maybe because we did stop. But through two seasons of television and a feature film, George and I never had an angry moment between us. Our friendship remained constant for 37 years.

George was consistently amusing; one of the few things he took seriously was his golf game. When I introduced screenwriter Winston Miller to George, I mentioned they had in common their passion for golf. George asked Winston if his wife was also a golfer.

"Yes," Winnie said, "but I never play with her. Women treat golf as if it were a game!"

George repeated that for years because it was exactly how he felt. Talking about his wife, he said, "Our marriage started out as a partnership and now I'm a wholly owned subsidiary."

He spent 60 years, man and boy, exercising his gift to amuse — or at the least, to keep us from getting sullen.

For that first season on television, I put together a writing staff that included Jack Douglas and James Allardice (a man I met at Paramount when he had adapted his play *At War with the Army* for Martin and Lewis); also Harry Winkler, a Chicago Ph.D. who had written several of the best routines in Gobel's nightclub act. I insisted Harry join our staff over the objections of Gobel's manager-slash-partner, David O'Malley.

Mr. O, as George and his family called him, seemed to run their lives, from deciding what and where George performed to where they lived and what furniture Alice bought. O'Malley was cautious about the money he invested, protective of the goose who laid his golden eggs and jealous of anyone other than priests or nuns who got too close to George.

Without consulting Mr. O, I rented a bungalow to write our scripts away from prying eyes at the network. I engaged Muriel Bermudez-Phillips, a beautiful middle-aged secretary who answered our telephone in such a cultured voice nobody suspected we were working out of a motor court in the Valley where other rooms could be rented by the hour.

John Scott Trotter wrote a theme song he called *Gobelues*, served as our music director and appeared on every show. Pretty, perky Peggy King was our vocalist who played George's wife Alice, a role that Jeff Donnell made her own after Judith Ames, Pat Carroll, Kay Ballard and Angela Lansbury each had a turn playing.

It was Angela's first attempt at comedy, she said. The only direction I had to give her was to deliver the lines without trying to be funny. She was so good, I got an immediate call from Mel Frank who wanted to know how she was to direct. I said she was an intelligent treasure, so he and Norman Panama cast her in *The Court Jester*, a Danny Kaye comedy they committed.

The camera director on our show as Alan (Bud) Yorkin and the stage manager was Walter Grauman, who later became a film director. Our property manager was Joe Rios, who made certain George was supplied with fuel brewed in Scotland.

Edward Sobel supervised the production, Gino Conte was the unit manager and Jean Messerscmidt was our capable production assistant who later became a network executive. Our art director was Jay Krause, technical director Joe Strauss. Audio engineer Howard Ialberg we quickly came to refer to on the air as Goofy Old Ialberg for reasons even Goofy forgets.

Fred MacMurray was our guest star on that first show and also our last. When he opened and closed our second season as well, he was known as Gobel's electronic zipper. We wished we had one the night tough guy Nat Pendleton accidentally played a scene with his fly open. That got Nat a lot of fan mail written on perfumed stationery.

After our third show, George was asked to do a spot on the biggest show of that year, *Light's Diamond Jubilee*, produced by David O. Selznick. The spot was a five-minute monologue, part of a two-hour show sponsored by the electric companies of America. It featured an all-star cast and George's monologue was written by Ben Hecht. But it was nothing that George felt comfortable reading for one basic reason — it was not funny.

To protect his star, Dave O'Malley convinced Selznick to hire me to rewrite it completely. I was amused by the irony of rewriting Hecht, who had rewritten me (and Lesser Samuels) at Paramount. I was also pleased that my five-minute spot became seven with laughs, stole the two-hour show and established my *iddy biddy buddy* as television's newest sensation.

Gobel's new celebrity attracted such major stars as Kirk Douglas, Jack Benny, Jimmy Stewart, Charlton Heston and my old friend, Peter Lorre.

When Peter worked with George for the first time, he discovered their mutual fondness for the grain and suggested George switch from Scotch to vodka because, "Vodka leaves no aroma, daddy, so nobody will know you've been drinking."

George considered that for a moment, then said, "No, Peter, when I walk up to a cop and hit him in the mouth, I want him to *know* I've been drinking!"

We finished the season Number One in the ratings, having produced 30 shows. I had also written several special guest shots for George on other shows and knew that Gobel would be picked up for another season at an increase in salary.

Gobel and O'Malley received a bonus from NBC — their Gomalco corporation would produce Gobel's summer replacement show. They hired Chicago's veteran radio comedian Ransom Sherman, and the fresh face attached to the used body of Jonathan Winters.

I was free to spend the summer recuperating but George was booked from east to west for fees Mr. O had never dreamed he would ever command. Yet, when O'Malley confronted Rosie to discuss my contract, he balked at meeting the increases my agent felt I deserved and knew that I could get anywhere else after that spectacular season. And when O'Malley offered an embarrassing token raise in salary, Rosie told me to walk. I probably should have, but I truly enjoyed working with George; he was the perfect vehicle for my sense of humor, so I agreed to another year at far less money than I could command elsewhere.

I was asked to write the whimsical introductions for a new TV show, *Alfred Hitchcock Presents*, but I declined and suggested Jim Allardice might like the job. MCA offered him a larger fee than he was making from O'Malley, so I lost Allardice to the master of suspense.

A housewife, Mary Agnes Liddell, wrote me a funny letter earlier in the year, saying she was a fan of the show who wanted to write just enough jokes to buy a new linoleum floor for her kitchen. I encouraged her to submit something and Mary Agnes contributed many wonderful domestic observations long after her new linoleum was installed.

My mother, dad and me with George Gobel.

Mary Agnes claimed that her husband was so absent-minded, on the days he drove in his company carpool, she pinned a note on his jacket that read, "Do not give me a ride home. I have the car today."

To replace Jim Allardice, I brought in old friend Howard Leeds and added Everett Greenbaum, a new friend who had been working in New York on *Mr. Peepers*, the gentle comedy that starred Wally Cox. We moved our office to an apartment in Sherman Oaks where Ms. Bermudez-Phillips continued to serve as our secretary and house mother.

On the last show of that first season, my daughter Donna and Gobel's son Gregg made their debuts in a scene with George. When I spent my vacation driving Lisa and Donna across the country, Donna was greeted as a celebrity by my family in Savannah. Lisa enjoyed her sister's stardom, a portent of the enjoyment she now gets from the achievements of her daughter, Kaleigh Megan Shafer.

Gregg abandoned performing after appearing on one film but Donna went to work in television as a writer, producer and director.

Our second season began with Gobel facing the formidable opposition of *Gunsmoke* on CBS, yet we avoided the "sophomore jinx" by remaining in the Top Ten. Jeff Donnell's Alice became such an important character, I suggested we spin it off into a show of her own called *That Alice* as a summer replacement, an idea that the network and our sponsors welcomed. Again, Rosie met with O'Malley to make a deal for me to own half of the show, a demand that brought Mr. O to the brink of apoplexy.

"He's not going to own anything," he managed to sputter. "Alice Gobel is a real person, not somebody he wrote."

"Then you do a show with the real Alice," Rosie said and walked out of the room. No matter how the network and O'Malley's own agents tried to convince him to change his attitude, Mr. O remained adamant, George remained in hiding and *That Alice* remained in limbo.

My relationship with my Iddy Biddy Buddy would have ended that day but RKO bought a screenplay from Goodman Ace called *I Married a Woman*, to star George and a luxuriously upholstered English blonde named Diana Dors.

It was produced by the very astute William Bloom, who engaged my services as director.

"I'm deteriorating on schedule." — Ben Gershman

38. *On Schedule*

When I returned to the studio as a director RKO had changed. Gone were stars like Ginger Rogers and Katharine Hepburn. The new glamour girl was a pneumatic British star, Diana Dors, George Gobel's leading lady in *I Married a Woman.*

The cotton candy blonde, whose real name was Diane Fluck, had never seen George but she was pleased to have Jessie Royce Landis playing her mother and the veteran Adolphe Menjou co-starring as Gobel's new boss.

Diana, an intelligent woman with professional work habits, had a naughty sense of humor and an instinct for self-promotion. Shortly before we began work, she gave a lavish brunch in Beverly Hills to welcome her equally skilled publicity hound, a flamboyant hairdresser named Raymond whom the British press dubbed Mr. Teasy Weasy.

Photographers had a field day shooting the stars who turned out to meet Diana and the unctuous Teasy Weasy. Both made international headlines when they fell — or were pushed — fully clothed, into the swimming pool, dragging along an irate agent who lost his toupee and an alarmed dressmaker who lost his dignity and shrank his shorts.

The picture that London papers printed was of Diana, her soaked white dress plastered to her generous figure, climbing out of the pool over the heads of Louis Shurr, the agent, and Howard Shoup, the designer (who once assured a starlet that "what God has forgotten, Shoup provides with cotton").

A few minutes before the splash, Doris and I had left the party to attend a Girl Scout ceremony where our daughter Lisa received a merit badge — for swimming.

Mr. Teasy Weasy dried out and went back to London. Diana remained in Hollywood, making several more pictures and marrying several more men before she returned to England. I never saw her again.

A woman I did see often thereafter was a beautiful young hopeful RKO had under contract. Her film debut was a bit part she never forgot. Years later, in the lobby of the Plaza Hotel in New York, she said, "Hello,

Mr. Kanter; do you remember me? I played John Wayne's wife for you," as if any man could ever forget Angie Dickinson.

Producer William Bloom had managed to lure Duke Wayne for a cameo role as himself in our picture-within-the-picture. It was a joke Wayne appreciated and a fee he enjoyed the rest of his life: an original Picasso. He also enjoyed Angie. She later co-starred with him in *Rio Bravo*.

Before I met my cast, Bill Bloom thought it would be beneficial for us to meet Lucien Ballard, whom he had already engaged as my cinematographer. I agreed. I knew his name because it was often in print when he was married to Merle Oberon. But seldom after she divorced him.

Lucien was a charming man whose younger brother Don was my fellow soldier at Lowry Field. Bill Bloom brought us together in a projection room at RKO to look at Dors' new British film, *The Blonde Sinner*.

"I want to be honest with you, Lucien," I told the man who was going to shoot my film. "I know nothing about cameras, lenses, f-stops or emulsion speeds and can't tell a zoom from a pan shot, so I'm going to leave it all up to you. I'll tell you what I'd like to get and will be completely at your mercy to get it."

"Well," Lucien said, "I'm sorry to hear that, because I don't know much about the camera, either. But I do know all about a director's job."

I knew from the twinkle in his eye that we would get along just fine. Lucien Ballard held my hand through our first few reels of film and nudged me along the rest of the footage and together we brought my first feature in a day under schedule.

George Gobel was, as always, a delight to work with and so was an actor I brought to Hollywood for his first role in films. I had seen him playing a detective in a TV mystery and when we were casting the film, I interviewed him in New York and was so enchanted, I signed him to come west for a guest shot on the Gobel show. His name was John McGiver. He was a riot with George and I got a phone call immediately after the show was seen on the Coast.

"It's Billy Wilder," my caller said. "Where did you find that man I just saw? He's exactly who I want for my new picture."

"You have good taste, Billy. But he's going to be in my first picture."

"When does your picture start?"

"In six weeks."

"I can have him back from Paris in six weeks," Billy said. "I must have him to play Audrey Hepburn's husband!"

Bald-headed, avocado-shaped, middle-aged John McGiver, already the father of eight, to play the husband of luminous Audrey Hepburn? What kind of perverted story was Billy going to tell?

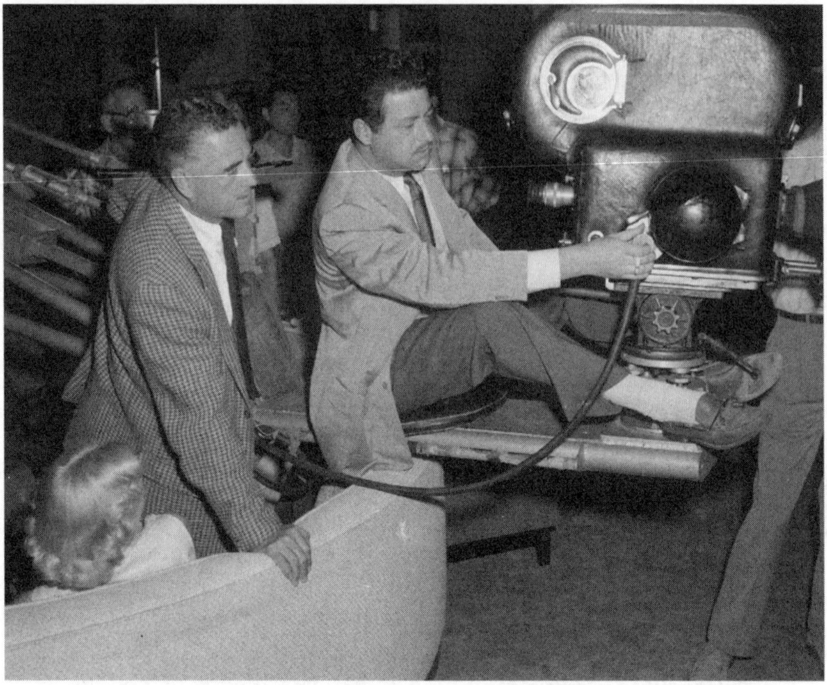

Lucien Ballard giving Hal Kanter lessons in operating a camera.

It was called *Love in the Afternoon*, Gary Cooper was to be Audrey's co-star, I. A. L. Diamond had written the script with Billy and I could not stand in the way of advancing my new friend John's career by denying Billy access to him. So, with great joy, John went to Paris, where he had served as an officer in the Army under Eisenhower. Way under.

While McGiver was in Paris for Billy, another producer saw some of Wilder's rushes and he hired John to co-star in a cinema with the rubber-faced French favorite, Fernandel.

By the time John came back to work with us, he was famous enough to afford two more children and bring them all to California from their upstate New York residence, a former church that housed their congregation of ten.

Another colorful comrade was that veteran curmudgeon and Beau Brummel, Adolphe Menjou. When he began work, the fashion plate brought his own wardrobe and even though all of it was at least 40 years old, it fit perfectly. Menjou's profile had not changed.

"I've had so many operations," he told me, "the only gut I have left is four inches of small intestine that goes straight down."

As fine an actor as Dolph was, he could be equally aggravating. We did not agree politically and by mutual, tacit agreement, never discussed politics. That suited Gobel, too, because George, always the first to avoid contention, never seemed to be aware that Americans voted.

Menjou was aware of everything, had opinions on everything and was never reluctant to express every one of them. He seemed to tell outrageous lies—yet every one of them turned out to be true!

On our set one day, there were some visitors who wore unfamiliar uniforms and when I asked an assistant who they were, he said, "Russians."

Menjou looked up from a newspaper and said, "Russian sailors!" He got up to approach them and I said, "Dolph, please, let's don't start an international incident."

"Don't worry," he said. "I am fluent in their tongue."

"You speak Russian?"

"Certainly," the arch conservative said. "How else can we know what our enemies are saying if we don't learn their language?"

Dolph approached the dour sailors and, to my relief, engrossed them in a Russian conversation that broke their silence and led to laughter.

Another day, while waiting for Lucien to light a scene, I went to the stage next door with Walter Keller, our art director, to check Menjou's office set. I invited him to come along because we were going to shoot there the following day. As I looked over the set, Dolph sat at his desk and went through the mail the prop man had provided. After giving Keller my suggestions, it was time to get Dolph back to work.

"Just a moment," he said. "I'm checking out these stamps."

"Why? You save them?"

"Oh, yes," he said. I should have known. When he saw a print of a Utrillo painting, he told me he owned the original; when I misquoted a line from *Hamlet*, he corrected me by reciting all of Act III.

"I've saved stamps for years," he told me as we walked back to our stage. "I have one of the finest stamp collections in the world."

"How nice for you," I said.

My daughter Lisa was anxiously waiting for me to get home that night to show me a package that had arrived. It was a starter kit for philatelists, containing assorted foreign stamps, a packet of hinges and a small album with a preface about the joys of philately. I opened the brochure to read that there were three great stamp collections in the world: King George of England's, Franklin Delano Roosevelt's and Adolphe Menjou's!

I groaned and slammed the album shut in exasperation, which may be why Lisa never became the stamp addict I still am.

Before we completed filming the Gobel picture, I had lunch at Lucey's, a popular restaurant across the street from Paramount, where I ran into Hal Wallis. He knew I was working next door and asked me if I could find some time to look at a screen test of a young man he had just made. Perhaps I could do a picture with him.

"What's his name?"

"Elvis Presley."

"Hal, you're kidding! You're going to do a picture with *that*?"

"Just look at the test," Wallis said. "Paul will set it up for you tomorrow."

I sat alone in a projection room at lunch the next day and watched some film of the young hillbilly, answering questions asked from a voice off-camera. He was better looking than I had remembered from his one television show I had seen but I supposed that was due to better lighting in film. I was also impressed by Elvis' sense of humor in his replies to his questioner.

Then, when it was apparent that the young man was not going to be cowed by the camera, the test switched to a scene from *The Rainmaker* and Elvis bowled me over. I don't remember the name of the actor he played opposite because Presley wiped him off the screen. I couldn't wait to tell Wallis how impressed I was.

"This kid is dynamite," I said. "He hurtles off that screen and grabs you by the throat!"

"Then you'll do my picture?" Wallis said.

"Yes, if we can make a deal. I'm directing now, you know."

Of course he knew. And he made a deal with Rosie while Bob Coryell was making another for me at Universal.

As soon as we completed shooting *I Married a Woman*, William Dozier, who was head of production at RKO, asked me if I would write and direct a remake of *Vivacious Lady*, a 1938 comedy that George Stevens was directing at the time I began working for Eddie Davis at the studio. We ran the picture that evening and when the lights came up, I asked Dozier, "Why would you want to remake this gem? You haven't got Jimmy Stewart, you haven't got Ginger Rogers and let's don't kid ourselves, I'm no George Stevens."

Dozier said, "We've two or three other stories I'd like you to consider."

"Okay," I said, "but first I'm going to do a picture with Elvis Presley."

"Now why would you want to do a picture with Elvis Presley?" Dozier asked.

Because my daughters would never have forgiven me if I hadn't.

"Without music, life would be a mistake."
— F. W. Nietzsche

39. *Without Music*

As it turned out, I wrote two films for Elvis and directed the first of them, *Loving You,* his first starring vehicle. He had a supporting role in a Fox Western entitled *Love Me Tender,* but he was modest enough to tell me, "I don't know no more about making movies than a bullfrog knows about buttermilk."

When he first swiveled to our attention, snake-slim, cat-quick and orchid-pretty, Elvis stood out like a red stripe on a zebra.

The young man with the ancient eyes and the child's mouth, the body as loose, unadorned and as unpredictable as a whip, awoke from the nightmare of poverty to find himself suddenly bathed in the brilliant sun of fame.

It started with his records. One after another they zoomed to the best seller lists; eight of them over a million. Then the television exposure: guest shots that decimated the opposition. Then personal appearances, where rabid thousands of squealing, shrieking, thundering, fainting, ticket-buying youngsters stormed the theaters and auditoriums and ball parks. Next, his first movie, a sudden burst of box office bonanza that soared his stock to even more dizzying heights.

And around and around whirled the constant controversy: a barrage of polemics that served only to increase the appetite of his seemingly insatiable adherents. Newspapers, magazines, television, churches and radio talkers hurled pros and cons while the lad leaped to legend. His likeness was affixed to postcards, pillowslips, banners and kerchiefs; he was molded in clay and cast in bronze; he endorsed clothing and cosmetics, books and bric-a-brac; the money rolled in and nothing seemed capable of slowing it down, much less stopping it.

In the eye of the hurricane, Elvis took it all with good grace and humility and was enjoying himself as much as the Presley he read about, the glamorous, exciting, romantic, soul-stirring self that evoked a powerful magic on audiences, whipping them into frenzies of appreciation no entertainer in his time had been able to match.

It was at that pivotal time of his career when I completed the first draft of my screenplay and Wallis sent me to meet my star and accompany him on a fruitful trip into the eye of the hurricane.

When I arrived in Memphis, Elvis and two or three others met me at the airport. I was never to be in his company when Elvis did not have at least two others present. Before driving me to my hotel, he insisted I come to supper at his home, where his mother had gone to some fuss to prepare a meal fit for a Hollywood celebrity they all held in awe. I tried to let Elvis know that I did not take the title of director as seriously as De Mille, Capra or others who equated their position with Divinity. But when he introduced me to others, he emphasized that I was his "movie director from Hollywood."

Gladys Presley presided over a table crowded with cousins and friends who were invited to meet her son's glamorous movie maker. This was not the mansion called Graceland but the modest home Elvis had bought earlier for his parents, decorated in a style that displayed more financial success than taste. The same applied to his father's wardrobe and his mother's meal.

Somewhere between the biscuits and the okra, Elvis' notorious manager, large, loud, loutish Col. Tom Parker, arrived with his assistant, Tom Diskin. They were just "passing through," Parker announced, en route to Shreveport, where Elvis was booked for his farewell appearance on *Louisiana Hay Ride*, the performance I had come to observe.

I got the impression that Parker had dropped in to look over the man who would put his golden egg-laying goose through his first starring movie. He did not stay long enough to sit down on that visit; he shook hands, made a few remarks, helped himself to a piece of Gladys' fried chicken and left with Diskin. I thought the colorful Colonel more interesting than his star.

After supper, Elvis dismissed his guests and took me to his play room, where the walls were lined with gold records he had already accumulated, and which featured a small pool table in the middle of the room. We were followed by his cousin Gene Smith and two or three others who began playing pool, as if it was their *raison d'être*.

Elvis asked me if he could read the script of *Lonesome Cowboy* and I told him the title of our picture had been changed to *Stranger in Town*.

"Good," he said. "I don't care too much about gettin' to be known as a cowboy. That's not what I'm gonna play, is it?"

"No," I said. I had been cautioned by Wallis not to bring the script to Memphis lest it fall into Tom Parker's hands. Wallis wanted no interference from Parker regarding the script, so I ad libbed a general outline of the scenario for Elvis and his pool players, who stopped shooting to listen. They were all impressed by the story but it was Elvis who asked questions that defined for me his studious approach to preparing for his new challenge. He wanted to understand the character he would be playing and—without using the term—what motivated his actions.

Then he asked, "Do I have to smile much?"

"What do you mean, smile?"

"I mean," he said, "you're gonna direct me, so are you fixin' to have me smile in the movie?"

"I don't recall right off if I've written, 'He smiles,'" I said, "but why do you ask?"

"Well," Elvis said, "I've been studyin' the actors the girls seem to like the most—Jimmy Dean, Brando, Humphrey Bogart—and they don't hardly never smile. When they do, it's like an *event*. So if I don't smile but once toward the end, I'm gonna get 'em!"

"Very astute, Elvis," I acknowledged.

This kid was no happy accident. I recalled a reporter who asked the 20-year-old rockin' roller if he was contemplating marriage and Elvis replied, "No, sir," with a wicked grin. "Why buy a cow when you can steal milk through the fence?"

The reporter printed that remark and the public outcry was a lesson in keeping his mouth shut to the press. Elvis attempted to burnish his public image from Country Yokel Casual to Man of the World Sophisticate but it didn't quite happen because he never seemed comfortable in that role.

Even after he became an authentic name-above-the-title movie star, Elvis avoided the social life of show business to hide from his peers under the security blanket provided by his home boys from the Delta country. Wherever he went to perform, record or relax, Elvis brought along his six-pack of personal go-fers and do-fers. With them he could remain a good ol' boy himself, wrapped in Dixie, shielded from what he perceived as the city slickers of the Nawth. Somewhere deep within, the King still considered himself a commoner, just visiting from Mississippi.

"Tupelo," he told me about his home town, "is so small, we didn't have a village idiot. We had to take turns."

The night we sat in his den, Elvis allowed that he might not be up to the demands of starring in such a big picture as the one I had described. I sensed his "aw shucks" shit-kicker's demeanor was no act and assured him he had nothing to fear.

"I saw the screen test you did for Wallis," I said, "and you knocked me out. That's how come I took this assignment. You're going to be a big, big star, Elvis, whether you want to be or not!"

"Oh, he wants to be!" his cousin Gene said. "Do that piece for Mr. Kanter, Elvis!"

"Mind your own fuggin' biniss," Elvis said.

"Aw, c'mon, man," the others said. "Tell the man the piece."

"What piece are you talking about?" I asked.

"Oh, something I wanted to see could I learn," Elvis said, "so I did."

What he chose to commit to memory was Gen. Douglas MacArthur's 1952 farewell speech to Congress and when he began reciting it for me, like a schoolboy in an assembly program, I was constrained to listen to the entire florid piece until "old soldiers never die" faded away.

The pool players applauded Elvis and I told him I considered his performance every bit as good as MacArthur's. He was pleased. I did not tell him what I thought of MacArthur.

The next day, Elvis, Gene and two others took me to see the sights of Memphis, a 20-minute tour they managed to cram into three hours. I realized why Elvis had recited the MacArthur farewell when he asked me again if I really thought he had done it well: He needed reassurance from someone other than his immediate family that he was better than the scalding reviews of *Love Me Tender* had been when the picture opened three weeks earlier. The critics had brutalized his acting debut. Only the box office saved his movie career from abrupt distinction. But Elvis was pained by the rude reception the nation's press accorded him.

That evening, we left Memphis in a two-car caravan for the monster farewell appearance in Shreveport, Louisiana. Elvis drove the lead Cadillac, with bass player Bill Black at the wheel of the second. His fellow musicians Scotty Moore and D. J. Fontana rode with Bill and their band instruments.

I sat next to Elvis while the back seat was occupied by his cousins Gene and Junior and a former ballplayer named Bitsy Mott, Tom Parker's pleasant brother-in-law, now working for him as a security guard for Elvis.

We raced through the chilly night, Elvis in high spirits, singing, cracking jokes, teasing his cousins until we came to a roadhouse where we stopped "for refreshments"—a piss, a pop and some barbecued pork. Elvis was welcomed by the proprietors as the old friend he was and proudly introduced me as his director from Hollywood, to share with Elvis another few minutes of celebrity.

Shortly after we left his friends, a souped-up Chevy pulled up beside us. Four men and three women were packed into the hot rod and one of the girls yelled, "Hey, Elvis!"

Elvis slowed his Cadillac and lowered his window to call, "Howdy, honey" and Bitsy Mott warned, "This ain't no time to stop for pussy, boy."

The ersatz cowboy driving the Chevy shouted, "Drag you for a tank of gas, Presley!"

"Is he kiddin'?" Elvis grinned, stomped on his accelerator and we zoomed from 40 to 90 m.p.h. Elvis loved that. I was terrified and he loved that, too.

Later, we stopped for gas in a tiny town. While Bill Black was filling the gas tanks, Cousin Gene came from the office with a skinny redneck who looked like the Southern distributor for acne and said, "Elvis, this guy don't think you are who you are."

"Well, mister," Elvis said as he looked over the mechanic, "like Popeye says, I yam what I yam."

"You ain't Elvis," the boy said. "The real Elvis is in Hollywood, makin' a movie show. It was just on the radio."

"That's where we're goin'," Elvis said. "To Hollywood, right after Shreveport. This is Mr. Kanter, my director."

The acne distributor sneered at me and said, "If he's Elvis, ask him to sing something."

"He gets paid when he sings," I said. "You give him $10,000 and name your tune."

Bill Black stepped up and said, "For another thousand, we'll throw in some accompaniment."

"I be damn!" the awed redneck said. "You're Bill Black!"

We all laughed for the next ten miles.

When the boys in the back seat fell asleep, Elvis and I continued our conversation. I learned more about him although he was full of questions about the actors he would be working with, Lizabeth Scott, Wendell Corey and the newcomer, Dolores Hart. They were just as curious about him, I said, and they would get along well.

He was excited to hear I had recently directed his mother's favorite star, John Wayne, and he asked about singers I had worked with: Bing and Bob Crosby, Judy Garland, Dean Martin, Peggy Lee, Rosemary Clooney, Frankie Laine, Tennessee Ernie Ford, Dinah Shore. He was particularly interested in Louis Armstrong, Ella Fitzgerald and Mahalia Jackson. He asked questions I had never been asked, about what they ate, where they bought their clothes, what did they do for Mother's Day, did they have private toilets in their dressing rooms.

If he ran out of questions, it was after I fell asleep.

Before dawn, we arrived at the Captain Shreve Hotel while the citizens of Shreveport were still asleep, so we joined them. I was awakened early in the morning by chants of "Elvis! Elvis!" coming from the streets below.

They subsided when Elvis went to the window and pleaded for them

At Paramount Studios, circa 1957, Hal Wallis has just presented Elvis Presley with a brand new bicycle as Hal Kanter looks on and wonders if Elvis will ever use it (he seldom did).

to allow him to get his rest for the big concert that night. He did go back to sleep but I could not. I put on a black velvet sports shirt, gray slacks and jacket and went downstairs for breakfast. Bill Black was already having his grits and bacon and whistled his appreciation of my wardrobe.

"Yo' mother sure dresses you nice!" he said and then invited me to ride with him to the fairgrounds, where he would check the setup for the evening. It was hours before the concert was to begin but the grounds were already crowded with ticket holders and disappointed hundreds who wanted to buy admission.

Bill drove the black Cadillac and, at his suggestion, I sat in the back. He carefully nudged the limousine through the crowd to the spot where he had access to the equipment. But getting out of the car was a challenge, because the minute it stopped, it was recognized as one of Presley's and a screaming horde surrounded us and began rocking it like Hammerstein's willow in a windstorm. I was frightened by the intensity of the attack but Bill laughed and said, "Shit, this happens wherever we go."

He managed to get out when some of the fans recognized him, but told me to keep the doors locked until he got back. When the kids realized they did not know me, they stopped rocking. While a few followed Black, others remained to take pictures of the car and of each other standing next to it.

One young woman unfolded her handkerchief, scraped some dust from the side of the car, shook it into the handkerchief, folded it neatly and tucked it between her breasts.

When we returned to the Captain Shreve, I went to my room to make notes on things I had observed that I wanted to put on the screen. Later, I realized I had packed a shirt with French cuffs but had neglected to bring cuff links, so I went to the haberdashery in the lobby to look for a pair. Elvis was there with his security and, like Bill earlier, admired my black velvet shirt and asked, "Where'd you get it?"

"Cy Devore's, in Hollywood," I said. "But here—" and I took it off and handed it to him, to his astonishment and delight. Instead of cuff links, I bought a shirt without French cuffs.

Weeks later, he reported to my office at Paramount to begin rehearsals and was wearing my black velvet. "That's a handsome shirt," I dead-panned. "Where'd you get it?" Elvis thought for a moment, then said, "A fan gave it to me."

The next time I saw that shirt, one of his cousins was wearing it.

"Although he's gone, the show goes on ... it doesn't change a thing."—Marie Cain

40. The Show Goes On

Tom Parker once had a carnival attraction that amused but frustrated many rustic innocents who tried to teach chickens how to dance. Col. Parker's Dancing Chickens were not talented; Tom was. He noticed that when poultry walked on hot gravel, they stepped livelier, so he put several handsome hens in a cage with a heater on the straw-covered tin bottom. When his customers assembled, Tom turned on the heat and a phonograph record of "Turkey in the Straw."

The best thing about that scam was that when business was bad, he could eat his act.

By the time we met, his lean days were behind the ersatz colonel and I was witness to a well-fed King Con in action. Backstage at the Shreveport fairgrounds, he was raking in dollars from everything from souvenir programs and tinted photos of Elvis to homemade sausages.

Parker never passed up an opportunity to feather his nest, although I felt that he was happier fleecing the world of its money than the actual making of it. When he offered me the opportunity to ghost-write his autobiography, he already had a characteristically cynical title: "How Much Does It Cost If It's Free?"

He assured me that the book would make a profit from the first copy sold. He would sell advertising in his book to cover all publication costs.

"RCA is buying the back cover," he said, "and I'm taking bids on the inside covers."

I thought the huckster was giving me one of his snow jobs but over the weeks we were filming *Loving You*, Parker proved to be serious and wanted me to write it on weekends, which I had no intention of doing. In fact, I was not going to ghost-write anything, but told him he should be thinking beyond the book to the film version of his life. That prospect intrigued him even more.

He had visions of Paul Newman playing him. My choice of the ideal actor to play Col. Parker would be W. C. Fields. When I—perhaps foolishly—told him that, his pink face turned magenta and he never again mentioned that book in my presence.

That night in Shreveport, I was witness to a nerve-shattering hour backstage where the Colonel demonstrated his genius as he skillfully moved Elvis through the milling scores who wanted to slap his back, shake his hand, "remember me" him, get his autograph, take his picture, even try to snip a lock of his hair—an attempt which infuriated Parker, who ordered the culprit out of the area.

"Come with me," Tom said and brought me out to the arena. "You're going to see something you never saw in Hollywood."

He was right. Elvis' introduction was drowned by the shout that went up at the appearance on stage of Scotty, D.J. and Bill, the musicians his fans recognized. On Presley's entrance, the shout became a shrill, roof-lifting scream that continued for the 25 minutes Elvis sang.

For those 25 minutes, there was an exhibition of mass hysteria that stunned me. Caught in a tidal wave of adoration that surged up from 9,000 fanatics, up over the wall of police flanking the platform, over the floodlights to the performers and beyond, lifting Elvis to frenzied heights of response, I turned to Parker and shouted, "You always have bodyguards?"

"*Got* to!" he yelled. "If I didn't have 'em, those sweet little gals out there would tear my boy to pieces. Tear him to pieces! That's why I got to protect him. You people in Hollywood don't know a damn thing about protection."

Instead of reminding him that he had never attended an Academy Awards, I provoked another response that provided me more insight to Parker's view of his associates: "I guess," I said, "Abe Lastfogel would get lost in a crowd like this."

"Abe Lastfogel," Tom sneered, "wouldn't know where to go to *find* a crowd like this!"

The crowd that found Elvis roared their approval of the star who, one wag said, wore out his underwear from the inside. With every thrust of the pelvis, every move of a leg or hip, they screamed such delight, they drowned out his music. It amused me later to read a newspaper wire service's criticism of Presley's performance because the reporter couldn't hear a word of the singer's lyrics or more than the thumping of Bill Black's bass shuddering through the amplifiers.

And during it all, the incessant popping of camera flashes illuminated the arena enough to read the small print on an aspirin bottle.

Never had I seen any audience respond like that one in Shreveport, and I remember newsreels of the thundering hordes of Hitler's rabid Nazi followers.

Hal Kanter gives Elvis Presley direction while Liz Scott wonders how that shadow got on Kanter's nose! On the set of *Loving You*, 1957.

I returned home to a barrage of questions about Elvis, not only from my family but from Wallis and many of my colleagues who were intrigued by the young phenomenon. Wallis was happy that the Colonel did not ask to see the script. Tom's concern seemed to be the number of songs he could place in the movie to be exploited profitably for himself, his client, publishers and RCA Records.

Wendell Corey and Lizabeth Scott were looking forward to meeting Elvis, Wendell because his own children were more excited about the kid than any of the actors Wendell had already starred with and Liz because she had never seen the young man all of show business was watching.

For Presley's love interest, I tested several actresses for the role before Paul Nathan brought us Dolores Hicks, a dewy-eyed student from a local Catholic university he had seen in a school play. Wallis was sufficiently impressed to invite her to test, even though she had no idea who Elvis Presley was at that point.

When she met him, she liked him. When we met her, all of us fell in love with the talented Miss Hicks; so did the camera. She won the part—and my respect as she stood up to Wallis when he wanted to change her name. She agreed to swap her father's name for her mother's but stubbornly clung to her first name and Dolores Hart went on to make several films before she gave up acting to become a nun.

Shooting the film was such a joy for most of us, Alice Corey, Wendell's wife, confessed to me that it was the first time in years the actor looked forward to coming to work. And Elvis was such an attraction, it was the first time Alice visited Wendell while he was working. And the first time my own wife came with friends, after she had brought our girls to meet Elvis.

Gaining entrance to our set was not easy because I wanted to give Elvis enough privacy to work without distractions. But I soon learned he was a fast study, had a photographic memory and enjoyed meeting his fans. Even before I relaxed my rules about a closed set, studio executives, major exhibitors and other producers used their clout to keep us over-supplied with visitors. Elvis willingly posed for photographs and shook hundreds of hands and kissed dozens of little girls and old ladies, but when he was called for the camera, he was on his mark, ready for "Action!"

For one of his longest and most difficult scenes with Liz Scott, we were shooting day-for-night, in a realistic graveyard set, dramatically lit by Charles Lang. While he was doing so, Elvis and Liz were playfully going over their lines although the scene was anything but playful. When Charles was satisfied, he called for the "first team" to replace the stand-ins.

"Ouch!" Elvis screamed and came into the scene rubbing his cheek, followed by a laughing Liz. But when he said, "That's not funny, dammit!" Liz apologized and tried to pat his cheek.

"It was just a little love nibble," she said as he brushed her hand away.

Her little nibble left such deep red marks on his cheek, we lost an hour while I restaged the scene to shoot the other sides of the actors' faces.

On the last day of the production, I played host to a wrap party to which I invited everyone who worked on the film, from the front office to the back lot. I borrowed a nightclub set Cornel Wilde built for one of his films and engaged the studio's Pauline Kissinger to cater from her commissary. There were a hundred people eating, drinking and dancing on the stage while we were making the last shot across the lot.

The final set-up was a two-shot with Liz and Elvis, who were, they both said, sad to hear me say, "Cut! Print! That's a wrap!"

When we arrived at the party that had cost me a bundle of cash from my own pocket, festivities were in full revelry and in the middle of the set was a booth with a large sign reading, *ELVIS AND THE COLONEL THANK YOU!*

Tom Parker stood in front of it, handing out printed autographed pictures of Elvis and selling raffle tickets for glow-in-the-dark plaster busts of Presley, plus some of his record albums that were promotional gifts from RCA.

What amused me first was that the Colonel was graciously accepting the thanks of all the guests for the splendid party. What angered me later was that I did not win a glow-in-the-dark Elvis.

Dissolve to Palm Springs, a dozen years later. Doris and I were spending a weekend at the spa when I went to have a drink while she dressed for dinner. Seated at the bar, I saw an older man who looked like Tom hobble on a cane toward the dining room with two women. When they were followed by a man I recognized as Tom Diskin, the maitre d' ushered them inside with courteous regard.

When he returned to his post, I summoned him to the bar and asked if that was Col. Tom Parker.

"It is," the steward sniffed. "Why?"

"Send him a bottle of Lancer's Rose, with the compliments of Hal Kanter, and put it on my bill."

"Do you know the Colonel?" he asked.

"I used to," I said.

"Then you should know that he does not drink Lancer's. He drinks —" and he named some wine I don't recall but which I do recall was much more expensive than the Portugal pink that came in a ceramic bottle.

"Then send him a bottle of that and charge it to me." I showed him my house key.

I was on my second vodka Gibson when Doris arrived. She did not join me in a drink because we had reservations across town, we were already late and she did not drink.

"Wait a while," I begged and told her what I had done. "I'm waiting to see how Parker will react."

I signed my bar tab and noted that the bill for the wine was already there, so I beckoned over the aloof maitre d' again. "Did you send the wine to the colonel's table?" I asked.

"I did," he said with the coolness of a servant who has not been tipped.

"What did he say?" I demanded like a customer who won't tip a surly bastard.

"Col. Parker said you must be an impostor. Hal Kanter would not send him a bottle of wine. Hal Kanter would send him a case!"

I never saw Parker again.

"Nobody wants to get into his grave still feeling frisky."—Quentin Crisp

41. Still Frisky

The next offer my agents presented was to write and direct an original screenplay based on a one-page short story in *Collier's* I had bought for $10,000 from its author, Henry Gregor Felsen. I wrote a 30-page treatment for Bing Crosby and Jimmy Stewart, who had never made a film together.

Cash-strapped Universal could not afford those stars but could afford me if I would make a comedy with a new team I had never heard of, Dan Rowan and Dick Martin. Bob Coryell urged me to accept this opportunity to establish a franchise not unlike Abbott and Costello, who had once saved the same studio from financial disaster.

The head of production, Ed Muhl, got me when he added another hyphen to my title as writer-director-producer. Before I attacked the screenplay, I thought it would be wise to meet my stars and see what they did for a living. They were then doing it in Chicago.

To go see their act, Doris and I combined business with a vacation we both needed. We had suffered the tragic loss of her father when Morris was killed on the highway en route to meet Katya for a weekend in Palm Desert. In her grief, Katya welcomed the time she spent tending the girls while Doris and I tried to enjoy Chicago.

We found Rowan and Martin attractive and pleasant gentlemen who had one routine that got laughs because of Dick's ability to drink an inordinate amount of beer as Dan was trying to recite a soliloquy from *Hamlet*. They were amusing but I felt I could make them funnier.

"If you can't," Doris said, "Universal's in big trouble."

One of Ed Muhl's executives was Dona Holloway, former assistant to Harry Cohn at Columbia and now in charge of talent at Universal. She began as a receptionist in the William Morris Agency where she befriended a frightened young girl who became Marilyn Monroe. Dona knew more secrets about more people than anyone in town and would have made a scandalous gossip had she been less scrupulous.

The lady helped me enormously, cutting corners to get what I wanted from all departments on the lot and dealing with agents in casting. She was rewarded with the associate producer credit on the film I called *Once Upon a Horse.*

When we were unable to cast Jane Russell as Dan Rowan's leading lady, Dona urged me to give the part to Martha Hyer. For Dick's lady, I called in the soubrette I admired in my first feature, the deliciously funny Nita Talbot. I also called back John McGiver and rounded up a posse of cowboy stars (Bob Steele, Kermit Maynard, Tom Keene and Bob Livingston) to ride once again with a sheriff played by Leif Erickson, a clutch of comics from the Keystone Kops, silent movie comedians Hank Mann and Snub Pollard, plus Broadway's brilliant Davey Burns, whom I was lucky to get between stage shows.

Dona brought me gorgeous Ingrid Goude to play opposite two former boxing champions, Max Baer and his brother Buddy. Dona also cast a refreshing chorus girl she felt was a candidate for stardom, but Universal was not signing anybody then. So Mary Tyler Moore had to wait — rather impatiently — for Sheldon Leonard to make her a star.

While I was writing the screenplay, my brother hosted a birthday party in Connecticut for Dad's sixtieth which Abigail and I attended, keeping a promise to take her on a trip as I had done earlier with her sisters. We went east by train, in a compartment where I continued to write and Abbe learned how to spell Colorado, which she can still do today.

Thanks to her, it was during the trip through that state that I wrote one of the most successful sight gags I ever put on the screen. The train was stopped near a stockyard, where some cowboys were branding bawling calves. As one calf got away, a young cowboy pursued it and I explained to my curious daughter what they were doing. Wide-eyed, Abbe said, "If I was a calf, I'd run away, too."

In my story, Rowan and Martin played would-be cattle rustlers. Dick attempts to bulldog a steer and the animal trots off with Dick hanging on to his horns. Dan calls to him, "Dig your heels in the ground!" and watches in awe as Dick's heels cut a trench in the dirt. The camera then follows Dan as he goes to rescue Dick, buried up to his waist.

The film was shot in black and white CinemaScope by Art Arling, a surly veteran who was chafed by the assignment "on a horse opera with a green director." My first thought was to replace him but decided to wait for him to say that to my face. Arling and I, accompanied by art director Robert Clatworthy and assistant director Frank Shaw, were driven to the Janss ranch in the San Fernando Valley to pick locations. Arling was silent during the 45-minute ride.

We found a broad stretch of prairie for the main title shot in which a lone horseman comes riding from the distance toward the camera. Framing

the vista with my hands, I stood with my back to the others and asked if any of them had a viewfinder.

"Yes," Arling said and handed his to Frank Shaw, who handed it to me. "Tell him I always carry it and a bottle of aspirin for my new directors."

Without turning, looking through his lens, I said, "He better get a big bottle, because he's going to take a lot himself every day he works on this horse opera!"

Before we began shooting on the first day, I made a presentation of a bottle of aspirin to Art in front of his crew, who laughed. They laughed a lot during the entire production and on the last day, Arling returned that bottle. Unopened. His wife came to our wrap party to meet the first director her husband ever had a kind word for. I don't know what the word was because Art never said it to my face.

Once Upon a Horse got mixed reviews from the trade papers: good and great. But when it was released a year later, inexplicably retitled *Hot Horse*, New York's reviewers rejected it with such vehemence, I would have been crushed had I believed them.

Dan Rowan, Dick Martin and the rest of the cast survived and did well in television, if not films, and Martha Hyer did even better in matrimony. She married the widowed Hal Wallis.

While the film was going through the long process of post-production, I had ample time to write a half-hour script that my old friend Jack Webb dared me to try. Jack occupied a bungalow across from mine where he produced, directed and starred in his enormously successful *Dragnet.*

Every evening, we would gather in Webb's dressing room with his co-star, Harry Morgan, a few of Jack's colleagues and several full bottles that had to be emptied before Jack dismissed us for the night. One evening, Harry mentioned the lack of humor in recent *Dragnet* scripts. Jack, who rewrote all of his scripts, said the stories they were doing were too grim to find levity. I argued that levity could be worked into any script, so Jack challenged me to write one for him. I agreed on the condition that I did so under a pseudonym I had registered with the Writers Guild, Henry Irving.

Jack's story editor, Bob Cinedar, offered me the grim crime of a hammer slaying and drove me down to police headquarters to meet the detective who had solved the case. I wrote the script in two days and both

Opposite: Top: **As long as they are in California, my parents visit the set (*Once Upon a Horse*, Universal Studios, 1957). Left to right: A. L. Kanter, Dan Rowan, Mrs. Kanter, Dick Martin, Hal Kanter. *Bottom:* On the Universal back lot, 1957, before we began production on *Once Upon a Horse*. Pictured are Dan Rowan (left), Dick Martin, Hal Kanter, and a complete horse.**

Cinedar and Webb greeted it with such enthusiasm, I agreed to do another. I chose one with built-in humor, a thief who trained a police dog to snatch purses.

By the time I finished that one, Jack had rewritten my first and extracted all the humor from it. He was a genius in that regard. He even wrote out the inherent irony in the purse-snatching dog. And to further exasperate me, the check for my first script arrived, made out not to Henry Irving, but to Hal Kanter. Cinedar swore that he had put only my pen name on the script and Jack vowed that only Henry Irving's name would appear on the screen.

Some detective work by Cinedar revealed that the studio's payroll computer read our Social Security numbers and, because Henry's name had Hal's number, Hal got his money for the next half-dozen *Dragnet* scripts he wrote until he gave up trying to make Jack Webb's Sgt. Friday less robotic.

Before leaving Universal, Henry Jaffe asked me to do a one-hour special television show for his client Dinah Shore, who was taking a week off. I agreed if I could use Rowan and Martin to plug my movie. He approved that, but said he also needed star names to hold Dinah's audience.

We signed Shirley MacLaine, Nanette Fabray and Bob Crosby to augment Dan and Dick, with music by Livingston and Evans, conducted by Paul Weston. Milt Josefsberg and I wrote the script, George Gobel and Fritz Feld did cameos and the show was such a roaring success, Jaffe gave me a bonus: my choice of any Chevrolet. I chose the brand new Corvette. I also chose to do another special for Henry. It was to be a satirical documentary with Groucho Marx called *Groucho on Laughter.*

Groucho and I spent many days together on the script, working with Bob Dwan, who did research for us. Working with Groucho was often fun but usually tormenting because of his incessant puns and outrageous jokes, most of which he would never say if given to him by a writer. I was not unhappy when Henry scrubbed the project for financial reasons. Other financial avenues were open to me.

One was a call from Jerry Wald at 20th Century–Fox, where he had gone after he and Norman Krasna had kayoed RKO. Jerry and Edmund Goulding, a venerable English director, were preparing *Mardi Gras*, a musical written by my friend Winston Miller. They wanted a rewrite to accommodate the limited talents of Pat Boone, Tommy Sands, Gary Crosby and a French souffle named Christine Carere.

Goulding and I got along splendidly. He told a lot of naughty stories about the early days of Hollywood and had many good ideas in reshaping the script I had inherited from Winston. He asked Jerry to keep me on salary and on his set while making the picture. Several times, Eddie told me to go to Christine's dressing room and go over lines with her, exchanging words she had difficulty with or we had difficulty understanding. Eddie thought he was doing me a favor, but Mlle. Carere was a lady who never once assaulted me sexually. It was an otherwise pleasant experience.

Watching Goulding coax a performance from Pat Boone and Gary Crosby, I was relieved at not having the burden of producing and directing. But then Rosie brought me a request from Milton Berle to supervise his new television series for Kraft. It would be a chance, he said, to restore Berle to the exalted position he once held as Mr. Television, so I agreed to have lunch and a discussion with him.

Milton Berle can be charming when he wants something. Sometimes even when he doesn't. He wanted me to take over as producer, director and head writer for a series of 39 half-hours on NBC. He promised that he would leave his notorious whistle at home, would not interfere in writing, casting, staging or lighting and would restrict himself to performing.

"I'll put my life in your hands," he promised.

And he did. For almost 48 hours.

"He was born with the gift of laughter and the sense that the world was mad."—R. Sabatini

42. *The Gift of Laughter*

Wednesday night, October 8, 1958, a silhouette of Bing Crosby appeared on the NBC network, singing "When the blue of the night meets the gold of the day, someone waits for me." An equally familiar voice said, "This is Ken Carpenter. A dozen years ago, on May 6, 1946, Bing Crosby closed the doors of the Kraft Music Hall, radio's all-time favorite variety program."

As Bing's theme song faded, doors closed on Crosby and Ken continued: "Tonight, 12 years later, the doors to the Kraft Music Hall opened on television—in living color—under the management of its new star—Mr. Milton Berle." Bing's theme segued into Milton's "Near You" and Berle entered to open the door. But it was locked. He pounded on it until it was opened from inside by Bob Hope.

"Here, boy," Bob said, "Bing asked me to give you the keys to the hall." And, "I'm leaving because I want you to make it on your own."

Milton did. Our first show introduced a "new" Berle to a large audience, but getting him there was not as calm as he had promised. His interference began when he balked at the first person I wanted to hire, Jack Benny's veteran writer, Milt Josefsberg, but he then reluctantly withdrew his objection when I added the team of Hal Goodman and Larry Klein to our writing staff.

We engaged Billy May as our music director, Jerry Hausner as associate producer and Selwyn Touber, who was later followed by Ben Tompkins as our camera director. Ben so loved my Corvette, he swapped it to me for his Cadillac, the only car deal where I ever came out ahead.

On our first show, the hysterical highlight was a troupe of colorful Russian dancers billed as "the world famous Prudovskya Ballet." They made a spectacular entrance with their spokesman, the extremely funny Lou Jacobi, whose heavy Russian accent was punctuated by shouts and stomps from the dancers as he introduced them.

"My dear American friends," he said, "we will dance for you the story of Katchinka and Gregori, a very old Russian folk tale.

"In certain village lives Katchinka, most beautiful daughter of a peasant farmer. One day, Gregori, a Cossack, steals her away from farm. Katchinka's father and brothers chase after Gregori and have big fight with all the Cossacks. This is the most exciting part of dance, the fight. Much leaping and jumping, with swords and whips. Music is very fast! We are working very hard, dancing with every muscle in our bodies. Is a difficult number to do and when we are finished, we are soaking with perspiration, wringing wet and we are going to our dressing rooms, where you are having this marvelous invention, air conditioning, here in America.

"We are lying down and the cold air is blowing over our soaking hot bodies. We are catching from this a cold and go to hospital where we come down with double pneumonia. The whole thing is a dirty capitalist plot to kill Russians — and if you think we're going to fall for that, phooey on you! We won't dance!"

Shouting, they stomped off to an ovation from the audience, which delighted me because my star had interfered so often with my staging of the scene during rehearsals. Poor Jacobi turned to me in tears and asked, "Which one of you am I supposed to listen to?"

"Lou," I told him, "do it the way you feel best, because you know more how to play comedy than anyone in this studio."

As Milton jumped up to defend himself, I said, "And Mr. Berle, in your scenes, try to be as funny as you used to be when you were popular."

Milton took out his frustration on others, telling Selwyn where to put the camera, Bill Levitsky when to crank up his audio, Jay Krause how to design his set, Joe Viera how to light it, Grady Hunt where to obtain his wardrobe. He even instructed Ken Carpenter how to announce.

But I already realized what I had stepped into when Milton insisted on auditioning an engineer who would provide recorded laughter for the show. We didn't need a laugh track; we had a live audience. I never needed one on the Gobel show, but Berle always used one on his Texaco series, as he said, "just to augment."

He assembled a medley of his favorite old jokes and we went into a small studio in Burbank to record a five-minute monologue. Milton told the engineer he would time his delivery for the laughs, which he did with surgical precision I admired.

Then we played back the tape. Milton nodded approvingly at the first laugh. He smiled at me at the second and joined in the laughter at the third joke. By the fifth laugh, Milton was slapping me on the back with glee, the engineer knew he had passed his test and I knew I was dealing with

Left to right: Hal Kanter, Larry Klein, Barbara Maltby, Milt Josefsberg, Hal Goodman. Barbara was our script secretary who came to work when there were no bridge tournaments in the vicinity of 11 western states!

paranoiac delusion when Berle's crazed eyes glistened and he exclaimed, "Listen to me! I'm killing them! Killing them!"

It was so close to masturbation, I suggested that he have his telephone bell replaced with a laugh track so he could have an orgasm whenever anyone called.

We had to use canned laughs—"just to augment"—the entire season, so I never really knew if our shows were as funny as we thought. Only the audience can tell you the truth about comedy.

Many of our shows were quite funny, thanks to superior writing for such gifted guests as Sammy Davis, Jr., George Jessel, Joan Davis, Edgar Bergen, Red Skelton, Jimmy Durante and Andy Griffith. Casual Andy had to wear a suit for one scene, so Grady Hunt went to a Los Angeles wholesaler to buy him one. We continued rehearsing with Andy, Milton and our rehearsal pianist, Dudley Brooks, but Milton kept blowing his lines and each time he blamed Dudley. Milton always blamed others for his own mistakes and when he continued to lash out at Dudley, I was provoked to defend the gentle black musician. In the bitter argument that followed, Milton stormed out of the studio and I dismissed the company for lunch long before noon.

An hour later, Grady returned to Andy's dressing room with a gray suit and called me to approve it. I used the visit to apologize to Andy for my outburst at Milton.

"You don't have to apologize," Andy grinned. "I appreciated every bit of it."

We did not know where Milton had gone until I got a call from Ruth Berle, who said, "So, at last, the snake's out of the basket! What did you do to my husband?"

"Look in the basket, Ruth, and ask the snake what he did to us."

Ruth Berle was a tactful, wise woman with a keen sense of humor who protected Milton without antagonizing his foes. He returned to work and did a great show. Andy's manager Dick Link asked me to let him keep the suit, because it was the best one Griffith ever had. It cost us $48.50.

A month earlier, when I invited our next guest, Milton's reaction stunned me. "Who the hell," he asked, "is Carl Sandburg?"

He found out who the poet was when the white-haired gentleman arrived to make his first appearance on a television variety program as a folk-singing raconteur. Our sponsors gave a cocktail party in his honor and all of Hollywood who could read turned out to meet Sandburg. Milton was so impressed, he was on his best behavior all week, basking in reflected intellect.

Instead of checking into the hotel that unit manager Jim Loren had booked for him, Sandburg accepted the hospitality of his friend Norman Corwin. It was in Norman's guest house that I first met the poet and went over the script we had prepared. Carl hated it.

Over the weekend, with Corwin tossing in suggestions and opinions, we rewrote every word that Josefsberg, Goodman, Klein and I had done as a first draft. That long encounter was probably deliberate on Carl's part. He loved to talk and Corwin's presence protracted our meetings. Any audience encouraged Carl to expand and both he and Norman shared an infatuation for puns which drew roars from them and groans from me.

At our first cast rehearsal, the actor Robert Easton came in with an anthology of poetry he asked Sandburg to autograph. Carl glanced at it and told the young man that he'd be happy to affix his signature after Bob had collected the autographs of all the others represented in the volume … Byron, Keats, Browning, Whittier, etc.

That afternoon, Easton returned from lunch with a volume of Carl's poems. Carl sat at the table, called everyone's attention to the book and announced in his orotund baritone, "This volume cost $4.50. It contains

Carl Sandburg and Hal Kanter, Beverly Hills, California, October 20, 1958, at a cocktail party for Sandburg.

over 500 poems. That is less than a penny a poem. To this grand bargain, I now happily affix my signature!"

That sums up my impression of the man: Had he no sense of humor, his ego would have strangled him.

He hated attention like ticks hate hounds. On a warm afternoon as he and I went to lunch, Carl strode erectly across a busy street with his white hair blazing in the sun and a woolen shawl draped around his throat. His long coat hung from his shoulders in the manner of a ham actor. The old man could make heads turn.

Carl had opinions about everything and almost everybody. He dismissed Burl Ives as a minstrel who never contributed anything to folklore, would not mention the name of Elvis Presley, held William Faulkner in disdain as "an overrated pornographer" and pitied Robert Frost not only for his political philosophy but for his family life. He did, however, consider some of Frost's poetry splendid, if not up to any of his own.

Despite the time it took us to arrive at a draft we could take to the rehearsal table, I enjoyed that first exposure to a giant whose work I admired and enjoyed sharing laughter with him. His laugh was robust and genuine but unpredictable. I was never sure what would elicit it.

I told him about a discussion held at dinner at our house a few days earlier. We were talking about racial prejudice when our five-year-old Abigail said, "I don't know why some people don't like black people; they're just like anybody else except they have a lot of freckles all pushed together!"

Instead of laughing, Carl nodded his head gravely and commented, "That is a worthwhile child, a child well worthwhile and a tribute to her mother."

When I suggested Abbe's father might share in that praise, he said, "You selected the mother." *Then* he laughed.

In rewriting our script, I asked Carl, "What one thing would you like to tell the 30 million Americans who may be watching this show?" After a moment's contemplation of the size of that audience, Carl said something to the effect that we could solve all our problems by turning our government over to the Socialists. As I got wet at the thought of his blurting that out over NBC on time paid for by the Kraft Cheese Company, Carl lectured on the values of Socialism and outlined his own career as the secretary to the Socialist mayor of Milwaukee around 1910.

He was, to quote him, a rare bird. I am grateful he accepted my offer to come out from Flat Rock, North Carolina, to do the show — and yet, I sometimes feel guilty that I lured him there, because he later returned to Hollywood, where he was so lionized, so quick to lap it all up, he seemed to lose dignity and became a caricature of himself, popping up at gatherings infested with people who had never read a word of his, people who regarded him as the newest cocktail party celebrity and a quaint old man.

When he came back to work on *The Greatest Story Ever Told*, I told an audience, "George Stevens said that what Hollywood needs is new blood, so he hired Carl Sandburg ... a writer who knew personally the original cast of the New Testament."

Both Stevens and Sandburg laughed heartily at my jokes and the next day, Carl called me to say he would be available for dinner, "just as soon as this great genius, Stevens, and I lick this God-damned Bible story."

The perversion of the artist was a sorry way to enter the sunset of his career. When he returned to North Carolina for the last time, I got the impression he realized it also, but too late.

My family and I were driving across the country when we heard the news report of his death. We were doubly saddened because Carl, who had always been a guest in California, had invited us to his farm in Flat Rock that he might be our host when we arrived in nearby Hendersonville, the summer home of my boyhood.

Today, Carl's albums are in our home to hear and his books for us to read. From one we get the richness of his voice, the cadence of his speech, and from the other we draw knowledge and inspiration. It is a comfort to remember him that way and recall the humor he exhibited in such exchanges as the time I introduced him to the head of the William Morris Agency, Abe Lastfogel.

It was in the dressing room right after Carl's appearance on the Berle show when Sandburg asked the origins of Lastfogel's name. The powerful agent said it was German, originally Lustvogel, and meant *bird of prey*, whereupon Carl said, "What an apt name for a man of your calling!"

Meeting Sandburg was memorable and worth the ordeal I suffered during that season with Milton.

Perhaps Mahalia Jackson, the brilliant gospel singer, summed up our star for many of us. The lady was booked as a special guest to sing a medley of Negro spirituals. It was a week when Berle was more obnoxious than usual. He demanded Mahalia reduce her medley to one song, carped about the one she selected, rearranged my staging, criticized Billy May's music, ordered Mahalia to change her dress three times, blew cigar smoke in her face and, in general, acted like Milton. After the show, I went to her dressing room to thank Mahalia and her accompanist for their performance and forbearance. Mahalia merely nodded for both of them. Then as I started out, she said, "Mr. Kanter! That Uncle Milty is sure a genius, isn't he?"

"Well, ma'am," I stammered in surprise, "I—yi—I suppose that in his field, some might consider him a genius. Why do you ask?"

"Because," she said, "if I ever come back on his show—which I seriously doubt—that man better not *genius* all over me!"

During one of those weeks, the genius and his wife Ruth entertained their friends, Larry Gelbart and his wife Pat, when they returned to California from England. While Pat and Ruth sat in the dressing room, Larry watched our rehearsal, appalled by Milton's behavior.

When it was over, Larry took me aside and said, "I want to ask you a question. Why does a man with your credits, your reputation and your talent put up with this monster?"

"Because," I said, "he pays me $5,000 a week. Now, let me ask you a question, Larry. Why are you his friend for free?"

In the almost 40 years since, Milton has mellowed to the point where I have given him what he always wanted from all of us: our love.

I also declare my respect and affection for Milton, a classic example of the irreverent Yankee attitude toward sham, hypocrisy and pomposity. He has become part of our native folklore. Our seminal stand-up comedian, he is the Thomas Edison of our comedy theater, and every comedian working in his giant shadow owes him an enormous debt.

If he ever reads this, I want him to know that I would rather spend just 15 minutes in Milton Berle's company than three hours in a dentist's chair.

"Some of us express ourselves by writing music or painting pictures or erecting buildings. Sheldon expresses himself by belching after meals." — Earle Hagen

43. *Expressing Ourselves*

The summer we built a swimming pool in our backyard coincided mysteriously with our daughters' discovery of the beach at Malibu.

My timing was better with my career. I had more offers than I could accept. Placing the Berle experience in its proper perspective, before the year was up I wrote a part for him in *Let's Make Love*, a Norman Krasna screenplay I rewrote for Jerry Wald.

Another offer I took was to satisfy myself, not my suspiciously Republican business manager. It was a salute to Harry S Truman that Irving Kahn televised as a tribute to the ex-president on his seventy-seventh birthday.

My contribution was a segment I wrote and produced for the closed circuit banquet in New York. It was a fund-raiser for the party, not for me or the three stars I presented from Hollywood, Jack Benny, Peggy Lee and Jimmy Durante.

Nineteen fifty-nine was also the year I joined Sheldon Leonard's annual Mexican fishing vacation. My roommate on that trip to Mazatlan was Milt Josefsberg, who stayed up all night, reading. When I mentioned that to Sheldon, he said with a smile the only reason he invited me was to share a room with the man nobody else would.

Two of our party, dentist Frank Greenbaum and insurance broker Al Ruben, forgot they shared wedding anniversaries, so I quietly ordered a bottle of wine to remind them. And to make sure it was cold, I emphasized to our Mexican waiter, *frito, muy frito*! The waiter gave me the kind of smile that suggested my Spanish left much to be corrected, so I appealed to *el Jefe*, "Sheldon, how do you say cold in Spanish, *frito* or *frio*?"

"*Frio, stupido*," he said. "*Frito* means fried."

I jumped up and cried, "Call that waiter back. I just ordered fried champagne!"

Sheldon never let me forget that. Nor did he ever tire of reminding others who joined us over the years in various Baja resorts of the time we came back to the bar at Punta Colorado after a hot day of dorado fishing.

Earle Hagen, Ray Jacobsen, Rocky Kalish, Sheldon and I were exchanging lies about the day's catch when a tipsy woman from the Midwest stumbled over to ask Sheldon for his autograph and then insisted she buy the next round.

After the third round, she began complaining about Mexican mosquitoes, which she declared are the biggest in the world. For reasons I can attribute only to frozen margaritas, I told the woman she was wrong. I said Georgia mosquitoes were much bigger.

"Especially the females," I said. "You can tell which are which, because the male mosquito has a small white spot between his eyes as big as your fist."

When she expressed skepticism, I said, "I know what I'm talking about, lady; my sister used to be a stewardess on one."

For over 30 years, the six days we spent in Baja, away from telephones and television, recharged our batteries, reinforced our fraternity and replenished our laughter.

Late summer of 1959, I flew to England to write a prestigious TV special starring Charles Laughton. It was Charles himself, I learned, who had asked producer Hubbell Robinson for my services. We had become friendly when he made his TV debut on the Ed Wynn show and later, when his wife Elsa Lanchester made a riotous appearance on the Gobel show.

My assignment was to meet Charles in Stratford-on-Avon, where he was appearing with the Shakespeare Memorial Theater as King Lear and as Bottom in *A Midsummer Night's Dream*. For *Lear* he had grown a luxuriant white beard, and on the days he played Bottom he dyed it a vivid pink.

On the flight to England, I read as much about Shakespeare as I could find, for my job was to write an amusing introduction to Peter Hall's celebrated Stratford production of *A Midsummer Night's Dream*. I was met in London by the debonair Fletcher Markle, who would direct our portion of the program, and from the beginning, I was beguiled and sensed I would enjoy this assignment. The next day, I knew it when Fletcher introduced me to a young, gap-toothed, loquacious Irishman named Denis O'Dell, our energetic production manager who proved to be an inventive and treasured companion.

In my happy reunion with Laughton, he armed me with a sheaf of material Elsa had researched on Shakespeare's life, work and the history of the neighborhood. Elsa concluded that *A Midsummer Night's Dream* was Willie's spit in the faces of local landowners. Using that as a point of view, I wrote a script that pleased Charles. O'Dell's gorgeous secretary, Donna, who typed my script, kept Fletcher's production notes and, when it was all over, became Mrs. O'Dell and bore Denis two beautiful children.

The evening I saw Charles' performance in *Midsummer Night's Dream*, I was smitten with the cast that included Vanessa Redgrave, Albert Finney and Ian Holm as Puck. But it was Laughton, with his great pink beard and the body of a manatee, who defined for all time Shakespeare's Bottom.

The following evening, Sir Laurence Olivier played *Coriolanus*, and at intermission I was invited to the director's office for cocktails with Sir Alec Guinness and Christopher Fry. They were amused when I said I was perhaps the only one in the room who was going back to see how the play comes out in the end.

The next night, after Laughton's stunning performance as King Lear, I confessed to him that I had never seen nor read the play. Charles roared when I said, "That's not the ideal evening's entertainment for a man with three daughters lying in ambush for him at home."

It took Fletcher and Denis five days to shoot my 15-minute script because it involved so many moves to locations in and around Stratford and places like Ann Hathaway's cottage, the Mary Arden farm at Wilmcote and Laughton's star residence at Avon Cliffe.

Every day I came into town from the Welcombe Inn, I passed a small gallery that featured a portrait of the artist's young wife. It was beautiful and reminded me of Donna, our middle daughter, so I asked Charles, a connoisseur of fine art, if he would look at it and tell me if it was worth what the gallery was asking for it.

Charles refused. "Are you buying it as an investor or as an aesthete? Whatever, buy what pleases you, what attracts you, what you see in art yourself without advice or opinions from others."

I bought the painting, which hangs in our living room to this day. I had it wrapped to bring home when Charles came to my room at the Mayfair in London to record some additional narration Fletcher needed after editing his film. Charles ripped the wrapping from the painting and said, "This picture is too lovely not to look at! Keep it in sight until you get on that airplane!"

Later that same day, he took me to a gallery to see two paintings. One he had sold and the other he just bought. I didn't tell Charles that I did not care for his modern art but did ask him why he sold the lovely Utrillo.

"To buy this one," he said. "I have lived with that Utrillo so long, I've memorized it. And I will memorize this DeStael before I make a profit. You see, dear boy, I am the investor who supports the aesthete."

He had a rollicking sense of humor. When they were shooting at the Shakespeare Memorial, I came by to watch. After the take, Charles said, "We have attracted a visitor," and looked at me. "How was that, Sir Hal? Do I make the author proud?"

"Enormously!" I replied. "That was the finest imitation of Charles Laughton I've ever seen."

"He's bloody right!" Charles bellowed. "We'll do one more!" And while Fletcher lined up the shot again, the actor addressed the crew: "You lads see how we Yanks speak to each other? Not like you prissy Limey sissies. We Yanks tell the truth!"

Had he remained in his native England, Charles would surely have become Lord Laughton. And I probably never would have met a man who gave me so much pleasure, even though the Ford Motor Company, who sponsored our *Dream*, never put it on the air. Somewhere, somebody has a rare reel of inestimable value to literature, drama and history in that *Midsummer Night's Dream* produced by Hubbell Robinson, directed by Sir Peter Hall, written by William Shakespeare, with my prologue starring Charles Laughton and directed by Fletcher Markle, all of whom are no longer able to tell us what happened.

After Charles' death, Doris and I were at a party for Elsa and I told her I had some snapshots of Charles I had taken the summer of our content and asked if she'd like prints. "Thank you, no," she said and turned away.

Hours later, saying good night to our hosts, John and Ruth McGiver, Elsa took us aside and asked to be forgiven for her earlier rudeness.

"You see," she explained, "all the years I was married, I felt like I was locked behind a door with only a peep hole that Charles had drilled for me to see the world. And the world I saw was that tiny"—she curled her finger to demonstrate—"because that's all he allowed me to see. When Charles died, it was as if someone had unlocked that door and I saw the world was not his—but *this*!" And she flung her arms wide, grabbed Doris and me and kissed us both.

Much later, when Elsa had become reclusive, she called me out of the blue and asked if I still had those pictures of Charles. I brought them to her when she turned down my invitation to meet me at the studio for lunch.

"I should like to," she said, "but I daren't leave this house."

"When my comedy succeeds, I'm happy; when it doesn't, other comics are."—Red Buttons

44. *When My Comedy Succeeds*

The 1960s were exciting as our girls became young ladies, Doris found time to study with the celebrated artist Sister Mary Corita, and I was increasingly involved in a career that now included frequent television appearances, university lectures, awards events, guild affairs and speeches for a plethora of civic charities and industry functions.

After I had presided at one awards evening, Doris was asked by Eva Marie Saint, "Is your husband as funny at home?"

"Only when I listen," she answered.

When she wasn't listening, I sneaked in a project called *Off His Rocker*, a comedy record album Milt Josefsberg and I wrote and produced for Pat Buttram, which Warner Bros. distributed and sold over a dozen copies worldwide.

Despite that vinyl disaster, I had confidence in Pat and wrote a pilot for him called *Down Home* that ABC bought two days after we completed shooting. I had brought the show to 20th Century–Fox to work with my Encino neighbor, William Self, the studio's new TV chief. When studio head Peter Levathes called to say ABC bought the series, Bill poured champagne for us and two beautiful women. Our wives.

I wrote five more scripts with Milt Josefsberg that nobody saw, then ABC changed their minds and canceled their order. I threatened to sue but Levathes and Self advised me not to jeopardize the studio's relationship with the network. Impelled by righteous anger, I sued all of them. Milt warned me I would never again work for Fox or the network … until, of course, I had something they wanted.

While my lawyer, Paul Selvin, girded me for battle, I received a call from Frank Capra. He wanted me to do a polish job on a script for his next film. I was thrilled at the prospect of working with the great director. We met to discuss *Pocketful of Miracles*, which he and Harry Tugend had fashioned from Capra's memorable movie *Lady for a Day*. He made that Damon

Runyon story from a Robert Riskin screenplay in the '30s and wanted to update it for the '60s.

His new script opened in Oregon, where ex-hoodlums had settled down to grow apples and adopt Korean orphans. The long premise was set in the present, then flashed back to tell the original Runyon story. When I read the ponderous script, my heart sank. Its length was enough for two films. Its sentimental treacle could cause cavities in plastic dentures.

As much as I wanted to work with Capra, I felt that if he made this picture he would have another failure, as were his last few films without Riskin's writing. Gingerly, I suggested his script was a tad too long and he didn't need the prologue because the story wasn't intriguing until he flashed back to Annie, the apple-vending harridan who Dave the Dude turns into a lady for a day. Frank surprised me. Instead of defending his script, he signed me to work with him in reshaping the new version and reducing the treacle.

For the next few months, we talked in the mornings and had lunch together, and in the afternoons, I wrote. One lunchtime, Maggie, Frank's secretary—this was when we had secretaries, not assistants—stopped him as we were leaving.

"Mr. Capra," she said, "you have a call from the White House."

"Who is it?" Frank asked and she said, "Vice-President Nixon."

"Tell him I'm not here," he said. I exchanged looks with Maggie and ran to catch up with him.

"Boy! If I wasn't impressed with you before, I sure as hell am now," I said. "Refusing to talk to the vice-president of a very well-known country!"

Frank grinned. "Why is Nixon calling me? He obviously wants something. If it's important, he'll call back. And if it's not, why should I give him some of my lunch time?"

It was during one of those lunches, at the Naples on Gower Street, that Frank solved his first casting problems. The part of Dave the Dude was played originally by dapper Warren Williams but now Frank couldn't find another star with his qualifications. As he faced me, with his back to the door, I saw the restaurant owner greet and seat a handsome couple, Glenn Ford and Hope Lange. I asked Frank if he knew Ford's work and Frank nodded and allowed that he was a possibility that United Artists should approve.

When we left the restaurant, Frank stopped at their table and asked Glenn what he was going to do next and Ford half-jokingly said, "I'm going to do your next picture."

Driving back to Paramount, Frank convinced himself that Fate had decreed that meeting and he called their mutual agent, Abe Lastfogel, to begin negotiations for Glenn to play Dave the Dude.

A few days later, Frank sent me to a screening room to see a new film called *Murder, Inc.* He wanted my opinion of an actor who played the menacing role of a killer. I found him frightening, feral and fascinating. His name was Peter Falk and I thought him too sinister to play comedy. A lot I know! Frank cast him as Joy Boy and Peter, who turned out to be a very funny man, stole the picture.

Some of the dialogue was neither Riskin's, Tugend's or mine, but came from visiting newspaper columnist Jimmy Cannon, who was hired to insert what Capra believed was "Broadway lingo." In his autobiography, a book that is a tribute to his creative memory, Frank wrote that he had instructed Cannon to "take Kantor's [sic] script and rewrite every line in your own lingo." If that happened, very few of Cannon's lines made it to the screen. Jimmy spent more days covering the Democratic Convention in Los Angeles and telling me who the Kennedy boys were banging than he did moonlighting on the movie.

Despite Frank's affirmations of love and affection for me and my work, he not only dismissed my contributions to his *Pocketful*, he misspelled my name. Years later, when I introduced him at a Masquers Club dinner in his honor, I referred to him as "the second Italian to have discovered America." He loved that so much, he forgave me for also saying, "Frank Capra is a legend in his own book."

While he was shooting *Pocketful*, Capra was battling severe headaches and the equally severe Bette Davis, who had developed a profound dislike for both Ford and Capra. In Frank's case, her dislike was requited.

I had my own share of problems working with Sylvia and Danny Kaye, who had succumbed to the blandishments of money to make Danny's first appearance on television. They engaged me to write the script. But first I had to go to Las Vegas to see Danny's show and hear Sylvia whisper.

His act at the Desert Inn was a marvel of showmanship and talent. Danny displayed a charm I seldom saw when we worked in radio. In his dressing room, I praised him with the admission of how impressed I was.

"Of course you were," Sylvia acknowledged. Danny merely nodded agreement and said something in exaggerated baby talk he frequently employed when undergoing an attack of the cutes.

My visit to Vegas lasted a week as I continued to monitor Danny's performance. I shared midnight meals with him and late lunches with Sylvia as we discussed his TV debut. Danny stayed clear of the creative process, leaving us to meet each day with ideas for sketches, and each day Sylvia found some way to twist mine into what became her ideas. It was a toil-

Mike Mazurki, Frank Capra, Hal Kanter at the Masquers Club in Hollywood, February 29, 1980.

some process to arrive at agreement on sketches I could write while she struggled with her songs. When Bill Foster came from New York to work out Danny's choreography and Norman Jewison to discuss directing the special, I returned home to write the first draft and also begin another job for Hal Wallis. I was back in my groove of writing two scripts at once — Danny's television hour and Elvis Presley's next film, *Beach Boy*, which was his biggest hit when it was released as *Blue Hawaii*.

General Motors, Danny's sponsor, was so pleased with his first show, they asked him to do another one the following year. Danny told me that if I came back, I would not be writing with Sylvia and I could work with any available director of my choice. Relieved, I suggested my former associate from the *Gobel Show*, Bud Yorkin, who had become an award-winning producer-director.

Bud accepted the challenge and urged me to work with a writer friend of his named Norman Lear. That turned out to be a marriage made in Hell. Mr. Lear and I did not agree on what was funny and his groveling sycophancy in Kaye's presence made me laugh more than anything he wrote. I turned in my work to Bud, wished him luck, said good-bye to Danny and went to London to write a screenplay with two old friends, Norman Panama and Melvin Frank.

Norman was busy directing Crosby and Hope in *Road to Hong Kong*, their last *Road* picture, while Mel and I worked on the script, *Five Pieces of Maria*. Norman joined us on weekends, most of which we spent driving around London looking for restaurants where Norman could find authentic Jewish food. When we discovered some matzo balls that were hard as hockey pucks, Norman said they had been made for Disraeli and brought them home to Marcia, his artistic wife who collected antiques.

The stars of *Maria* were to be Danny Kaye and Sophia Loren, and about the time we wrote FADE OUT on the latest draft of our comedy, Miss Loren won the Academy Award for her performance in the drama *Two Women*. Almost immediately, Sophia's husband Carlo Ponti summoned Mel to Paris and informed him that his wife would not do the film with the American clown, Danny Kaye. Stunned, but still pragmatic, Mel offered to make the film with any leading man of her choice.

That offer missed the point. What Ponti told Mel was that Sophia would not make his comedy. Period. Panama and Frank were free to cast any leading lady Danny would approve. So until they found one, I was free to go home and await the casting of Melina Mercouri, Claudia Cardinale or any number of others who never did make that film.

Nobody waits long in this business. I accepted another gig soon after I got home. It was to work at Fox again, and with another celebrated film director, George Cukor. Producer Jerry Wald had Gregory Peck and Marilyn Monroe ready to star in a Norman Krasna original called *The Billionaire*. Krasna had moved to Switzerland when Cukor asked for some changes in Krasna's script, so Jerry called me in for emergency dialogue repair.

After reading the script, I had a meeting with Cukor in his elaborate suite of offices at Fox, where he usually ate lunch from a picnic basket he brought from home in his Rolls-Royce. As I shared some cold chicken and room temperature wine with him, I alarmed George by asking if Monroe was really going to play this part. "She has only four or five scenes in the whole script," I pointed out.

George expressed his new concerns to Wald. Jerry scoffed and assured him that Marilyn would do the film, then called me and told me to start writing and stop talking to Cukor because he was getting more and more nervous. George knew that Krasna had told Marilyn the story and had already gotten her approval even before he went to Switzerland to write the screenplay.

Krasna, who had a genius for selling a story to actors, had also told this one to Peck. Norman was a gifted writer but did not always write the story he ad libbed. Peck read his first draft and approved it. Evidently Monroe had not seen it yet.

Within a week, I made the changes Cukor wanted and he flew to New York, where Marilyn was being Mrs. Arthur Miller *pro tem*. He went there with Lionel Newman, the studio's talented, bawdy director of music, and songwriters Sammy Cahn and Jimmy Van Heusen. They were to demonstrate for the Millers the score they wrote for the film.

The day after they arrived in Manhattan, I was preparing to check out of Fox when I was summoned to Wald's office. He asked if I had any ideas on how to expand Marilyn's role. Apparently, Mrs. and/or Mr. Arthur Miller had read the screenplay for the first time shortly before Cukor had arrived. The lady was distressed. Jerry called the Millers and mollified them with the promise that a brilliant comedy mind was already addressing the script problems. He also cried "Help!" to Switzerland.

Working rapidly, I got several new scenes written when Cukor returned. Jerry encouraged me to keep going while Krasna read the pages in the Alps and Cukor went over them at a lower elevation. Wald also sent pages to the Millers to show them he was living up to his word and, to be evenhanded, he also sent the rewrite to Gregory Peck. That gesture led to another meeting in Wald's bungalow with the producer, the director, the star, his agent and me.

Mr. Peck was not happy and his agent, Lew Wasserman, said that *he* was also not happy with the changes that were being made. The story Krasna told Peck clearly indicated that it was to be his film, with Monroe in support, but the new pages indicated it would be Monroe's with Peck in support. That was unacceptable.

Greg withdrew from the project and my original week on the script turned to months while Jerry tried to recast and I kept rewriting.

I enjoyed my sessions with Cukor, who was a skilled raconteur, and we spent more time discussing his famous friends and exchanging anecdotes than we spent on the script. That was just as well, for we had no leading man until, after a long search, George arranged a clandestine meeting in his lovely home where Marilyn met Rock Hudson. Evidently they got along well, Miller approved and it looked like Rock would replace Greg. But this ideal casting hit a snag.

Universal had Rock under contract and refused to release him to Fox. So the search continued. Then Jerry discovered a charming French actor who was already an international star. He was Yves Montand and accepted Wald's offer to co-star with Marilyn Monroe. While they apparently had fun getting to know each other, it entailed another rewrite to accommodate the Frenchman.

Now Cukor was getting suggestions from Arthur Miller. The playwright wrote some gags that proved what a great dramatist he was. But there was one joke that Cukor instructed me to put in the script: Montand, walking with Monroe, says to a nightclub doorman, "Call me a cab," and the doorman says, "All right — you're a cab."

While Cukor chuckled, I stared at him. "You're not serious about using that, George. That joke is ancient." George said he never heard it before. No, I supposed, his friend Willie Maugham never told jokes like that, but everyone else had.

"How could they?" George said. "Arthur Miller just told it to me."

"That's not an Arthur Miller joke," I said. "It's *Joe* Miller. Please don't do that to me, George. My name's on this script!"

So he allowed me to leave it out. He also allowed me to make some casting suggestions that worked out well for the show. When we lost Frank Sinatra for a cameo, we got Bing to fill in. In place of Jack Benny, I wrote a funnier routine for Montand and Milton Berle.

By the time the film went into production, I was at MGM on another assignment and had not been on the set while they were filming. I had forgotten about "Call me a cab" until Doris and I saw the finished film, retitled *Let's Make Love* the week it opened in Los Angeles.

In a poorly attended matinee, I cringed when I saw a doorman sweeping a sidewalk as Monroe and Montand approached. George wouldn't dare do that, would he? By God, he did. And by God, it got a huge laugh from even that small audience.

From George Cukor and Frank Capra, I learned why a writer should never trust a friend — no matter how much he respects him — if he's a director.

"Pay no attention to what critics say; there never has been set up a statue in honor of a critic."—Jean Sibelius

45. *What Critics Say*

It was Bob Hope's custom to hand the first draft of his screen scripts to his radio/TV writers and have them sprinkle the pages with additional jokes. When he got the first draft of *Bachelor in Paradise*, which I wrote with Valentine Davies for MGM, Bob paid us the tacit compliment of not asking his staff to sprinkle.

Metro-Goldwyn-Mayer had lost its luster by the time I got there but I welcomed the chance to work with Val Davies, one of Hollywood's most admired citizens. George Seaton once said of Val that he had become rich by serving as a dollar-a-year man on 100,000 committees a year.

Despite the distractions of Val's abundant involvements, we completed a screenplay for Hope and Lana Turner that eventually restored some of the studio's luster. Val proposed that we team up for other assignments, which I welcomed. But first we both had to discharge previous commitments. He to Paramount and I to a special for Jack Benny and a screenplay for Edward Small at the Goldwyn Studio.

That comedy, *Sigrid and the Sergeant*, was one of several scripts I have been paid to write that never received the amber light to proceed to film. But during my stay on that lot, Small loaned me out to work on William Wyler's remake of Lillian Hellman's *The Children's Hour*. I did not add enough to John Michael Hayes' excellent screenplay to receive credit, but I relished watching Wyler work with Audrey Hepburn, Shirley MacLaine and James Garner.

One day, Samuel Goldwyn dropped in on Wyler's set and asked, "How do you like working with Willy?" Before any of us could answer, Goldwyn put his arm around Wyler and said, "Oh, I know he's a son of a bitch, but he's *my* son of a bitch!"

I had almost forgotten my lawsuit against ABC and Fox by the time Paul Selvin called me to his office to monitor depositions by network executives Oliver Treyz and Tom Moore. Following several more months of delays by their attorneys, both ABC and Fox settled with me "on the courthouse steps."

In addition to cash, my settlement included a guarantee for three pilots, one of which had to be ordered for a minimum of 13 episodes. The one the network chose to go forward with starred Tony Franciosa as Valentine Farrow, an editor in a New York publishing house, and Jack Soo as his dauntless majordomo. I called it *Valentine's Day*, naming Tony's character after my suddenly departed partner Val, who died while our representatives were arranging our impending production entity. His loss had sent our film world into mourning.

Doris' art classes inspired me to resume my own attempts to create, and I made several large abstract pictures by dripping acrylic paint onto board, one of which I hung in my office at Fox. It was there that I tried to talk a matronly opera star into playing Franciosa's mother. She had never done a TV series and her husband, who was also her manager, was skeptical she should attempt comedy. But she asked, "How can we turn down anyone who has an original Jackson Pollock on his wall?" Only after she got congenial notices for her performance did I tell Helen Traubel I was the forger. She laughed with delight and asked me to forge a smaller one for her, which I did.

When Jack Soo was offered his role, he refused because "I don't play stereotypes like Oriental houseboys." I promptly flew to Las Vegas, where Soo was starring in *Flower Drum Song*, and handed him my pilot script in his dressing room. "Read this," I said, "and then let's talk."

He read a description of his character, then a few lines of dialogue and the stage direction, "Rocky mixes two martinis, sits down with one and indicates the other is for his boss, Val."

Jack grinned, stood up and said, "You got me."

The pilot was directed by George Marshall, who later did several episodes until Tony heard George refer to him as "that Wop" and to Soo as "the Chink." Nobody gets away with that sort of obscenity in Franciosa's presence. I engaged directors like Bruce Humberstone, Leslie Goodwins and a few others who had also become guilty of committing the unpardonable Hollywood sin: They got old. But they knew how to make audiences laugh.

I brought Murdo MacKenzie into TV to join Bernard Weisen as an associate producer. Bernie had been my assistant director on the first pilot I directed with Louis Nye that the network rejected, although Louie was their choice to star in a show I conceived as *The Marx of Time* for Groucho. They had heard that Groucho was ill, and they would not take a chance on a man his age. That was utter rubbish, based on rumor. Groucho was in good health and a close friend with whom we socialized. He lived a good 15 years after the network nabobs were long gone from their posts.

Tony Franciosa tweaks my nose behind my back.

As they were deciding which of my pilots to pick up, I began writing a comedy for Doris Day with Dick Breen, a screenplay being another part of my settlement with the studio. Dick and I were just getting started when Bill Self pulled me back to TV because ABC had selected *Valentine's Day* and wanted it on the air in six weeks.

While Bernie Weisen showed the pilot to a lot of freelance writers, I was scrambling to get out the first few scripts to make the air date. The underlings at ABC demanded more unnecessary meetings than I could afford with my accelerated schedule and when I told them so, they marked me down as uncooperative. It never occurred to them that they were being even more so, having ordered a new show at the last minute and questioning every decision we were making in order to get it done.

My acrimonious complaints that Douglas Cramer, Burt Nodella and Adrian Samish were trying to tell me what to write and how to do it resulted in arrival from New York of another future mogul, Edgar Scherick. He could "handle" me, he convinced his bosses, because we had in common Long Beach High School, which Ed attended with my sister Saralea.

He reminded me of another executive about whom Ed Wynn once

Hal Kanter with Bernard Weisen, his associate on two shows and three pilots.

said, "There are only two things about him I don't like. His face." Scherick's diplomatic tactic was sympathy with my plight while planning to cancel my show at the first opportunity.

He had to wait because *Valentine's Day* won the night for the network, topping Carol Burnett's first variety show on CBS and *Bob Hope's Chrysler Theater* on NBC. Despite that success, ABC dropped us at the end of the season and put on a series called *Honey West*.

Tony Franciosa, a conscientious, dedicated and diligent actor whose film career was resuscitated by TV, was immediately grabbed for several

Producer Kanter on the set of *Valentine's Day* at 20th Century–Fox, with Jack Soo and veteran director George Marshall.

features. I went to work for Bob Hope, producing the *Chrysler Theater*, a show that had been our competition the season before.

My one regret at leaving Fox was losing the peerless services of Myra Stuté, my devoted secretary, who had even helped my 16-year-old Donna get a summer job as a travel agent in Switzerland.

Among the Hope shows was an hour I wrote, produced and directed that got the highest rating any Chrysler hour had ever garnered. It starred Don Knotts and Arthur Godfrey and had the intriguing title of "The Reason Nobody Hardly Ever Seen a Fat Outlaw in the Old West Is as Follows."

One of my most enjoyable experiences was working with Don, whom I consider a comedy genius, and Godfrey, who considered himself one.

Having dinner with our family, Arthur advised Lisa that she could learn to do anything as well as he did — play the ukulele, fly airplanes, sing, dance the hula, ride horses, sail a yacht, shoot a rifle, barbecue steaks or perform surgery if she'd just do what he did: spend 15 minutes a day studying the subject she wanted to master!

When *Honey West* failed to win the audience that *Valentine's Day* had

Hal Kanter, left, found skinny Don Knotts perfectly suited to star in "The Reason Nobody Hardly Ever Seen a Fat Outlaw Is as Follows," a satirical Western to be presented on *Bob Hope Presents the Chrysler Theatre*," on NBC.

done, the alarmed network acknowledged that they had acted too hastily in canceling us. Tom Moore asked Bill Self if they could bring it back. Too late; Tony was committed to his feature films and it would be some time before he could return to the small screen.

But I went back to work for 20th Century–Fox, back to the big screen and again with Myra Stuté, who, before she abandoned her career for motherhood, hand-picked Dee Staley as her sterling replacement for the next few busy years. Dee's loyalty proved, over the years, equal to her superb skills, her diplomacy, and a sense of humor that endeared her to me.

One morning I arrived at work to find Dee laughing as she hung up the phone.

"What's so funny?" I asked the daughter of the former mayor of her Ohio home town.

"That was my sister," Dee said. "I just told her the news that Boris Karloff died last night, and she said, 'Boris Karloff! Is he still alive?'"

A few years earlier, Fox's *Something's Got to Give* was a film that had been in production until it was shut down while Marilyn's demands for script changes were met. That was my job and before I completed it, the world and I were shocked by the news of Marilyn's apparent suicide.

When the script was reactivated for producers Aaron Rosenberg and Martin Melcher, they assigned Jack Sher to join me in rewriting it for Melcher's wife, Doris Day, and James Garner. Our version was directed by Michael Gordon and co-starred Polly Bergen and Thelma Ritter. Added to that mix were my friends, Don Knotts, Elliott Reid and John Astin.

My other contribution was a new title, *Move Over, Darling*, which provided the film's title song written with established lyricist Joe Lubin and thus won me membership in BMI. Every time I hear the song, I think not of Lubin but of Lisbon, because long after the film was a hit, the song lingered. A few years later, with Doris in Portugal — where she wanted to buy rugs at the nation's semi-annual going-out-of-business sale — our driver turned on his radio and joined Doris Day in singing *Move Over, Darling*.

I was ashamed that I didn't remember the lyrics but so flattered, I tipped the driver five escudos.

Over the years, my one song has paid so many small dividends, it's little wonder Johnny Mercer's many paid him such huge ones. My fellow Georgian and I went back home in 1972 to stage a variety show celebrating the opening of the new Savannah Civic Center. I enlisted many Hollywood friends to make a comedy film saluting the city, Mayor John Rusakis and Alderman Leo Center. Twenty-five years later, they still show that film to anybody who stops — or even hesitates — in Savannah.

Today, the auditorium where Johnny sang a medley of his hits on that indelible night is called the Johnny Mercer Memorial Theater. Miriam Center lured me back to emcee ceremonies dedicating that with a program of Mercer material sung by Rosemary Clooney, Rose Marie, Helen O'Connell and Margaret Whiting, four artists Johnny respected.

His brilliance as a writer, performer, record executive and amusing companion is unmatched. Through his songs alone, the millions who never enjoyed my personal contact with him are nonetheless Johnny Mercer's huckleberry friends.

"Hamlet's experiences simply could not have happened to a plumber."—George Bernard Shaw

46. *Hamlet's Experiences*

"Kanter," my caller asked, "how do you feel about free speech?"

Assuring him that I consider it one of our most precious heritages, he said, "Great! We'd like you to come downtown and make one."

For decades, I made too many of them before I discovered how to avoid the inconvenience of platform popularity. An executive of a small film company asked me if I would fly to Toronto as their guest and address a conclave of theater owners. On impulse, I said I might if he would give me $5,000.

"Five?" he gasped. "I can get Henny Youngman for *one*!"

"Get him," I said, and hung up.

That gambit has served me well ever since and, while I still deliver free speeches for a few charities and industry affairs, making a speech is usually easier for me than listening to one.

An exception was one in the summer of 1967 I attended as the guest of Jack Valenti, an erudite, eclectic orator who lets none of his thoughts go unpublished. Yet it was not Jack who moved me so much that afternoon but the speaker he introduced, Roy Wilkins, an adherent of Walter White who had succeeded him as executive director of the NAACP.

Wilkins spoke with dignity and passion on the plight of the black man in the social, economic and cultural structure of American society. Without rancor or bitterness, he urged us to consider more positive and more meaningful ways to support his organization's practical agenda.

Leaving the luncheon, I wondered how I personally could help realize the American Dream for us all and recognized the one weapon I knew most about: that enemy of fear, pretense and pomposity—laughter.

I reasoned that if I could create a television show that featured black characters as people first and black only incidentally—in time a white audience would see blacks as people, not as black people … and if they could laugh *with* and not *at* my characters, as we once laughed at Stepin Fetchit, *Amos 'n' Andy* and *Beulah*, sooner or later some of the verities of African-American life would become apparent, some of the myths exploded.

In the 1960s, that was a bold dream and it would take a bold network to implement it.

The usual procedure a writer takes before submitting his dream to anyone is to set his characters, background and basic theme, describe them in great detail, then outline half a dozen stories for future episodes and write the pilot script.

I approached my dream differently. I wrote no descriptions of characters, backgrounds or themes. Instead, the reader is pulled right into this:

FADE IN:

INT. BAKER APT.—COREY'S BEDROOM—DAY

A small, neat room. COREY BAKER, not quite six years old, gets out of bed, pulls a robe over his pajamas, dons his slippers and pads out to—

THE KITCHEN

Small but spotless. Corey takes two oranges from the fridge, places them on the table. He has to use a chair to get a knife, two glasses and a juicer from the cupboard. He slices an orange and begins squeezing it.

JULIA'S BEDROOM

Not much bigger than Corey's. JULIA BAKER, 27, is a beautiful woman even in her sleep. Corey enters, carrying the two glasses of juice. He stands at the bedside for a moment, admiring his pretty mother.

As the dialogue begins, we see the warm, natural and amusing relationship of the boy and his mother and discover that she is a widow, they have recently moved to Los Angeles from the Midwest and that Julia is going to be interviewed for a job that morning.

At no point in describing the characters did I mention the color of their skin. Nor did I mention it in describing the others Julia encounters as she goes for the interview. The reader discovers her color only when she challenges a bigot, "Should I have written in bold, black letters on the top of my application, 'I am a Negro'?"

Two readers admitted that they dropped the script in surprise at that point—on page 12. Because many scripts are discarded after five pages, it was significant that they had read that far and were sufficiently intrigued to keep reading.

Of course, that was my hope, for had I stated my purpose immediately, the chance of getting my dream considered would have been significantly reduced.

It took me a week to decide what to write and two days to write a 35-page first draft I called *Mamma's Man*. I had no idea if it was good, bad, funny or not. All I knew is that my Julia and her son had grown very real to me and very dear. I gave it to my severest critic to read. To my relief, my wife liked it.

Doris did say that I should not allow a small boy to use a knife but I said I needed it for a plot point and she said "change the plot point" and I said why and she said to keep a knife out of a child's hands and I said don't tell me what to write and she said you asked for my comments and I said I did not want comments, I wanted praise.

The next step, after I brought Doris some flowers, was to send the presentation to my agent.

Two midnights later, Meta Rosenberg, Rosie's wife and partner, apologized for calling that late but she had just finished reading *Mamma's Man* and was so excited by it she couldn't wait to discuss what to do with it. I thought we might find any one of several production entities to finance a pilot, but Meta reasoned that we should take it to a network first. They decide what goes on the air and if no network was willing to take this bold step forward, we would be wasting our time shooting a pilot.

Meta chose NBC as our target. They had already proved their courage putting *I Spy* on the air, fighting and winning the battle with some Southern stations who, at first, refused to broadcast a show co-starring dark Bill Cosby with pale Bob Culp.

From the day Mort Werner, vice-president of programs for NBC, read the script, he expressed his determination to put it on his network. We brought his offer of a pilot to 20th Century–Fox and asked Bill Self if his company would like to become our partner. Bill took his own sweet time to read the script and make his decision, dragging his feet for almost two hours.

To cast my leads, I wanted a young, brand new pretty face to play Julia, but the network wanted a name. I was willing to compromise with Lena Horne, but Miss Horne was not to be compromised. Dave Tebet of NBC suggested Diahann Carroll. I did not know the lady or her work, so a meeting was arranged for lunch in the Beverly Hills Hotel's Polo Lounge. There I met Miss Carroll, who was chic, beautiful, warm and delightfully witty enough to overcome her proclivity for arriving a half-hour late, which, I was to find, was almost early for Di.

It was a frequent pleasure to be in business with her, and when Diahann went back to New York with a contract that made her an equal partner in *Mamma's Man*, I began assembling the rest of our cast while she earned headlines as the first black leading lady in a TV series. That pub-

Kanter and Diahann Carroll discussing the *Julia* TV show, 1968.

licity resulted in a plea from her friends James Baldwin and Harry Belafonte to change the name of *Mamma's Man* to refute the canard that black women dominated the males in their families.

"What do they suggest we call it?" I asked her representative, Martin Bregman, who answered, "*The Diahann Carroll Show.*"

"While I respect Baldwin's and Belafonte's points of view," I said, "this show is not about Diahann, it's about a woman named Julia, so that's what we'll call it. And please remind Di that her mission is to entertain, not to become the spokeswoman for her entire race. She's Julia Baker, not Joan of Dark."

Bernie Weisen, again my associate producer, interviewed platoons of 10 and 12 year olds whose parents swore they were six-year-old boys in our search for Corey and his white friend, Earl J. Waggedorn. We tested several. Among them was an under-six year old whose father had given him the wrong script to memorize. But little Marc Copage so enchanted all of us I asked him to learn the scene and come back the following day. John Copage said his son was a quick study who could learn the three pages in half an hour, which he did.

Red-haired, freckle-faced Michael Link, a toy Huck Finn, came into my office alone, wearing a Chiquita banana sticker on his nose. He was almost six, adorable, and while I never mentioned the sticker, he didn't either, and kept it on his nose throughout our interview. Later, we tested four boys and picked "Quick Study" and "Banana Nose."

For the crucial role of Julia's boss, a young agent named Mike Medavoy suggested Lloyd Nolan, a star who wanted to read my script before even considering an offer. He had, Mike said, been burned before and was twice cautious about another television job.

Nolan loved the script and breathed life into his role of Dr. Chegley. He and Diahann got along splendidly, even though Lloyd was so Republican we had to shoot around him when he went to Washington as the president's guest for Nixon's inauguration. Di was not.

With other regular cast members, Lurene Tuttle and Betty Beaird, we gathered in my temporary offices, formerly David O. Selznick's suite in Culver City, to rehearse the final draft of the pilot script.

As the cast sat down for the first reading, little Mike and Marc stood, nudging each other when their cues came up. They were letter perfect, which seemed to annoy Nolan, an ominous omen for the future, I thought.

After the reading, I approached Lloyd on a coffee break to ask if he had any comments. "Yes," the gentleman said. "Why'd you let those kids embarrass me by learning their lines?"

"Don't be ashamed, Lloyd. They had to memorize them because neither one of them can read yet."

"Oh! Of course," Nolan blushed. His reaction was a relief because when I signed him, an agent named Joe Narr warned me that Lloyd never learned his lines when he played in the detective series *Martin Kane*. In our second season of *Julia*, I asked Lloyd about that.

"Did you ever see *Kane*?" he asked. "I never learned a line of that dialogue lest it escape from my mouth and embarrass me in a social setting!"

When shooting was completed, the distinguished composer Elmer Bernstein added his music score and our pilot was screened for Mort Werner and his phalanx of networkers who flew in from New York to sit in judgment.

Their initial reaction was silence until I said, "Well? Who talks first?"

Diahann Carroll (center) gets her "Golden Globe" from Kanter as Lurene Tuttle wishes one for herself as well.

"You did," Bill Self said. "Now it's Mort's turn."

"It's okay," Mort said, whereupon a chorus of voices agreed that it was all right. "But it's not as funny as I thought it would be."

"No, not as funny," said the chorus. "The script was funnier."

"Can we make it funnier?" Mort asked.

"Funnier!" said the chorus.

Then Bill spoke. "Maybe we should add a laugh track," he said.

I had neglected to mention that I left out that ingredient that seemed so essential to other television comedies. Without the raucous laughter of an anonymous audience, many an executive is unable to tell what will amuse an audience and what won't.

"Yes," Mort said, "let's try a laugh track."

"Sure," I said, "you tell me how big a laugh—if any—do I drop in after Julia tells off the bigot. And at exactly what point and what volume of laugh I should insert at the end of the first act, where Corey and Earl J. Waggedorn have become friends and the white kid meets Julia for the first time.

"Earl says, 'You know something? Your mother's colored' and Corey said, 'Sure. So am I!' and Earl says, 'You are? Oh, boy!' and the two of them start wrestling like two puppies.

"Now, gentlemen," I said, "you tell me where the laughs are: 'Your mother's colored' ... 'So am I' ... 'You are?' ... or 'Oh, boy!'? And how big a laugh?"

There was more silence in the room until Mort said, in effect, "You win."

Fox's loquacious young salesman David Gerber carefully exposed *Julia* to General Foods, whose advertisers exulted when it was seen by a larger audience than any new show of the 1969-70 season. Even though some red-neck station managers refused to air it, their bigoted boycott lasted three weeks before they capitulated to public demand.

Julia enjoyed international celebrity and when the actors who dubbed our show in Japanese visited our set from Japan, Marc Copage refused to come out of his trailer to meet the Asian who dubbed Corey's dialogue because she was a woman.

Marc's mother had abandoned him and his older brother when Marc was an infant, so he seemed to have difficulty relating to women. When I accompanied him and his father to receive an award, the presenter asked him how he liked having such a pretty woman as Diahann Carroll as his mother and little Marc said, "She's not pretty. Before she gets her makeup on, she looks like a monkey!"

Copage and I cringed in embarrassment at what may have been the biggest laugh the boy ever got.

In the three seasons we were on the air, we employed many blacks both in front of and behind the camera. Several writers received their start with *Julia* and some their stop. One handsome young actor who had struck out trying to write for *Peyton Place* talked his way into my office to tell me he was miscast on that soap opera because he was a comedy writer. His name was Gene Boland and when I gave him a chance, he wrote several scripts with veteran Ben Gershman until he claimed Ben was a burden he could do without. He was mistaken.

Ben worked successfully with others while Boland's sorry attempts could have gotten him arrested for loitering in front of a typewriter.

One day he approached me on location and said, "You know, baby, I used to think all my troubles would be gone if I was white."

"Now that you are," I said, "you know that's a load of crap."

There were others who wrote well, such as the very literate Ferdinand Leon, a street-smart Harry Dolan and a lady named Blanche Franklin who wrote one good script, cashed her check and disappeared.

Lurene Tuttle, Milt Stark, Hal Kanter on the set of *Julia*. Milt's mustache was false, but he was a true friend.

Ezra Stone directed many *Julia* episodes and also brought us several African-American actors. One who made his debut on our show was Robert Guillaume, who became a good friend, and another was the former football player Fred Williamson, a showboat who later became a successful writer, director, producer and star of his own films.

Another gridiron great who worked with us was Nate Barragar, our unit manager and former All-American from USC. He asked me to write a small part for a personable young SC player so Nate could get him in the Screen Actors Guild and earn enough money to support his wife and stay in school. Nate assured me he would become a household name. For Nate's sake, I accommodated the young man who did indeed become a household name but, thankfully, not in mine. He was O. J. Simpson.

A much more talented man was Paul Winfield, whom I wanted to build as a leading man for Diahann until Herb Schlosser, NBC's West Coast program head, suggested I find an actor "who's better looking." Against my better judgment, I began the quest.

That's when Fred Williamson showed up to tell me he was the black

On location for *Julia* in Century City: Bernie Weisen (associate producer), Diahann Carroll, Hal Kanter. Bernie also directed several episodes when he wasn't smoking his pipe, which the kids didn't like to smell.

Clark Gable, which I sincerely believe he sincerely believed. Sports writer Mel Durslag quoted me in a story he wrote for *TV Guide* in which I said that if he could find a bottle large enough to contain Fred's ego, he'd need a redwood tree for a cork. When he read that, Fred congratulated me for recognizing the well-deserved truth.

To help sustain our ratings, I enticed several friends to appear on *Julia*. The first one I approached was Groucho Marx, who accused me of having an affair with Diahann and said the only reason he would come on the show was to find out if it was true and if not, would she consider going to bed with him instead.

Phil Silvers was a guest star one week and Don Ameche was another. I was so impressed with Don's knowledge of film, I talked him into becoming a director for one episode. Reluctantly, he agreed and did a fine job but when I offered him another script, he said he was going back in front of the camera.

Bob Hope came in one afternoon, knocked off a whole day's work in two hours for speedy director Ezra Stone and left everyone laughing.

Handsome Cesar Romero came in for one guest shot and came back several times as one of our favorite characters who, in our third season, we married off to Lurene Tuttle.

The elegant Romero told us that he was then 72. When a wizened 55-year-old prop man said he could hardly wait until he's 72 to look like that, Cesar fell off his chair laughing.

Baseball player Jim Piersall, comedian Benny Rubin, John McGiver and Nick Stewart, who had played Lightnin' on *Amos 'n' Andy*, worked for us.

Another star I persuaded to do a cameo role was also named Stewart, but was not related to Nick. This Stewart was my old friend, James, and his appearance evidently pleased the cautious gentleman enough to consider entertaining the possibility of maybe attempting to try the chances of finding a television series of his own!

That was just about the time my agents brought me an enticing deal to create new shows and feature films for Warner Bros. With Bernie now directing some *Julia* episodes and Bob Cinader acting as a competent story editor and Diahann fast losing interest in television, I moved my office and Dee Staley from Fox to Warner Bros., where I soon began another series with Stewart. Jim, not Nick.

"If you want to get to Hang-chou before Fang Li, feed gravel to his oxen."—Christopher Buckley

47. Feed Gravel to His Oxen

There was competition in the attempt to sign Jimmy Stewart to his first TV series in the '60s; after writing the screenplay of *Dear Brigitte* for him at Fox, I tried myself but failed. I had to wait until 1970 when Jimmy succumbed to a succulent offer from Warner Bros.

"What's Jimmy Stewart really like?" was the second question I was then most often asked, after "Have you got a job for me on the new Stewart show?"

"First," I answered the second question, "you better remember that he was a general in the United States Air Force—because *he* does."

James Stewart was probably the best motion picture actor who ever worked in films. He knew what he wanted, what he liked and what he didn't, what was good and what wasn't and while he could be obstinate, I found him unfailingly polite yet unfailingly forthright in expressing his opinion.

As dignified as he was, his wry sense of humor allowed him to respond to the esoteric nickname Bones without losing his dignity or his temper.

Herb Schlosser of NBC was elated to meet Jimmy. We had come with Warner Bros.' Jerry Leider to make a pitch to the star and his agents, who were then entertaining television proposals. Herb, who stopped only a few inches short of idolatry of his fellow Princeton alumnus, was eager to seize Jimmy for his network.

Stewart's agents seemed more disposed to a proposal from Universal for an hour drama than our half-hour comedy. I agreed with them that Jimmy would be better than anyone for the Universal project even though any number of actors would be adequate. However, there was no leading man who could hold a candle to Jimmy playing comedy—and situation comedy is the caviar of television.

My argument was bolstered by my idea for a show which appealed to Jim, and when we left his agents' offices, Leider was certain a decision would be made in our favor. Herb hoped so, but expressed his concern.

"Stewart looks old," he worried. "How old is he?"

"Late fifties," Jerry said.

"Very late fifties," I said. "Sixty-three!"

"How old will he photograph?" Herb asked.

"About 73," I said, tongue-in-cheek, and watched them both jump.

"Even if he wears a toupee?" Herb groaned.

"No matter how old he looks," I reminded them, "he's the only old-looking Jimmy Stewart in the world."

A few days later, Warner Bros. made a deal with Stewart, who became 1971's highest-paid TV actor at $33,333.33 per half-hour. I settled for less.

Even before I shot our first episode, Warners' TV sales executive, Charles McGregor, congratulated me. *Julia*, he said, was a huge hit in Japan and, on the basis of my name coupled with my globally adored star, he had just made the most lucrative foreign sales of *The Jimmy Stewart Show* in the history of Asian television!

Gratifying as that was, the predatory studio's bookkeeping never allowed Jim or me, who shared ownership of our show, to profit from any foreign or domestic sales. As close as I ever came to explaining how studios arrived at their bottom line was that they took the money that came in from the first and second runs, all foreign and syndicate sales, added them up and then kept it all.

For two years I had been writing a novel in my spare time and the week *Snake in the Grass* was published by Delacorte in 1971, I brought a copy to the studio, showing it to anyone with eyes. That day, Stewart came to my office to discuss the casting for our series, which NBC had bought even without making a pilot. I showed the book to Jim, who congratulated me and dashed out with it. He returned in a moment, grinning and said, "Thanks; I put it in my car."

"Bones," I said awkwardly, "that's the first copy off the press. I just wanted you to see it."

"Aww ... ch-cheeze," he sputtered, turning crimson, and loped back outside to fetch it. He apologized so profusely, I was equally embarrassed and autographed the book, insisting he accept it as a gift to him and Gloria.

He had come to talk to me about his wife. Jim thought she might be the ideal woman to play his TV mate. He asked me to come to their home and screen Jack Benny shows in which he and Gloria were guest stars.

Mrs. Stewart was an attractive, vivacious and intelligent non-professional with a keen sense of humor who probably could handle the role if we crafted it to accommodate her, so we made a screen test. Before we signed anyone, we tested all of our cast except John McGiver, for whom I

Hal Kanter, writer John Lee Mahin, and Jimmy Stewart.

had written a co-starring role which Jimmy welcomed; he had worked harmoniously with John earlier.

Gloria's test was adequate and I was happy to accept her. Jim and I both felt she would improve with experience and Gloria gamely welcomed the challenge. However, Mort Werner sent word from New York through Herb Schlosser that she was simply not acceptable to NBC and would therefore not appear on *The Jimmy Stewart Show*, which was to star James Stewart.

Jimmy accepted that decision but James never forgave the men who made it. He allowed to me that he would not work for them beyond that first season. His wife was played by the elegant Julie Adams, although I found a way to put Gloria on the tube in our first episode.

I wrote a script that explained how Jim's family had settled in our fictional small town. In a flashback, Jim played his own grandfather, Gloria his grandmother. He was funny and she was charming. But he was adamant that I rewrite his grandfather's character, an illiterate coward who made a fortune. Jim did not object to his illiteracy, but he was damned if his granddaddy was a coward!

"Jim," I argued, "this isn't your family we're having fun with. This is fiction, not fact!"

"What's fiction to you is fact to an audience," he said, "and when fact makes fiction look bad, fuck fact!"

Yes, sir, General! Rewrite coming up!

Earlier, while assembling a crew, a veteran assistant director named Dave Silver gave me a helpful caution about working with Stewart. "He's the most punctual star you'll ever see," Dave said. "If he has a 7 A.M. call, he'll be on the set, in makeup at 7 and you better be ready to shoot no later than 7:05."

Jimmy surprised me when I told him that I was thinking of hiring Dave as a first assistant and he said no. Jim also said he wanted Frank Westmore to do his makeup, but Frank tried to take advantage of their friendship and made such excessive demands, Jim surprised me again by saying we should find someone else.

That surprised Frank, too, so he came to terms we could all live with. Then Jim told me why he would not work with Dave Silver. Years before, Dave was an assistant on a Western they were shooting in Arizona. The location was an hour's drive from Yuma and Jim had to get up at five in order to be on the set by seven, but was not called for his first shot until after eight. This happened twice. Dave would never work with Stewart again.

I had hoped Gloria would work again following her brief appearance on our first episode, but she occupied herself with her favorite charities, animals and the Los Angeles Zoo. When she went off on an African safari, Jimmy sheepishly confided that he was so lonely he took a flirtatious bit player who expressed her worship into his dressing room. Just as he was about to yield to her libidinous invitation, she purred, "I've wanted you ever since I saw you play Sgt. York!"

"Coop never knew what he missed," Jimmy grinned, referring to his pal Gary Cooper, who played Sgt. York. If Bones ever encouraged another liaison, he never mentioned it to me. He may have amused Coop with that anecdote but I doubt that he shared it with Gloria, even though she may have laughed. Perhaps *because* she would have.

The last time I saw her she was laughing. We were guests at Bob Hope's ninetieth birthday party, where Gloria was charitable enough to contribute a laugh to a rare *bon mot* from Gerald Ford.

During production on our series, we employed many mutual friends and favorites such as Arthur O'Connell, Gloria DeHaven, Cesar Romero, Jackie Coogan, Eddie Quillan and Nita Talbot. Jimmy even found Beulah Bondi in Colorado and brought her out of retirement to play his mother in an episode written by John Lee Mahin.

My daughter Abigail took her first steps toward retirement when she joined the Screen Actors Guild and played a variety of roles. A fine actress, Abbe also became a dialogue coach during one vacation from college in Ohio, where she studied theater at Antioch. Donna was then working as a TV journalist and Lisa was teaching second grade minority children in Los Angeles' inner city schools. Lisa had married handsome fireman Anthony Shafer in a beautiful backyard wedding that was attended by our widely scattered family.

Before we wrapped production on the *Stewart Show*, Jim and I chartered a Santa Monica boat to take our company out for a day of deep sea fishing. Jim arrived carrying a small boy's rod and reel. I offered him some of my best tackle but he elected to stick with his own and, of course, caught the most fish.

"Do you think," actress Ellen Geer whispered to Westmore, "even the fish recognize him?"

When we completed our twenty-fourth episode, I knew it was to be our final one. Jimmy remembered NBC's brusque manner of rejecting Gloria and when he finally attempted another TV series, it was a 90-minute drama for CBS, written by my passionate friend, David Karp.

John Y. Brown, Jr., wanted to talk to me. He was the politically ambitious entrepreneur whose Col. Sanders' Kentucky Fried Chicken had become as ubiquitous as heartburn. On his nickel, I flew to New York to meet with Brown and Robert Strauss, the boisterous Texas lawyer who chaired the Democratic party. They wanted me to work on a national telethon to raise money for the upcoming elections. No political fund raiser of the magnitude they envisioned had ever been attempted, so they were seeking advice on how to go about it.

During dinner at "21," I gave them my thoughts but turned down their offer to produce the show. I suggested others they might interview, including Barry Shear, who was directing a film in New York at that time.

Barry was full of ideas and bowled over Strauss, Brown and their staffs in a meeting the next day, but he, too, turned down their request to produce the marathon. Politicians admired show business more than show business admired them.

I told Strauss, a man I found amusing, intelligent and devilish, and Brown, a man I found naked in his thirst for celebrity, that I would help whomever they found to produce their extravaganza when I returned from Europe. They engaged the soft-spoken, industrious, independent producer of TV variety programs, Bob Banner.

After I wrote the forty-fourth Academy Awards show with Leonard Spigelgass and Bill Ludwig and once again performed the audience warm-up for producer Howard Koch, Doris and I flew to London with, as I mentioned earlier, Oona and Charlie Chaplin. While they went on to Switzerland, we remained in London to see some shows, visit museums and galleries with our friends Barbara and Max Wilk, have dinner with NBC correspondent Ray Scherer, Barbara Eisenhower and S. J. Perelman, spend a day with Donna and Denis O'Dell at their country home and dine with Mark Nichols, the Wilks and Ken Shipman, who invited us to sail on his yacht with him to Nice. Instead we continued our itinerary to Amsterdam for more museums, Dutch paintings, food and windmills.

In Paris, Doris took great pleasure guiding me through my first visit to the city she had visited with Abbe. We were entertained by the charming Madame Marie-Blanche Pathé, the daughter of the pioneer French filmmaker, and her brother Peter.

The city was more fun than Lisbon, our next stop where our hotel was luxurious, the food poor and where every other Portuguese we met on the street tried to sell us the same watch.

From Lisbon to Nice, we checked into the Negresco, where I had worked for a week with Mel Frank on the Danny Kaye–Sophia Loren script that was never made. After a day of shopping with Doris, we returned to receive a call from Bob Banner in Hollywood. Regarding the Democratic Party telethon, he was checking to make sure I would participate. I looked forward to it, because by that time I had seen enough museums, menus and money changers.

We continued to travel to Florence, Venice and Rome, where I got another call from Bob Banner, who was then in New York and anxious to meet me there as soon as possible. We were booked to sail from Naples the following day, so I told Banner I could see him a week from the following Sunday.

At dinner in our Naples hotel rooftop *ristorante*, we encountered an acquaintance from Hollywood, actor Jay Novello. He and his wife were dining with their friends, Mr. and Mrs. Dan Cohen, who would also be sailing home on the *Michelangelo* with us. Our voyage was made more pleasant by the friendship we established with Jay and his wife Pat, and Dan and his wife (who was known as "Your Honor" to those who appeared before Judge Maxine K. Duberstein of the Supreme Court of New York). It was the beginning of a friendship that has flourished ever since.

When we arrived in New York, we received courtesy of the port, thanks to Maxine, and were rushed through immigration ahead of others. Then I discovered one of my bags was missing. By the time it was found, we were among the last to leave the ship.

We checked in at the Plaza Hotel and Bob Banner called almost immediately. I went to his suite at the Park Lane to hear his plans for the telethon and meet some of the people I would be working with, writer Lou Solomon and political expert John Stewart.

We returned to Los Angeles and I started working with Banner and his associate Carolyn Raskin in her office. Lou Solomon joined us and the writing team of Bernie Kukoff and Jeff Harris. Ruth Berle volunteered to cast celebrities for whom we wrote speeches, comedy bits and pleas for cash.

Dick Dunlap was sent to Florida to direct celebrities who would appear from Miami Beach. I was elected to accompany him as the head writer and Doris came along to help me. I needed all the help I could get because our production headquarters at the Doral Hotel was complete chaos.

While most of the big name politicians were in Hollywood, I was asked to provide material for Wilbur Mills, Larry O'Brien, Joan Kennedy and film stars Shirley MacLaine, Lorne Greene, Marlo Thomas, Jack Carter, Betty Furness, Andy Williams, Bess Myerson and Alan King, who was the Florida emcee.

Evidently, the telethon was successful enough for the Democrats to do it again and they asked me to work with the executive producer Brown and Strauss engaged to replace Bob Banner, who chose other ways to celebrate Democracy. His name was Nick Vanoff; he was more organized and I was happy to work with him.

Among others Nick hired was Tom Whedon, a gifted comedy writer with whom I enjoyed working, and an officious production manager named Eric Leiber with whom I did not.

Eric was neither the first, worst nor the last person I found difficult to work with, because I foolishly went on to work with Norman Lear again.

He engaged me as executive producer of Yorkin and Lear's already successful *All in the Family*. In that position, I hired Milt Josefsberg, Mel Tolkin and Larry Rhine, the three writers who would stay with the show long after I left it.

"Life is only the overture; stand by for the big show." — Fred Allen

48. *The Big Show*

The day I completed the preceding chapter was July 2, 1997, and I planned to call Jimmy Stewart to ask Bones if he felt like accepting my long-standing invitation to come out of the house for lunch. But before I made that call, I received the distressing news that he had died that morning.

Jimmy's death began three years earlier, when Gloria died. I never knew a man who loved his wife more or was more dependent on her for enjoyment of life. He seemed almost anxious to join her for what I'm sure he believed, along with Fred Allen, was much more to come.

Thoughts about Jim evoked memories of my father, who had recovered from a severe stroke in 1970 and was able to join Mother on a previous visit with us. They both enjoyed meeting Jimmy, who was gracious and charming the afternoon they spent on our set. And Jim enjoyed Dad's stories of his recovery, particularly the time a young nurse's aide came to his hospital room to take a urine specimen. Dad indicated a small glass of apple juice on his nightstand and said, "Here it is — but let me run it through one more time," then, to the girl's dismay, drank it.

On St. Patrick's Day, 1973, the bright flame of my father's fun flickered and, alone in his New York apartment, he died. Mother was in Flower 5th Avenue hospital with severe back trouble, from which she never fully recovered, and was unable to attend Dad's funeral. Mother lived for a dozen years more, confined to a wheelchair, but at 93, was still as alert — and as stately — as a lioness.

Stewart's death brought gloomy memories of other colleagues like Freddie Prinze, the young meteoritic comedian who took his life the hard way with a bullet through his brain.

Then it was Elvis, who did it gradually, but too soon, and Groucho Marx, who took longer, but too long to suit him. Plagued by illness the last few years of his long life, Groucho said he was "waiting to get this foolishness over with."

But George Burns relished his even longer life, still smoking cigars, sipping martinis and reminiscing about sex throughout his nineties.

Left to right: Billy Barty, Groucho Marx, and Hal Kanter rehearsing what was to be one of Groucho's last TV appearances, a special for Bob Hope called *Joys*.

Bing Crosby left suddenly. Quickly. On a golf course in Spain. Once the most popular singer in the world, Bing finally got what he had wanted for the two decades I knew him: to be left alone.

Sheldon Leonard went reluctantly because he had things yet to do at 90, among which was waiting for me to complete this manuscript, so he could suggest improvements.

Years ago, Sheldon invited me to work with him developing a TV comedy adventure series that he would shoot in exotic locations but I was too involved with movies at that time and thus missed participating in his gold mine called *I Spy*.

When I did return to TV, I was lured back by Carroll O'Connor. He and Nancy had been our friends before Carroll had enough weight to throw around. Now that he was the heavyweight champion of the tube, he was able to make demands of his putative bosses, Bud Yorkin and Norman Lear. Among his demands in 1976 was a new director — Paul Bogart — and a new producer — me — for his hit series, *All in the Family*.

Norman and I met on a neutral battleground, agreed to let bygones go by and struck a deal for me to assume the duties of executive producer of the show.

January 20, 1978: Studio City, California. Bing Crosby congratulates Hal Kanter when he received an award from the Pacific Pioneer Broadcasters.

At CBS, Lear's tiny lieutenant, Al Burton, made me comfortable in a suite of offices that Norman visited the next day to make sure I had everything I needed. Then he struck a resonant chord when he tried, with transparent awkwardness, to change my position.

"You know," he said, as if it had just occurred to him, "Carroll is dying to produce this show, so we better fill that spot now, because he can't produce. He just wants another credit on the screen, so maybe you should take that job before he demands it."

"But if I become producer," I asked with what naivete I could muster, "won't he want the exec credit?"

"No," Norman said. "I'll have that."

"That's not the deal we have, Norman, so forget it. We'll make Lou Derman the producer."

"Lou writes. He can't produce!"

"Anybody can produce!" (A statement I still believe to be true.)

Our debate ended when Norman allowed Lou to co-produce with another writer, Bill Davenport. With Milt Josefsberg, Mel Tolkin and Larry Rhine, we met our first challenge, the new season's opening show, without having the character of Gloria to write for. Sally Struthers, the actress who played that pivotal role, was a holdout for more money until Norman made his peace with her.

Lear, my earlier adversary, seemed to have grown and become a capable executive; his demands for improving every draft of our scripts forced all of us to work harder and write better.

By the time we satisfied Lear, who hovered over every move I made, the first script we brought to the table for rehearsal was a gem. Paul Bogart was pleased, Carroll satisfied and Jean Stapleton elated, but Rob Reiner, who regarded me as an interloper, rephrased his opening lines from our first reading.

Bogart looked at me but said nothing. Nor did O'Connor, Stapleton or the writers, who were all frowning. After the second line change Rob made, I interrupted and asked him to please read what's on the paper and to give us all a chance to decide if anything needed rephrasing, rewriting or regurgitation.

Rob finished reading in a sullen pout and then left the studio. Carroll said Rob always had line changes and Lou Derman said it was about time somebody said something to him because Norman never did and Jean said he's a good boy and he'll come back in a minute and Carroll said we should start with Rob's changes and then make a few of his own he wanted.

Rob did not come back. Norman called to ask me what I had said to Rob that upset him so, he had gone home. He asked me to call and apologize to him. I said I would and hoped Rob would apologize to all of us.

I did. Rob didn't. It became increasingly clear to me how *All in the Family* was written: Six writers slaved over several drafts of each episode before the script went down to the rehearsal stage, where Jean Stapleton invariably praised their work to the writers, while Carroll, Rob and Sally Struthers rewrote it all to suit themselves, their egos and their director.

"Bernie West used to do the audience warmup," Lear told me. "Think you can handle that?" I could, I thought, so he said he'd stand by and let me bring him out to introduce the cast. We did two shows. The first was the dress rehearsal, taped before dinner, the second followed dinner and any changes made between shows to improve it.

Our first "dress" got such laughs, the show did not require adjustments, but the warmup did. I had amused the audience for ten minutes before I introduced Norman, who lectured them for five, then asked if anyone had any questions.

"Yes," asked a man in the first row. "Can we have that other guy back?"

Norman's reaction to that was as nervous as a trout in a washing machine. At that moment I knew that he and I were destined to get along like Caesar, who knew no superiors, and Pliny, who knew no equals. It would be a hopeless collaboration and after six splendid episodes, painfully arrived at, I confronted him with the admission that our relationship was too uncomfortable to continue. He felt the same and confirmed that he had, in fact, already spoken to Carroll about replacing me.

My sly friend O'Connor obviously did not object but had not mentioned that to me, perhaps feeling my departure would allow him to step into that spot. In time, he did and eventually killed Edith, the character Jean Stapleton played, said good-bye to Rob and Sally, changed the name of the show to *Archie's Place* and ruled it like a tyrant.

Rob, of course, went on to even greater glory in films as a writer, director, producer, actor and executive who is very kind to his mother.

The Hollywood Reporter's Will Tusher cornered me at a party to ask why I left Lear's *Family* and I rashly said, "I'm too old and too rich to put up with that shit." Tusher printed that verbatim and I got clippings from around the world with cheers from many people I had forgotten, or never knew. To some, I was a hero; to others, a fool. I regarded my position as a hero to fools.

I went on to NBC as a tyrant myself on *Chico and the Man*, a then-floundering comedy that starred Jack Albertson and Freddie Prinze. It was the year series creator Jimmy Komack added Della Reese to the cast that included Scatman Crothers. Scat was a former musician who brought to the show a willingness to try anything for a laugh or smoke anything for a high.

For years, Scatman repeated a joke I gave him to use at a benefit: "I could've been white, but my Momma outran the dude."

Chico's ratings rebounded that season and Della became such a hit with the audience, Komack asked me and Michael Morris, the show's veteran story editor, to write a pilot to spinoff for a series of her own. Mike and I had written several reasonably good *Chico* episodes, so I undertook the task of working to expand on the character he, Komack and I had created for Della.

That was one of the many pilots I have written over the years, alone and in collaboration with others which, if they were not stillborn, never managed to get out of the maternity ward.

In the case of *Della*, the pilot was lost when Freddie fired that fatal shot at 4 A.M. on the morning of January 28, 1977. He died at 1 P.M. the next day and around 3, Jack Albertson called to beseech me to write Freddie's eulogy for him.

The next morning I telephoned Jack to read what I had written. He cried. At Freddie's funeral in Forest Lawn, Jack broke down again while reading the eulogy to an overflow crowd of mourners. Tony Orlando took over the services and as I sat there, thinking how much Freddie disliked Orlando, Scatman whispered to me, "Freddie's whirlin'."

Two weeks later, I was writing another eulogy that made me cry. My dear friend, Jack Wormser, had giggled his last.

During this period of mourning, we continued writing comedy — the Della pilot — and the rest of the *Man* series *sans* Chico. Jimmy and Paul Mason, his associate, were resolved to find a younger *chicano* to replace Freddie and we continued to assign scripts to George Bloom and Beverly Bloomberg while Mike and I rewrote others.

As gifted as Jack Albertson was, and as sweet, Freddie's gruesome death seemed to change him; he was less joyous and more argumentative about his scripts. Jimmy, too, had problems with his other shows and became testy with all of us. He cheered up when the new little Chico worked out well enough for the show to be renewed for another season.

I chose not to return because there were other things I wanted to do. Among them was to escort my daughter Abbe to the patio in our backyard, around the swimming pool, to a gazebo under which our friend, Judge Joe Chandler, made Michael Jaye my legally wedded son-in-law.

Michael was an advertising copy writer who wrote songs on the side and who now is a songwriter who writes ad copy on the side.

Before their June marriage, Doris and I returned to Savannah to help the city celebrate renaming their Civic Center auditorium the Johnny Mercer Theater. After the wedding, I wrote several specials, more pilots and a brief series of hour comedies for George Schlatter called *Just for Laughs*, which is all we got, when what we needed was an audience.

It was on that aborted series that we first saw the potential of an intelligent young comedian from Boston named Jay Leno and a merry-andrew from the Los Angeles Dodgers, Tommy Lasorda.

Despite guests like those and many other of somebody's favorites, the critics who found fault with our show were equally divided into two categories: those who watched it and those who turned it off.

I was turned on by an offer from Hector Crawford, brought to me by my friend, Mort Fine, of a trip to Melbourne. There I directed Australia's first indigenous comedy, written by Terry Stapleton and starring a superb cast who spoke what I assumed to be English.

"If you liked Lincoln, Nebraska, in 1938, you're going to love Melbourne, Australia, in 1974."—Mort Fine

49. *You're Going to Love Melbourne*

Doris and I found our friends Down Under to be warm, hospitable and a choice audience for jokes like my observation, "Australia seems full of crime, pollution, dirty politics, juvenile delinquency, alcoholism, pornography, obscenity, murder, mayhem and madness—all the things that make America great!"

We also found good friends in the Crawford family and the Stapletons, Terry and his beautiful wife Ann. Terry had written a sparling comedy script called *The Last of the Australians* and was amenable to most of the changes I felt should be made. His excellent cast, headed by Alwyn Kurtz, Rosie Sturgis and Maury Fields, embraced me and our pilot went off with "no worries, mate."

It was their first attempt to tape before a live audience, and even with the primitive tape equipment available to the Crawfords at that time, the experience was more enjoyable than the pilot I shot in Rome with state-of-the-art film equipment. *Three Coins in the Fountain* may have looked better, but it never went to series. My Aussie show was sold to a network immediately after we delivered the rough edit.

The Crawfords asked me to stay on to help Terry with the first 13 episodes ("eps" they called them) but I had other obligations at home, so recommended Larry Marks to help with the writing. My neurotic friend Marks had a conspicuous list of writing credits and loved to travel in a vain attempt to get away from himself. (I once asked a mutual friend how Larry was and Ed Jurist answered, "I don't know. I have been relieved of his friendship.")

Larry, a huge man, took his tiny wife Nora to spend a year in Melbourne, helping Terry turn out several successful shows. The year after their return, I, in what turned out to be a case of erroneous euphoria, teamed up with Larry to write a comedy pilot for Paramount. While I agreed with his concept that comedy comes out of conflict, I never felt that

Kanter and Terry Stapleton, who wrote a comedy script called *The Last of the Australians*, in Melbourne, Australia.

the conflict should start in the office while you're writing. It was our first collaboration and I found it so agonizing, it was our last. Fortunately, the studio shelved the project.

It was during this time we built a beach house in Malibu. Our architect, A. Thomas Torres, was also our builder and found ways to cut corners to such an extent, we went way over our budget.

But the two-story house near Big Rock was a spacious aerie nestled over waves crashing below and Doris would have been elated with it had not the kitchen floor sloped seaward and her bathroom sink been built so high she had to stagger to her toes to reach the faucet. Tom claimed the floor was level and said it was our imagination, so we imagined he would not receive the last installment of our fee until he made corrections.

Donna lived there for a year, then we rented it to a French couple who rapidly multiplied into an army of foreign students. The following year, we sold the house at a sizable profit, which Jim Harper, our business manager, invested in desert real estate, wherewith we promptly lost our ass and Jim two clients.

Before Donna moved into our beach pad, she had been producing the evening news at KING-TV in Seattle, where we visited her the week the Seattle Mariners baseball team played their first American League game. Danny Kaye was one of the owners of the Seattle club. Their first opponents were the Angels, which were owned by Gene Autry.

The afternoon of the game, I was in the lobby of the Olympic Hotel when I saw Autry sitting with Don Drysdale, who was then broadcasting the Angels games. I thought I would have some fun.

"Gene!" I called. "Don! What are you guys doing up here?"

"The ball game!" Don said, surprised at my naivete. "Tonight's our season opener." And Gene asked, "What the hell are you doing here?"

"I came up for the game, too," I said, "but it's a sell-out, so it's lucky I ran into you. Have you got an extra ticket?"

"Jesus Christ, no," the cowboy said, patting his pockets. "You got any, Don?"

"No," Don said. "There's not one to be had."

"Well, maybe I'll just have to come up to your room and watch it with you, Gene."

"My *room*?" Gene said, alarmed. "I'm not going to watch my ball game in my god-damn room!"

"Oh, that's right," I said. "You own the team. Why don't I go with you to the ballpark?"

Autry squirmed and said, "Too late, Hal, I got a box full of V.I.P.s coming to the game."

"Well, maybe I can sit in the booth with Don."

"Hell, no," Drysdale said. "There's six other guys in there now."

"Well, in that case," I said, "I'll just have to sit in Danny Kaye's box and root for the Mariners this season."

I wished them luck and went chuckling back up to our room to get ready to join Donna's KING colleague, Bob Royer, who had invited me to be his guest at the Kingdome for the game. Bob's brother Charles, who worked with Donna as a political commentator, had resigned from KING-TV to run for mayor of Seattle. He had a block of seats and a busload of campaign workers whom he was treating to the game. The Mariners lost, but Charlie won.

I never became an Angels fan, but I continued to be a devout Dodgers follower, thanks to the glossy voice and velvet vocabulary of Vin Scully, the sports announcer who consistently comes closest to perfection. When Cedars-Sinai Hospital paid a tribute to Scully, I had the honor to be the master of ceremonies and introduced, among others, a man who "must have a sense of humor because he's talking about running for president." That man was the Scullys' neighbor, Ronald Reagan.

As we were leaving the affair, Reagan stopped us to congratulate me on my handling of the evening and asked if I would write some lines for his campaign rhetoric. I declined on the grounds that I was a Democrat.

"So was I once," Ron grinned.

In retrospect, perhaps I should have written for him. I wrote political humor for Adlai Stevenson, Walter Mondale, Henry Jackson, Hubert Humphrey, Jerry Brown, Lloyd Bentsen and a few others who lost their bids for the presidency. I also contributed humor to Bobby Kennedy, who might have won, and Jimmy Carter, who did.

Between other assignments, I helped George Stevens, Jr., salute two recipients of the American Film Institute Lifetime Achievement Awards. The first was Henry Fonda and the second was Alfred Hitchcock. Among the many stars Stevens enlisted for the Fonda tribute was Lucille Ball.

Knowing Lucy, I thought we could have fun if she played a movie fan whose favorite star is Hank Fonda. George endorsed the notion and we called Lucy to get her approval. She laughed at the idea and told us to have the script at her house when she got back from Las Vegas, where she was just heading to a backgammon tournament. She must have lost; when she returned, she read my droll monologue and called George in a rage. "Who wrote this crap?" she demanded. "I'm no damned housewife from Wichita! I'm a star! How dare you ask me to do this shit!"

George signaled me to get on the phone with them and try to mollify the lady. She demanded we both report to her house for a discussion. When we hung up, George, still in shock, asked me if Lucy drank — or had *we* been drinking? The answer was both. She could drive others to drink.

I wrote another spot before George and I were admitted to Lucy's home (across the street from Jimmy Stewart's) by Gary Morton, who said Lucy would be down in a few Scotch and sodas. When she did appear under a cloud of cotton candy pink hair, I apologized for our "misunderstanding" and offered her my new pages. She read them aloud and said, "Now, that sounds more like me, baby."

"Can't you toss in a couple of laughs?" Gary asked and Lucy gave him a look that sent him out of the room.

Perhaps, in the wee horizontal hours of the morning, Gary convinced her to get at least one laugh because Lucy had a change of heart again and accepted a funny line or two.

Preparing the Hitchcock tribute afforded me the joy of spending time with the incandescent Ingrid Bergman, a woman with whom I could have easily fallen in love. In fact, I did. I called Doris from Ingrid's hotel room and told her I'd be a few weeks late for dinner but that I could be found wherever Ingrid Bergman was.

The day of the show, I was found in Alfred Hitchcock's suite at the Beverly Hilton. He had invited me up to thank me for his acceptance speech, which he said he would read as written. Herb Steinberg, Universal's public relations maven and Hitchcock's temporary baby sitter, warned me not to drink in his presence lest he be tempted to fill his generous stomach before the banquet.

Mr. Hitchcock and I exchanged anecdotes for an hour before we went downstairs to rehearse with the cue cards that director Marty Pasetta had prepared. Marty asked Hitch to wear his tuxedo and astutely taped a good reading, filling the seats behind him with dress extras. Hitch returned to his suite and, it seems, to some wine an admiring waiter had smuggled to him behind Steinberg's back.

When the time came to respond to the plaudits heaped upon him that evening, Hitchcock managed to rise and begin reading his speech, then abruptly plopped down where he could no longer see the cue cards. Those who thought he had premeditated that sudden gesture laughed, but those of us who knew otherwise began to pray that he could extemporize a graceful or even a logical ending. He managed to rise from his chair again to find his place on the cue cards, then sank down again to recall another line or two of mine before he ended with one of his own. After George and Marty edited the tribute that aired on CBS, observant viewers noted that Hitchcock sat, stood, sat and stood — and when sitting, the people behind him were not the same as those behind him when he stood.

Otherwise, the show went smoothly, with Ingrid as hostess introducing Cary Grant and many other of Hitchcock's internationally recognized stars.

Not all film stars are. When I went to China in the winter of 1982, I discovered there were people who had never heard of Ingrid, Cary, Hank Fonda or any of America's icons, except for two.

I was in the People's Republic with two other Americans, producer Bruce Kerner and journalist John Peer Nugent. We were engaged by Tom Sarnoff to prepare an ambitious trio of TV specials, an adventure to star Danny Kaye, a variety show and a documentary of the Chinese railways.

During our 7,000-mile journey on their rail system, our host in the city of Nanjing was an official who expressed interest in a small pocket knife I had brought along. It was a gift from Bing Crosby, inscribed with Christmas greetings and bearing his caricature. Our Communist host was intrigued to learn, through our interpreter, that exchanging gifts is a custom of our Christmas season. He asked why a man would put his picture on a gift. Who is he?

Somewhere in China: John Peter Nugent is studying a newspaper; Hal Kanter is listening to Mr. Lu telling him he (John) should be studying diplomacy.

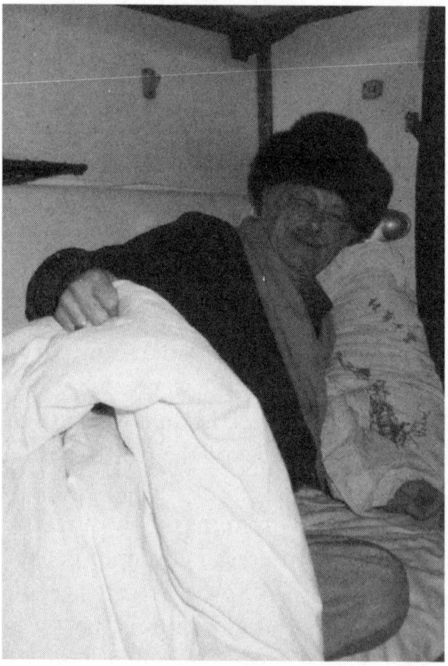

How I slept one winter night in China in a railroad compartment.

"A great actor and singer," I replied. "Bing Crosby." The Chinese in our party looked puzzled, including Mr. Lu, our interpreter. They had never heard of Bing. From then on, I made it a point to uncover which of our film stars were known in the People's Republic in 1982. That handcrafted survey disclosed that the only two stars most Chinese could name were Charlie Chaplin and Mickey Mouse!

In Kweilin, one of the world's most beautiful scenic areas, our hosts served a dish Nugent, Kerner and I had never encountered but which was exceptionally tasty. Helping myself to a second portion, I asked what it was.

"Wild game," Mr. Lu translated. When Kerner took another

Top: **John Peer Nugent and Hal Kanter in a Chinese zoo on their trip to the People's Republic.** ***Bottom:*** **Bruce Kerner, Kanter's traveling companion on the 7,000-mile rail trip.**

piece from the huge platter, Mr. Lu said, "Mr. Bruce is the lucky one. He has the tail!"

Our chewing stopped simultaneously. The end of the tail quivered from Kerner's lips as his jaws locked and Nugent asked, "Precisely what wild game is this?"

Lu engaged in an animated discussion with our hosts before he turned back to Nugent and smiled.

"Rat," he said.

Nausea *can* be instantaneous.

Tom Sarnoff invested a lot of money in the China projects which, to my knowledge, are still available for development because he and his late associate, George Cahan, were left holding the bag their Sino-American backers emptied of money.

However, my investment of time and energy provided me with priceless memories, knowledge and good friends in Bruce and JoAnn Kerner.

On the morning of June 12, 1984, Lisa Kanter Shafer checked into Santa Monica Hospital and around six that evening, via Caesarean section, Kaleigh Megan Shafer joined our family, weighing eight pounds, 15 ounces, making Anthony David Shafer the second happiest man in the cosmos. The happiest was the man who said he would never be the kind of boastful grandfather he invariably derided. But that was before he held that precious, beautiful, alert infant in his arms.

At that moment, I became a cliché.

"If you live long enough, eventually you'll be wrong about everything."—Russell Baker

50. If You Live Long Enough

I will never forget 1987 and the good Lord knows I've tried. So have the others.

Sid Smith, a personable, gregarious director, had a production company with three partners, Chris Hart, Pam Rosser and Larry Patterson. They gave it the acronym Harps and had the television rights to Kaufman and Hart's *You Can't Take It with You.* Sid asked me to write and produce a pilot. Because I loved the property, I liked Sid and felt they offered a civil contract, I rashly went to work for four executive producers, all of whom answered to their sponsor's representative, Procter & Gamble's Jack Wishard, and none of whom agreed on anything.

The only thing we all did agree on was casting Harry Morgan as our star. Harry was the most talented, cooperative and consistently pleasant actor for whom I have ever written. From *About Mrs. Leslie* and co-starring in *Dragnet* to his leading role as Grandpa Vanderhof, Harry never delivered anything but his best, which was always superb.

However, despite Chris Hart's attempt to emulate his father, the apple of Moss Hart's eye fell far from the tree. Instead of relying on him for any viable contribution to the scripts, I brought in reliable Milt Josefsberg and two refreshing young writers, Steve Barker and Daryl Busby. In time, we augmented the staff with veteran Larry Rhine and a number of freelancers of various ages, sexes, colors and dispositions, all of whom contributed to the constant confusion fomented by our producers, sponsors and directors, who were getting conflicting suggestions from me and some inept, hostile executives who were ruining my health.

To be fair, I admit that I was not the most tactful diplomat in trying to protect my staff; my scorn for several of my antagonists was as palpable as an earthquake.

Doris, who had written scripts for *Valentine's Day, Chico and the Man* and *Julia*, came to my rescue with one of our best and last episodes, but it

The set of *You Can't Take It with You.* The front row is me and the cast. Those behind us are our producers.

was too late. The damage, as I was to find out, was done. Only my admiration, loyalty and affinity for Harry Morgan kept me from changing my occupation.

Aches and pains are the language your body uses to tell you something. I devoutly prayed mine would shut up.

I thought it had for a few quiescent months after *You Can't Take It with You* faded to black. But then one Sunday morning in 1988, I went down to breakfast where Doris was already at the table, cheerful as usual. Before I had my coffee, which I no longer drink, I could never stand cheerful. I didn't even want to see a box of Cheerios on the breakfast table. Or Rice Krispies. I dislike any food that provides its own soundtrack. Dry toast. Celery. Radishes. Beans.

Doris greeted me with a few bars of "Oh, What a Beautiful Morning" and I grunted something I thought was, "And a good morning to you, too, Mary Sunshine." Concern replaced cheer to question if I was feeling well, still full of sleep … or what?

I stammered that I was fine, grunted that I was awake and where in hell was the orange juice? Doris didn't understand a stammer or a grunt. Neither of us knew it then, but I was displaying a classic case of aphasia.

When my deficiency in communicating continued — a condition alien to my garrulous self — I fell silent. Doris was sufficiently alarmed to call our family doctor, Jerry Schaffer, a man who was licensed to practice medicine in some states.

Jerry recognized the symptoms of a mild stroke and instructed Doris to get me in bed for a day of rest. He would see me at his office the following morning.

My efforts to converse with my wife frustrated me and frightened her. Doris couldn't understand what I was saying and I wasn't able to make myself understood. For over 50 years, it seemed to me that she could read my mind. Now she couldn't read even my lips.

Early Monday, Schaffer hurried me into Encino hospital for a complete check-up by a team of so-called specialists — many of whom were medical school graduates. Two of them gave me advice that could have cashed in my Veterans Insurance, were it not for my wife and daughters, who insisted on the second opinions that brought me to the UCLA Medical Center.

By then I knew what had happened: It was a playback of my father's stroke. I remembered how I cried when I flew to his hospital and saw that tall, handsome man, temporarily crippled, bravely smiling and trying to communicate with me.

Dad survived that stroke and, through long, painful therapy, he regained his speech and his mobility without ever losing his sense of humor.

Lying in my hospital bed, I invoked the laughter we shared over the years. I needed those memories because my check-up resulted in some unwelcome news. An X-ray revealed a spot on my lung that had not been there six months earlier.

As late as it was to heed my doctor's and my family's pleas to give up cigarettes, I stopped smoking so suddenly, I left skid marks on the linoleum. Further tests by specialists at UCLA confirmed the spot to be malignant.

Before I could have any cancer treatment, I had to recover from my stroke. Remarkable Marlys Meckler, a speech and language pathologist, began working with me from my first day in the hospital.

Ms. Meckler said that my progress in regaining my language skills and reading comprehension was remarkable, enhanced, no doubt, by my sense of humor and my inherent optimism. I had no doubts that I would recover.

During that time, Donna and Abbe investigated the Wellness Community in Santa Monica, a non-profit organization that helps cancer patients and their families through the battle for survival. We attended an open house at the Community and were impressed with their philosophy and their goals.

The lunch bunch mentioned on the first page of my book, Beverly Hills, circa 1996: Around the table from left to right are Sheldon Leonard, Charles Isaacs, Seaman Jacobs, Hal Kanter, Austin Kalish and Aaron Ruben.

Doris and I applied and were assigned to groups that met in separate rooms every Thursday night from seven to nine, me with fellow patients and she with family members. I had never been in any kind of therapy session before and was not prepared for the great comfort, camaraderie, knowledge and emotional support that I got from my group.

Despite a bumbling facilitator the wonderful group members helped me face the procedure I was to undergo. My wife and children, the group and I teamed with my doctors to combat the enemy called cancer.

The renowned chief of the pulmonary department at UCLA Medical Center, Dr. E. Carmack Holmes, a personable lung surgeon whose native Tarheel accent endeared me to him immediately, removed the upper lobe of my left lung. Instead of brooding, I congratulated myself for having had the lucky stroke which led to early detection of my tumor. And I consoled myself by telling me that I was now breathing one quarter less polluted air.

My spirits were further buoyed by the news that I had been elected by my peers to the Board of Governors of the Academy of Motion Picture Arts and Sciences. None of them knew that I was in the hospital, for we kept my condition secret at the time. In Hollywood, major illness is a ticket to limbo.

While I was recovering, our four-year-old Kaleigh asked me if I had stopped smoking. "You bet your Barbie doll," I said. Her little voice quavered as she said, "I don't like to come see you in a hospital."

Doris took me home and helped me begin a new adventure called macrobiotics. She even arranged a private session for us with the guru of the macrobiotic movement, Michio Kushi, an Asian gentleman who laid down my new regime. No cocktails before, during or after meals; no vodka or tequila even on fishing trips; no more meat, cheese, coffee, butter or candy. Lots of rice, beans, steamed vegetables, a little broiled fish, gallons of miso soup and seaweed.

Kushi fascinated me. All the time he spoke, he nibbled on cashews with stained teeth that looked like they were on loan from a Peruvian. But his diet made me feel better and lose weight rapidly.

One of our Wellness group, Bob, told us that after he had lost some weight, many people commented on how well he looked. "I guess," Bob said, "cancer agrees with me."

Loretta Levenstein's husband Marty told us after one meeting that my wife had made those in their group laugh when she told one chronic complainer, "You take all the fun out of cancer!"

No doubt about it: You must have a sense of humor to survive.

Fifteen months after lung surgery, I did another Oscar show, won another Emmy and was working on a new screenplay with Mel Frank when my sense of humor was put to another strong trial. I had a seizure on the night I was to emcee a Writers Guild awards dinner. Instead of getting laughs in Beverly Hills, I got oxygen in an ambulance and eventually wound up in the UCLA Medical Center again.

This visit, I spent time in the sepulchral chamber of the MRI machine where the pictures revealed that I had a tumor in my brain. It had drifted there from my lung.

So, on April 1, 1990, I was back in the operating room. Some April Fool's joke.

The brilliant Dr. Donald Becker and his festive team of neurological surgeons went into my skull. They removed my malignant tumor. Dr. Becker told me later that, before they began, I had quoted the tomcat who was making love to a skunk: "I've enjoyed about as much of this as I can stand."

And Doris amused me when she said how much she admired Dr. Becker's skill and asked, "How much do we tip for a thing like this?" Becker had taken the time to reassure her and our girls that the procedure went well, he had gotten out all of the cancer and I would soon be as good as new. Or, more realistically, as good as used.

To review my progress, doctors Becker and Holmes put me in the care of Robert Figlin, a respected oncologist, whom I continued to see for monitoring through chest X-rays, blood tests and MRI pictures. While my lung and a half continued to prove cancer-free, a new MRI revealed that my brain was playing host to another small guest spot Dr. Becker thought we should get rid of before it started growing larger. So, in 1991, I told my group that I would miss a couple of Thursday night sessions because I was going back into UCLA. When they asked why, I gave them an answer that our facilitator, Malcolm, quoted forever: "For routine brain surgery."

That did turn out to be routine — for the doctors and physicists. They did get out that damned spot with routine surgery, followed later by radio surgery. That was a procedure that brought me to the hospital in the morning, bombarded my head at noon and sent me home three hours later with a bandage, a headache and a lollipop.

The headache lasted longer than the lollipop but follow-up MRI results proclaimed that I was both headache and cancer-free. I still see my doctors every three months for X-rays, MRI scans, blood tests and reading last year's magazines in their waiting rooms.

So far as we know, I'm in remission. I'm one of the lucky ones who did not have to undergo chemotherapy.

At one meeting, Jack Pill, a kindly man in his seventies, grumbled about some setbacks in his battle and Malcolm asked him if he was angry at his doctors, his cancer or himself. Jack said he wasn't angry at anybody or anything. Imre Molnar, a veteran member of the group whose devotion to canned tuna fish was redolently evident, doubted Jack's assertion. He loudly proclaimed that Jack *had* to be angry. Jack insisted he was not the kind who harbored anger.

"Bullshit!" Imre said, refusing to accept Jack's sanguinity. "Everybody gets angry some time, at something or someone!"

Jack declared himself to be the exception; he wasn't now nor had he ever been angry. It was amusing to see Imre's own anger come to a boil at Jack's stubborn defense.

"God-dammit, man!" Imre shouted, "You're human! Don't sit there and tell me that you're some kind of fucking saint! In your whole life, were you *ever* angry? Not *one* time in your entire fucking *life*?"

In the accusatory silence that fell over the room, Jack nodded. "Twice," he said and bit his lip. "Only twice?" Imre badgered him, to the growing discomfort of the rest of us.

"Twice," Jack repeated, tears forming. "Once when they told me I had cancer" — his voice broke — "and on the day I was told my son was killed in Vietnam."

The shock of that revelation was a blow, but before any of us could censure Imre for tormenting Jack, Imre himself expressed his own apology and our collective compassion by bursting into tears.

Another time, a single man named Lyle lamented the death of his cat earlier that evening. Alfie, an eccentric Englishman who had recently joined our group, advised Lyle not to bury the animal but to freeze it. We stared at him.

"I have six cats in my freezer," Alfie explained, "so whenever I miss my little pussies, I take them out and play with them."

As others shuddered, Lyle said, "Thanks, but cold pussy is why I'm divorced."

Some of us were disappointed the night Malcolm announced that four of our group were no longer welcome to share the hospitality of the Community.

My good friends Loretta Levenstein, prolific author Tom Coffey, talented writer/director Parke Perine and I were unceremoniously dumped, along with our "significant others," for the sin of becoming "victors" over cancer.

Parke and I, who were now too healthy for Wellness eligibility, got together to write a TV pilot, a joyous experience even though nobody had the foresight to buy it.

My services were bought by a producer from New York who needed an attraction to fill six weeks at the Westwood Playhouse, a lovely theater within walking distance from the UCLA Hospital. The producer was Eric Krebs and in association with manager Larry Spellman, they put together an attraction they billed as "A comedy concept by Emmy Award winner Hal Kanter, *Laughing Matters*."

Their billboards described the show as "a rollicking evening of fun with Marty Brill, Hank Garret, Jackie Kahane, Frankie Pace and Hal Kanter" and it was, indeed, quite funny. For six weeks, I presided over those antic clowns six times a week and had more fun than anyone.

I consider myself a fortunate man. I was born with a compulsion to amuse and was admitted to an arena that permits me to earn a living for a loving family while doing so.

Looking back, there have been more laughs than tears; looking ahead, my wife, my children and the work that's still waiting to be done will continue to provide more fun than fret.

If any of my work over the past 60 years has inspired, encouraged, or motivated any young person to write comedy for radio, motion pictures or television, I apologize.

Index